THE REFERENCE SHELF

Vol. 20

No. 7

SHOULD THE COMMUNIST PARTY BE OUTLAWED?

B   43

Compiled by
JULIA E. JOHNSEN

THE H. W. WILSON COMPANY
NEW YORK

1949

1986

PREFACE

The proposal to outlaw the Communist party in the United States is increasingly important. Congressional investigations, attempts to bring Communists or reputed Communists to account in the courts, the challenging of Communists in various public institutions and organizations—labor, education, government, and others—have highlighted the deep concern of public officials and informed citizens.

The question here treated is not, predominantly, that of communism itself, but the intrinsic nature of the Communist party and of its impact, for good or ill, should it be permitted to penetrate further into American ideals and life.

The war left a legacy not only of national problems but of a wide range of international ones as well. In this setting the Communist party is in a larger sense a world problem, for communism has spread strongly in many countries. International basic ties among Communists have, in fact, constituted a major reason for the greater apprehension against them domestically. The fundamental American freedoms are invoked by the Communist party to protect its concepts, ideals and actions here, and in this basic liberty to act at will it is supported by many non-Communist liberals as well.

In keeping with the tradition of the Reference Shelf series the attempt has been made to present a wide variety of views. It has seemed advisable to limit material in the main to the more recent literature.

The compiler gratefully acknowledges copyright permissions and other facilities so courteously extended, which have contributed to the preparation of this book.

JULIA E. JOHNSEN

April 25, 1949

CONTENTS

GENERAL DISCUSSION

A democratic state faces no problem more delicate than that posed by subversive minorities dedicated to the task of supplanting the existing government with an incompatible form of government. Control of subversive activities of Communists is difficult because either too much or too little restraint can be fatal to the liberties of the people. . . .

On the one hand, suppression of subversives may lead to oppression of mere political nonconformists; in an aggravated form, this is no more desirable an alternative than that presented by the subversives themselves. On the other hand, it is equally dangerous not to protect our liberties from extraconstitutional destruction by subversive elements. Hindsight reveals that we have occasionally made invasions of individual liberties which were not justified by the threat to the existence of democratic institutions from subversives. The existence of a present threat, however, cannot be discounted solely on the basis of past experience. . . .

The difficulty of resolving these two competing considerations was abundantly illustrated by the variety of measures proposed to the Eightieth Congress for the purpose of controlling Communist activity in the United States. With the notable exception of the non-Communist affidavit provision contained in the Taft-Hartley Act, none of these proposals was enacted. But certain techniques emerged—particularly those embodied in the Mundt-Nixon Bill—which are likely to be reconsidered in the future. Other changes in existing legislation have been suggested since the adjournment of Congress. The purpose of this note is to appraise the most significant proposals from two standpoints: first, the need for such legislation in light of existing means of

[1] *Stanford Law Review*. 1:85-107. November 1948. Reprinted by permission.

controlling subversive activities; and, second, the possible constitutional infirmities of the suggested measures. This treatment is designed to serve only as a foundation for policy considerations which must determine the ultimate desirability of any proposal, but which are beyond the scope of this note.

I. EXISTING METHODS FOR CONTROL OF COMMUNIST ACTIVITIES. Proposals for additional legislation in the field of subversive activities involve a preliminary inquiry: Are the needs adequately covered by existing legislation? The measures presently available to combat the threat from Communists in this country can be classified as having one of four objectives: to reduce the number of subversive individuals in the United States; to keep them out of vital and influential positions; to scrutinize and publicize their activities; to restrict their activities by direct criminal sanction. Constitutional considerations will be discussed where they bear on the availability of a measure for use against American Communist activity.

A. Measures available to reduce the number of Communists in the United States. The immigration laws have been actively utilized in the campaign against subversive groups in this country. Action may be aimed at exclusion, deportation, or refusal of citizenship. The following classes of aliens, among others, are excluded from admission to the United States: those who believe in, or are members or affiliates of, organizations believing in sabotage, assassination, or forceful overthrow of the government, or those who publish or affiliate with publishers of material advocating such action. Intelligent administration of this provision by immigration authorities may impede any influx of alien Communists. However, persons with dangerous subversive designs will probably conceal their aims and affiliations carefully.

Perhaps more important is the provision for deportation of any alien who was at time of entry or becomes at *any time thereafter* a member of one of the above classes. Deportation was a device readily available against alien Communists under decisions allowing deportation upon a showing of Communist advocacy of forceful overthrow of the government together with party membership or affiliation on the part of the alien. The Supreme

Court in a recent case somewhat restricted the availability of the device by holding that actual adherence to the unlawful purpose of an organization must be shown, despite the statutory specification that mere affiliation is sufficient.

Grounds for exclusion and deportation also prevent naturalization. In addition naturalization certificates have been revoked on the grounds of fraudulent or illegal procurement in a large number of cases where a person's subsequent conduct or affiliations indicated lack of attachment to the Constitution. The number of successful denaturalization proceedings was greatly reduced after the criticism of guilt by association in the *Schneiderman* decision in 1943. The Supreme Court held that a showing of active membership in the Communist party before and after naturalization was not sufficient to sustain the burden of proving lack of attachment to the principles of the Constitution. What remained of the denaturalization program was further hindered a short time later when the Supreme Court in *Baumgartner v. United States,* dealt a sharp blow to the "relation back" device of using subsequent acts or utterances to show mental reservations at the time of naturalization.

The statutes appear to provide for elimination of subversive aliens who can be even loosely identified with advocacy of forcible interference with the government. But the courts have required closer identification and have correspondingly decreased the potency of the immigration laws for use in control of subversive activities.

B. *Measures available to keep Communists out of vital positions.* The memory of fifth column feats in the last war and speculation concerning a clash with Russia in the near future have induced special concern over the possibility of Communists gaining vital positions in government or industry. Existing legislation is directed at federal employees, candidates and parties in state elections, and labor union officials.

1. The first step to keep subversives off the Federal Government payroll was the Hatch Act of 1939, which makes it unlawful for a federal employee to have membership in any organization which advocates the overthrow of our government. Between 1941 and 1947 there were 101 dismissals under the

Hatch Act as a result of 6,193 investigations. In addition, it has been standard practice since 1941 for Congress to include riders on all appropriation bills forbidding payment of funds to anyone advocating the overthrow of the government by force.

Of far more practical importance is the controversial Loyalty Program established by Executive Order 9835 in 1947. The program provides for the investigation of federal employees and applicants for government jobs. Employment may be terminated or refused wherever "on all the evidence, reasonable grounds exist for belief that the person involved is disloyal to the Government of the United States." The potency of this measure as a device for use against subversive persons in the government stems from its departure from the usual formula of "overthrow of the government by force and violence." Six considerations are suggested by the Executive Order in connection with the administrative determination of disloyalty. They are not only sufficiently broad to include any persons who could conceivably constitute a threat to our democratic processes, but also broad enough to permit serious abuse in the hands of inexpert or intolerant administrators. From the standpoint of the present inquiry as to adequacy, however, it can scarcely be doubted that the degree of success in eliminating the threat from subversive federal employees is limited only by the skill and vigor with which the Loyalty Program is prosecuted.

2. State action to prevent infiltration of Communists into vital positions has been exercised primarily through control of the ballot. Inability to satisfy petition requirements for a place on the ballot or to poll a sufficient number of votes to qualify automatically for successive elections keeps the Communist party off the ballot in a number of jurisdictions. On occasion, Communist nominees have been excluded from the ballot, without statutory authority, by administrative action on the theory of inability to take the oath of attachment to the Constitution which would be required upon election.

Sixteen states have enacted legislation to suppress directly the political activities of subversive groups and individuals. All of these statutes are addressed in general terms to parties and persons who advocate violent overthrow of the government or other unlawful interference with its functions. Parties falling within the proscribed category are excluded from the ballot and from recognition as a political party. Affiliates of the proscribed parties are precluded from being candidates for elective office or from holding public office. The constitutionality of these statutes has been sustained by the courts.

Some of the statutes are also addressed specifically to parties or persons affiliated with the Communist party as such. These provisions also exclude parties from the ballot and from official recognition, prevent an individual from appearing as a candidate for elective office, or disqualify persons from holding public office. But this more direct means of identification is of doubtful utility since it has failed to clear the constitutional hurdle whenever passed upon. Several states require parties or individuals to file affidavits that they are not within the purview of the statute denying the ballot or public employment to designated groups.

In view of the political impotence of known Communists, state statutes controlling use of the ballot offer little actual protection. Use of such statutes to prosecute individuals and parties concealing their affiliations is rendered difficult by the burden of proving the "violent overthrow" formula. Any utility of these statutes seems offset by their undesirable tendency to give underground activities the appearance of being necessitated by political persecution.

3. The alleged infiltration of Communists into positions in labor unions where they can incite paralyzing strikes in vital industries has caused special concern. The non-Communist affidavit provision of the Taft-Hartley Act is designed to combat indirectly such a threat to our economy and national security. Unions are given access to the National Labor Relations Board only if each union officer files an affidavit stating that he is not a member of, nor affiliated with, the Communist party and does not believe in, nor belong to, an organization advocating the overthrow of the government by force or other unconstitutional means.

This section of the Taft-Hartley Act has been sustained by three Federal District Courts and by the United States Court of

Appeals for the Seventh Circuit, but there is still considerable dispute as to its constitutionality. The provision is variously attacked as a denial of due process to union members and officers, as a proscription of mere belief which infringes upon the guarantees of the First Amendment, and as a bill of attainder. In *National Maritime Union of America v. Herzog* and *Inland Steel Co. v. NLRB,* each of these constitutional objections was considered and dismissed. Both courts reasoned that Section 9(h) was not a bill of attainder because no punishment was involved, and that the provision did not infringe on constitutional guarantees of the First Amendment. This reasoning is open to challenge and the validity of the non-Communist affidavit provision will remain uncertain until passed upon by the Supreme Court.

C. Measures available to publicize and keep track of the activities of American Communists. Disclosure-type legislation represents an increasingly used technique in the struggle to control subversive activities. In theory, measures designed to force probable subversive individuals to disclose their status have three advantages: (I) subversive organizations and persons lose much of their potential threat when the truth is known about their activities, policies, members, connections, etc.; (2) misapplication of this legislation is less dangerous to nonsubversive minorities since disclosure does not impair the opportunity for such minorities to strive for acceptance in the market place of ideas; and (3) the nondisclosure furnishes a prosecution device against these subversives, since presumably only those with something to conceal will refuse to make the required disclosures.

The McCormack Act of 1938 adopted the disclosure approach by requiring agents of foreign principals to register. Definitions of "agency" and "foreign principals" are very inclusive, but exemptions from the application of the Act seriously reduce its possible effectiveness. Registrants must disclose rather complete information concerning organization, activities, financial affairs, identity of foreign principal, extent of control by foreign government or political party, and identity of employees. Provision for publicizing the information acquired is contained in three requirements: registration statements are open to public inspection; as a prerequisite to distribution, all political propaganda of registrants must indicate the identity of the foreign principal and the fact of registration as agent thereof; copies of all such propaganda must be filed with the Librarian of Congress and be opened to public inspection. In evaluating the McCormack Act as a device for dealing with the Communist movement, it is noteworthy that the Communist party of the United States has neither registered nor been prosecuted for failure to register. It is not clear whether this results from lack of diligent enforcement, absence of proof, or deficiencies in the Act.

The Voorhis Act of 1940 is aimed more directly at subversive organizations. It requires the following organizations to file detailed registration statements: (1) organizations subject to foreign control which engage in political activity (activity the aim of which is control by force *or* overthrow of the Government of the United States); (2) organizations subject to foreign control which engage in military activity; (3) organizations which engage in both political and military activity; and (4) organizations the aim of which is the control or overthrow of a government by force, violence, or threats thereof. Exceptions in the case of exclusively religious, charitable, scientific, literary, and educational organizations decrease the effectiveness of the Act, as does the failure to place responsibility for registration of an organization on its officers. Because the registration requirement depends on proof of purpose to overthrow the government, the Communist party of the United States has not been persuaded or compelled to register.

The Alien Registration Act of 1940 furnishes a useful protective device in so far as the presence of aliens may increase the threat of subversive activities in this country. The Act provides for registration, which includes disclosure of activities and fingerprinting, by every alien now or hereafter in the United States. While this furnishes information which has been found especially useful in connection with control of enemy aliens during time of war, the act of registration itself attaches no stigma to the individual.

A summary of disclosure devices would not be complete without mention of the highly controversial investigations of the

House Committee on Un-American Activities. While the avowed purpose of these investigations is the formulation of legislation, they have regularly brought widespread publicity to the activities of allegedly subversive groups and individuals.

The California Subversive Organization Registration Law, passed in 1941, appears to be the only state legislation directed at subversive activities which employs the disclosure technique. This law requires the registration of organizations which advocate overthrow of our government by force *or* which are subject to foreign control. A California District Court of Appeals has expressed doubt as to its constitutionality, apparently on the ground that the field has been occupied by federal legislation such as the Voorhis and McCormack Acts.

Disclosure legislation is most often commended because it is said not to threaten the democracy which it seeks to protect. However, the "pitiless spotlight of publicity" furnished by such legislation may unleash economic sanctions as severe as any direct suppression. This results from the subversive label which the public may attach to all registrants. The danger lies in the fact that administrative characterization and the tenor of the legislation may control the public appraisal of registrants more than the facts disclosed. Thus, unwise administration of apparently harmless disclosure laws may create the same potential for encroaching upon the liberties of nonsubversive minorities as do other types of measures.

D. *Measures available to restrict Communist activities by direct criminal sanction.* Statutes have long proscribed the extremes of possible Communist action, i.e., revolution or active assistance to the Soviet Union in the event of war with the United States. As defined in the Constitution, it is treasonable to levy war against the United States or give aid and comfort to its enemies. It is also a criminal offense to incite or aid an insurrection, or to conspire to overthrow or oppose the government by force. But reliance on prosecution of such drastic activities may only serve to bolt the door after the theft. The Espionage Act of 1917 strikes at somewhat earlier stages of subversive activities. It provides heavy penalties for obtaining or disclosing information affecting the national defense "with intent or reason to believe that the information . . . is to be used to the injury of the United States, or to the advantage of any foreign nation. . . . The difficulty of proving the required specific intent seriously impairs the possibility of prosecuting persons who supply vital information to American Communists. Another section of the Espionage Act makes criminal all wilfully false statements made in time of war with intent to interfere with the military success of the United States or to promote the success of its enemies. The constitutionality of this latter provision has been upheld, but its application is limited to situations where there is a clear and present danger of substantive evils which Congress has a right to prevent.

Perhaps the most drastic federal legislation employing criminal sanctions to eliminate subversive movements is the Smith Act. The outstanding section of this Act makes the following unlawful: (1) to advocate overthrow of any government in the United States by force or violence; (2) to disseminate written or printed matter advocating such forceful overthrow of the government; or (3) to organize or join any group advocating overthrow of the government by force, knowing the purposes thereof. While the constitutionality of the Smith Act has been sustained by a Circuit Court of Appeals, it probably will be narrowly construed and its application limited to activities presenting a clear and present danger to national security. The outcome of recent indictments under the Smith Act against twelve leaders of the American Communist party may determine whether the statute will remain dormant or will spring into active use.

To aid the enforcement of the various provisions considered in this section, Congress has made criminal the use of the mails to transmit printed matter advocating treason, insurrection, or forcible resistance to laws of the United States, or matter violating any of the provisions of the Espionage Act of 1917.

A large amount of state legislation has been enacted to impose criminal sanctions on subversive activities. The prevalent provisions against treason, and against insurrection and rebellion, largely overlap the corresponding federal provisions. More important are the state statutes proscribing criminal syndicalism and criminal anarchy. The former are directed at the advocacy of crime, terrorism, violence or sabotage as a means to accomplish industrial or political change. The latter apply to advocacy of the doctrine that organized government should be overthrown by force, assassination, or other unlawful means. Legislation of these two types has been before the Supreme Court on several occasions. An Oregon statute broadly proscribing participation in any meeting of a society which advocates criminal syndicalism was struck down as an unconstitutional invasion of the right of peaceful assembly. In an earlier case the particular application of a criminal syndicalism statute was held unconstitutional without invalidating the statute. On other occasions, never expressly overruled, the Court sustained both the statute and the application. Insofar as the wording of a statute of either of these two types applies to activities not presenting a clear and present danger of criminal acts, the legislation itself appears to transcend constitutional restrictions. While such a statute does not preclude a constitutional interpretation, its application would seem to be constitutional only in situations presenting such a danger of criminal acts.

Summary. The outstanding characteristic of existing legislation available to combat the Communist threat is that most of the devices hinge on identification of a group or individual with the idea of overthrow of the government. This type of legislation has been characterized as "an uncritical acceptance of a formula devised during the days when the Communist manifesto represented the technique of revolution. Communists have become very adept at changing their color to fit varying situations, and in this country they carefully avoid advocacy of unconstitutional change in the government. Many persons are certain, however, that the Communists in this country are very willing to resort to extraconstitutional means of change whenever it becomes profitable to do so. In view of the difficulty of meeting the "violent overthrow" formula of proof, it is natural that other methods should be sought.

II. PROPOSED METHODS FOR CONTROL OF COMMUNIST ACTIVITIES. Existing legislation is largely phrased in terms of a result which we seek to avoid, i.e., forceful overthrow of our government. But American Communists may be dangerous even though they do not advocate overthrow of the government. They constitute a threat primarily because of the disadvantage at which they could place the United States in the event of war with the Communist dominated nations of the world. To restrict subversive activities without impairing civil rights of loyal citizens is difficult. Yet, by exercising the ordinary civil liberties of free speech and right of assembly or in occupying important government positions, disloyal persons could constitute an appreciable element of danger in case of a conflict.

To cope with this problem, new methods of identifying and defining communism are being sought. Bills introduced in the Eightieth Congress identified the Communists in two ways: by name and by characteristics.

A. Regulation of the Communist party by name. Designation of Communists by name is intended to make prosecution easier by eliminating the necessity of proving advocacy of violent overthrow of the government. However, the burden of proof probably would be lightened only in the cases of the relatively small number of presently identifiable members of the Communist party in the United States.

The Sheppard Bill would have made it unlawful for any individual to be a member of the "Communist party." In addition to the oft-raised objections that such legislation would drive the Communists further underground and make them martyrs, there are serious constitutional objections to this type of outlawry. Implicit in such a measure is a legislative finding that the nature and purposes of the Communist party threaten national security. Congress may then exercise its inherent power to protect the existence and integrity of the state. Such a finding appears to violate due process since the statute presumes a state of facts which may not be true. Similarly, the measure appears to be within the constitutional prohibition against bills of attainder as interpreted in *United States v. Lovett.* The Supreme Court declared that "legislative acts, no matter what their form, that apply either to named individuals or to easily ascertainable members of a group in such a way as to inflict punishment on them without a judicial trial are bills of attainder prohibited by the Constitution." Punishing individuals on the basis of membership in the Communist party also constitutes an imputation of guilt by association. Constitutional doubts about the use of guilt by association as a basis for criminal prosecution have been raised by a recent dictum of the Supreme Court.

Two bills introduced in the Eightieth Congress would have forbidden Communist members to run for elective office in any state or federal election. Objections to the above proposal would apply equally here. There is the further objection that our Constitution permits the states to determine the necessary qualifications for the appearance of parties or individuals on the ballot.

The Rankin Bill, (in addition to banning Communists from the ballot) proposed to make it unlawful in the course of teaching in public or private schools "to advocate, or to express or convey the impression of sympathy with, or approval of, communism or Communist ideology." Without a more explicit definition of "communism or Communist ideology," the proposal seems to violate the due process requirement that a criminal statute must be "sufficiently explicit to inform those who are subject to it what conduct on their part will render them liable to its penalties." The most serious deficiency, however, is the obvious infringement upon the guarantees of the First Amendment. The proposal would apply to any statement in the mails or the classroom which approved of theoretical communism even though it did not threaten the security of our government. Suppression of opinion unconnected with incitement to overt acts is void on its face.

Although there were other proposals which would have dealt with the Communist party by name, they raised no further significant issues.

B. *Regulation of the Communist party by characteristics.* The second class of proposals sought to define their application in terms of the characteristics of the Communist movement. For example, one provision of the Sheppard Bill sought to proscribe membership in any organization engaging in political activity which is affiliated with, directed by, or aided by a foreign government or foreign political party. Since the proposal did not limit its application to foreign affiliations inimical to our national security, it is difficult to find a constitutional basis for this provision. If protection of the existence of the state be advanced as the legitimate objective, the lack of a reasonable and rational relationship between the proscription and the object would make the provision a violation of due process.

The Hobbs Bill sought to supplement existing federal legislation which is designed to keep advocates of forceful overthrow of the government off the federal pay roll. The bill would have made it a crime for anyone who had engaged in activities "subversive of the government" or who had affiliated with any organization with aims "subversive of the government" to accept or retain federal employment. The vague and inclusive definition of the phrase "subversive of the government" would have rendered federal employment a hazardous occupation. The proposal seems clearly invalid under due process requirements of certainty for penal statutes. The factors suggested for the determination of employee disloyalty under the President's Loyalty Program have many of the same qualities of flexibility and indefiniteness. But there may be a distinction between denying government employment to persons of doubtful loyalty and depriving the same persons of liberty and property.

The most significant proposal before the Eightieth Congress for the control of Communists was H.R. 5852, popularly known as the Mundt-Nixon Bill. Because it represents a more thoughtful approach to the problem than the proposals above considered and because a similar measure may be introduced at the next session of Congress, the bill deserves special attention. The bill contains provisions of three different types: (1) it would place heavy criminal sanctions on activities directed toward the establishment of a foreign controlled dictatorship in this country; (2) it would require the registration of subversive political organizations which fall within definitions contained in the bill; and (3) it would deny certain privileges to those organizations and their members. These provisions are preceded by an extensive legislative finding of fact with respect to the world Communist movement. The final finding is that this movement presents a clear and present danger to the security of the United States and to the existence of free American institutions.

Section 4 of the bill provides that it shall be unlawful "to attempt in any manner to establish in the United States a totalitarian dictatorship the direction and control of which is to be vested in . . . any foreign government, foreign organization, or foreign individual. . . ." Although the element of force necessary under the Smith Act is no longer required, prosecution of subversives will probably not be facilitated. Proof that acts are done for the purpose of establishing a foreign-controlled dictatorship will be extremely difficult to obtain. In nearly all cases such proof would be sufficient under the Smith Act to show that the acts were done for the purpose of aiding the forceful overthrow of the government. However, the Smith Act proscribes only conduct related to advocacy and not all acts directed toward the forceful overthrow of the government. Thus, a Communist who incites a labor dispute with intent to aid ultimate Russian conquest would not be within the terms of the Smith Act. While such a person might fall within Section 4 of the Mundt-Nixon Bill, proof of the essential intent would be virtually impossible to obtain.

The registration provisions constitute a more significant addition to existing legislation. The Department of Justice has apparently thought that the Communist party of the United States could not be compelled to register under either the McCormack Act or the Voorhis Act. The Mundt-Nixon Bill seeks to solve this stalemate. An organization is required to register if it is reasonable to conclude from ten specified considerations "(i) that it is under the control of such foreign government [in which is vested the control of the world Communist movement] or foreign governmental or political organization, or (ii) that it is one of the principal instrumentalities utilized by the world Communist movement. . . ." The ten considerations are all factors which would tend to identify an organization as part of the world Communist movement centered in Russia . Included in the considerations are control of policies by Russia, similarity between the policies of the organization and those of Russia, support of the principles of Marx and Lenin, financial aid from Russia, reports to Russia, recognition of disciplinary power of Russia, secrecy of operation, and allegiance to Russia.

The proposal also provides for an administrative determination that a particular organization must register. The Attorney General would be empowered to investigate, to hold hearings, and to subpoena witnesses and records for this purpose. If the Attorney General concludes as a result of an investigation and hearings that the organization under scrutiny is a Communist political organization or Communist front organization, an order requiring registration would be issued. The organization is entitled to a judicial review of such an order, but the Attorney General's finding of the facts is conclusive if supported by a preponderance of the evidence. Thus, an organization may be compelled to register if it is reasonable to conclude that it is an instrumentality of Russia or some part of the world Communist movement. However, this proof should be sufficient to compel registration under the existing Foreign Agents Registration Act. The important additional factor is the provision for an administrative determination supported by the power to compel testimony and evidence.

Further disclosure is required. Printed matter or radio broadcasts issuing from registrants or organizations which have been ordered to register must be appropriately labeled as issuing from a Communist organization. The bill would also make it unlawful to become or remain a member of an unregistered organization while knowing, or having reasonable grounds for knowing, that the organization is of the type required to register.

The third type of provisions contained in this proposal includes those which would deny certain privileges to organizations which have registered or been ordered to register. These organizations would be denied exemption from income tax payments under Section 101 of the Internal Revenue Code, and contributions to such organizations would not be deductible for federal income tax purposes. Members of a "Communist political organization" who have reasonable grounds for knowing it is such an organization are prohibited from holding nonelective office "under the United States" without revealing their membership. It is further made unlawful for members to apply for passports.

There are many doubts as to the constitutionality of the Mundt-Nixon Bill, but it bears the marks of a careful attempt to avoid unconstitutionality. Objections may be made that the indefinite standard which determines the application of the registration provision violates due process. However, no penalty depends on this standard except where the individuals and organization concerned should know that the organization is required to register.

Provisions relating to members of the Communist political organizations are open to objection as employing standards of guilt by association. However, the weight and extent of this objection have not yet been crystallized in the courts. Although the bill applies only to organizations connected with the world Communist movement and not to all organizations of a possible subversive character, this would not seem to violate the due process clause of the Fifth Amendment. The most difficult constitutional question is whether the proposal violates the First Amendment. If freedom of speech includes the freedom to remain silent, the validity of a compulsory registration provision is questionable. Furthermore the weight to be given the legislative finding of a "clear and present danger" is an open question. Although the bill raises constitutional issues, a strong case for the validity of the bill is made possible by its careful drafting.

The difficulty of drafting effective legislation is apparent from the above survey of existing and proposed legislation. The picture is further complicated by the existence of variables which no survey can adequately take into account. The administration of legislation can vary its effectiveness and its dangers within wide limits. Constitutional treatment likewise may vary with the personnel of the courts. Furthermore, public hysteria may encourage distorted administration of legislation in force.

The great diversity in existing and proposed legislation for the control of subversive activities indicates that no final answer has been found. It is appropriate to consider in which directions our search for improved legislation should lie. This suggests a re-examination of the need for regulation of Communist activities.

The advocacy of theoretical communism gives rise to no such need. Indeed, our Constitution would guarantee the right to advocate the peaceful substitution of communism for our democracy. Neither is the need found in present danger of a Communist-incited domestic revolution. At the present time Communists are not capable of engineering a successful internal uprising or *coup d'état* in this country without external aid. Our present statutes, however, have been influenced by fear of violence by Communists in America. In the decade following the Russian Revolution, the Communists in the United States openly espoused violence and destruction. State criminal syndicalism and criminal anarchist statutes were geared to this danger. But the Communist party of the United States today carefully avoids advocacy of forceful methods.

Today, the real incentive for legislation to control Communist activities is the danger that domestic Communists will render us more vulnerable to the threat from Russia.

Domestic Communists could impair our national security (1) by furnishing important military and scientific information to the Soviet Union; (2) by controlling policy-making positions in the United States Government; (3) by occupying vital positions outside the government, where discord may be caused by provoking labor disputes and racial disturbances; (4) by committing actual acts of sabotage. Exposure of the Communist spy ring in Canada and recent investigations in this country have aroused us to the possibility that native Communists with their allegiance abroad can appreciably threaten our national security. This danger is aggravated by the growing possibility of war with Communist-dominated nations.

Several observations can be made concerning the immediate problem of control of Communists. First, the identifying characteristics of *dangerous* Communist groups today is subversive to the policies of a foreign power. Communist ideology is important because those who embrace it may aid a foreign power in threatening our national security. This fact found expression in the Mundt-Nixon Bill. Future legislation should recognize it. Second, our energies and our legislation should be directed at the problem of keeping Communists out of vital positions in our government and economy. A registration provision is the most effective technique yet to emerge for coping with this menace. Third, part of the problem can only be met by alert enforcement of existing statutes dealing with espionage and sabotage.

LOYALTY AMONG GOVERNMENT EMPLOYEES [2]

Mounting tensions in our society have brought us to a critical point in the matter of political and civil rights. The stresses are in large measure internal. They grow out of the accelerating movement to effect far reaching changes in our economic and social structure, a movement which evokes ever increasing resistance. As the conflicts sharpen, there is rising pressure to discard or undermine the basic principles embodied in the democratic concept of freedom for political opposition.

Maintenance of free institutions in a period of deepening crisis would be difficult enough if the struggle were confined to our shores. But the domestic problem is only an element of the world problem. Large areas of the world have abandoned the system of capitalism in favor of socialism. Other areas are far advanced in economic and social change. Everywhere there is struggle, uncertainty, fear and confusion. Protagonists of the more militant economic and social philosophies are organized into political parties which have their offshoots and counterparts in other countries, including our own. As a result, the preservation of political freedom, the right to hold and express opinions diverging from the opinion of the majority, is often made to appear incompatible with the overriding requirements of "loyalty," "patriotism," "national security" and the like. The danger of "foreign ideologies," "infiltration," "subversion" and "espionage" are invoked to justify the suspension of traditional rights and freedoms.

If we look to our basic traditions and attend the counsel of our wisest forbears, the path before us should be reasonably clear. Recognizing that no political organism can survive without evolution and change, we must face change with courage and imagination. The journey towards a new destination must be undertaken within the framework of the democratic process. We must seek to plot our course through rational and intelligent discussion. We must encourage the fullest participation of all elements in

[2] By Thomas I. Emerson, Professor of Law, Yale Law School, and David M. Helfeld, Graduate Fellow, Yale Law School, *Yale Law Journal.* 58:1-8. December 1948. Reprinted by permission.

our society. We must be willing to compromise when the road ahead is obscure and to advance firmly when the road is clear.

There are tragic signs that this is not our course, that we have lost the path. The opponents of change have resorted increasingly to the delusively simple expedient of cutting off political opposition or of hounding it out of existence through appeals to irrationalism and prejudice. For ten years now the House Committee on Un-American Activities has spearheaded a drive which, while largely failing in its announced objective of exposing the activities of "subversive groups," has undoubtedly succeeded in arousing fierce and emotional opposition to progressive ideas and organizations. In the Alien Registration Act of 1940 Congress enacted an anti-sedition law comparable in sweep with the Alien and Sedition Acts of 1798. In Section 304 of the Taft-Hartley Act Congress undertook to emasculate the political power of labor by prohibiting expenditures for political purposes by labor organizations. The dangerously increasing ascendancy of the military in our national life is not only a threat to representative government but reflects a serious weakening of democratic vitality. And recent proposed legislation, aimed ostensibly at the Communist party, threatens the existence of all political organizations not adhering to orthodox views.

These and other manifestations of the trend have aroused a number of open minded citizens to warn publicly against the rising threat to democratic institutions. And certainly the danger is real. The suppression of political opposition is opposed to every tenet of democracy. It entails, among other things, the retention of outworn institutions, the elimination of every possibility of compromise and mutual adjustment, and the fomenting of class hatred, racial and religious prejudice, and allied social disorders. It must lead inevitably to an internal explosion in the form of revolt or an external explosion in the form of war.

The fear of "disloyalty" and "subversion" among the government bureaucracy is a modern aspect of the problem, brought to the fore by the greatly expanded function assumed by the executive in recent years. But the underlying issues are not new to America. Our history has been marked by a never ending struggle between the ideal of freedom in political expression and the efforts of temporarily dominant groups, particularly in periods of crisis, to demand rigid political orthodoxy. An invariable attribute of the struggle has been the stigmatization of the nonconformists as "disloyal." This is the typical behavior of standpatters, moved by fear and hostility toward the forces of change. Its malignance has been accentuated in the United States by the constant flow into a new and developing country of people and ideas from foreign lands.

The founders of our government, successful in their revolution against established governmental authority, embodied the principles of free political expression in the new Constitution. Two features of that document are noteworthy here. The provision on treason was designed to insure that the government's right to protection against treasonable acts would never be perverted, as it had been in England, to a weapon for the outlawing of political opposition. Secondly, the First Amendment constituted an express guarantee that the rights essential to the exercise of political freedom would be protected.

Within a decade after adoption of the Constitution these principles were put to a severe test. The period was in many respects similar to our own. Relations between the United States and France were critical. When President Adams publicized the notorious X.Y.Z. papers, anti-French and anti-foreign hatred was aroused to a frenzied pitch. The pro-British Federalists, who despised French libertarianism, fanned the flames with wild stories of French invasion plans. Federalist teachers, preachers and judges aroused the people with clamor for war. The Federalists contended that the French government was spreading pro-French propaganda through paid agents and sowing revolutionary doctrine. This hysteria even seized some of the Republicans, normally pro-French and anti-monarchist. Thus divided, the Republicans were easy prey. Denouncing all opposition as "disloyalty," the Federalists forced through Congress the Alien and Sedition Laws.

The Alien Act was designed to harry the revolutionary Irish immigrant as well as the French, both of whom were attracted to the libertarian Jeffersonian party. It provided for the imprisonment or expulsion of "enemy aliens" at the President's

discretion. The Sedition Act was even more severe. It provided
fines and imprisonment for the publication of any "false, scandalous and malicious writing" against the government, or which
brought officers of the government "into contempt or disrepute,"
provisions which would effectively seal opposition lips, even including members of Congress.

Even the hardbitten arch-Federalist Hamilton was amazed at
the ruthlessness of the measures. But his counsel of moderation
was ignored and the acts were vigorously enforced against indignant and alarmed Republicans. One major objective of the
campaign was to eliminate Republican office holders. Thus the
first prosecution under the Sedition Act was against a Republican
member of Congress running for reelection.

The constitutionality of the Sedition Act was sustained in the
lower federal courts and by three Supreme Court justices sitting
in circuit, but the issue of constitutionality never reached the
Supreme Court. Jefferson and Madison, in the Kentucky and
Virginia Resolutions of 1799, attacked the laws as unconstitutional. Regardless of their legality, the harsh enforcement of
the acts stunned the American people, and the legislation seems
to have been a major reason for the defeat of the Federalists in
1800.

Upon the accession of the Republicans to power, the Alien
and Sedition Acts were repealed and Jefferson pardoned the persons—all Republicans—convicted under them. In his inaugural
address Jefferson boldly reaffirmed the ideal of political freedom:

If there be any among us who wish to dissolve this Union, or to
change its republican form, let them stand undisturbed, as monuments
of the safety with which error of opinion may be tolerated where reason
is left free to combat it.

Thus the first experiment with "loyalty" as a weapon in political struggles came to a happy end. But the issue arose in another
form shortly afterwards. Nativist anti-foreign bias flared up
again with the addition of Louisiana to the Union in 1803. The
different national loyalties of the polyglot population of the new
territory created much concern. Fortunately this was short lived.
But in the 1830's nativism fastened upon the Catholics from Ire-
land and Germany. The legend spread that the Leopold Asso-

ciation, an Austrian missionary society, was "pouring gold into America to undermine the Protestant faith." Prominent citizens denounced Catholic immigrants, the Papacy and the church hierarchy; mobs rioted at Catholic churches; there was a demand for a twenty-one-year probationary period before immigrants could become citizens. The loyalty of the foreign-born and especially of Catholics was impugned and it was suggested that these groups be denied access to political office. When a well-known Catholic was appointed Postmaster General by President Pierce the vituperation of the anti-Catholic Know-Nothings reached a new pitch. It was asserted that Catholics in the Post Office would become members of a spy ring for the Pope, and it was solemnly claimed that Catholic immigrants were not and could not be loyal to the nation.

With the coming of the Civil War loyalty to the Union once more became a crucial matter. Congress passed stringent legislation granting the President discretionary power "to suspend the privilege of the writ of habeas corpus in any case throughout the United States." Harsh accusations of disloyalty were levelled against Democratic army officers because many Democrats at home opposed continuation of the war, and there were demands for stern measures of repression. But even in the heat of war "disloyalty," short of actual treason, was not invoked to bar government employees or elected officials from office. The wise and tolerant leadership of President Lincoln was a significant factor in minimizing infringements on democratic liberties.

In the bitterness of reconstruction following the Civil War, Congress and some of the states passed legislation requiring various forms of loyalty oaths as a condition to practicing certain professions. These laws were struck down by the Supreme Court as bills of attainder and ex post facto legislation.

The issue of disloyalty among government employees and office-holders was not seriously raised again until the first World War. Indeed, affirmative steps were taken under the Civil Service Act, passed in 1883, to assure political independence among government employees. Civil Service Rule I, issued in 1884, required that "no question in any form of application or in any examination shall be so framed as to elicit information concern-

ing the political or religious opinions or affiliations of any applicant, nor shall any inquiry be made concerning such opinions or
affiliations, and all disclosures thereof shall be discountenanced."

In World War I military tensions again inflamed suspicion
and distrust of those who might hinder the war effort. Public
attention centered on foreign-born groups, particularly the Germans, even though many were citizens and had been assimilated
into the American culture. Government activity concentrated on
aliens, who were suspected of potential disloyalty, and numerous
deportations took place. While government employees as a class
escaped notice, certain elected officials did not. In the early
stages of the war Victor Berger, elected to Congress as a Socialist,
was denied his seat because of his opposition to war.

The Berger affair gave impetus to the doctrine that "disloyalty" was a legitimate basis for barring duly elected representatives from public office. Shortly after the war the New York
Assembly expelled, without hearing, five members elected on the
Socialist slate. The grounds were that the five were "disloyal"
to the American government, and that the Socialist party was not
a political party but in reality a subversive organization which
adhered to the revolutionary principles of Soviet Russia. A half-
hearted allegation was made that the five had violated the Espionage Act, but the charge was not supported. They never
regained their seats.

Political suppression reached flood tide with the widespread
raids of A. Mitchell Palmer, U. S. Attorney General, whose drag-
net swept thousands of "disloyal" aliens into prison. At the same
time, the Lusk Committee in New York, which fathered the expulsion of the Socialists from the New York legislature, forced
the enactment of legislation drastically curtailing political expression. Teachers, usually the first group of government employees
subject to attention, felt the sting of the Loyalty Oath and those
suspected of radicalism were dismissed.

The reaction to these moves was not long in coming. The
Bar Association of the City of New York protested the expulsion
of the Socialist Assemblymen and issued a memorial, written
principally by Charles Evans Hughes, later Chief Justice of the
United States Supreme Court, strongly condemning the action of

the legislature. Most of the victims of the Palmer raids were released and the charges against them dropped. The fever of the postwar years slowly ebbed. In 1923 Governor Smith signed the repeal of the Lusk Anti-Sedition statutes. The country seemed to take to heart, at least for the time being, the words of Justice Holmes reaffirming the American tradition:

> But when men have realized that time has upset many fighting faiths, they may come to believe even more than they believe the very foundations of their own conduct that the ultimate good desired is better reached by free trade in ideas—that the best test of truth is the power of the thought to get itself accepted in the competition of the market. . . .

It is in the light of this background that one must consider the current programs and proposals to maintain a constant and intensive check on the loyalty of all government employees. The specific issues raised by the loyalty check are particularly significant for a number of reasons.

The problem is important, first, because of the number of persons involved. During the war the civilian payroll of the Federal Government included over 3,000,000 employees; it is now somewhat over 2,000,000. To this number must be added 3,400,000 state and local government employees. Together with their families these civil servants represent a substantial segment of the population. Postwar reductions have now ceased and the number of government workers is again on the increase. With the development of government owned plants for the production of atomic energy, not to mention the possibility of nationalization of certain basic industries, the numbers involved would be even larger. Furthermore the loyalty program directly affects many thousands of employees of private employers operating under government contract.

Second, the standard set by the government in this area has an incalculable effect upon the attitude of the country as a whole. Calm and intelligent action by government sets a healthy example. Witch-hunts officially sponsored must breed imitations throughout the nation. In a period of rising tension the government has a special obligation to hold firm to a reasoned course in the best tradition of political democracy.

Third, the issue posed is one that goes deep into the foundations of political freedom in a modern industrial state. The political theory of our founding fathers predicated freedom of political institutions upon a groundwork of economic freedom. The vast accumulations of capital which have marked the growth of modern industry have largely removed this underpinning of economic independence. Hence the basic problem of modern democracy is to preserve political independence for large masses of citizens who do not have a source of strength in the ownership of small units of productive enterprise. This problem is particularly acute in the case of the government employee, who is peculiarly lacking in economic independence. Establishment of a firm foundation of political freedom for the government worker would constitute a significant advance toward solution of the broader underlying issue.

Finally, the loyalty program must be considered in its effect upon the morale and efficiency of the government service. The government bureaucracy is an indispensable tool in the modern world and the quality of its performance becomes more and more vital to the welfare of all. Forces are constantly at work in any large organization seeking to dull, to ossify, to strait-jacket its activity. Only a thoughtful and continuous effort can prevent government bureaucracy from degenerating to a moribund level where it becomes incapable of handling the novel and complicated matters with which it must deal. Our government has the exacting task of recruiting competent men and women and the equally difficult task of retaining the services of its ablest officials. A loyalty program which gives rise to fear and uncertainty places a premium upon conformity and mediocrity. It will determine, as much as any single element, the capacity of government to function as a vigorous, effective force in modern society.

OUR POLITICAL COMPETENCE [3]

This year is a fateful one because of the breakdown of order throughout the world. Two world wars left a social vacuum.

[3] By William O. Douglas, Associate Justice, United States Supreme Court. *Vital Speeches of the Day.* 14:645-9. August 15, 1948. Reprinted by permission.

In the Soviet Union the small select group of rulers proclaimed
that their philosophy alone was destined to fill that void. They
proclaimed this so loudly that many became convinced.

Meanwhile we, the democrats of the world, had begun to
drift. Only now are we beginning to recover balance and
direction.

Our present danger is that we may see the issue too narrowly,
as a choice merely between appeasement and war. But the choice
is not so limited. There is still another way. It is for the democrats of the world to fill the social void and dispel the chaos
throughout the world. Against a living democracy, the assaults
of the Communists will be unavailing. Before we consider how
this may be done, let us first be certain that we understand the
nature of the Communist philosophy. . . .

Dictators have a way of setting down their programs and
purposes for all to read. Democracies, for some reason, have
a way of ignoring or disbelieving the dictators. We recently
had our lesson from the totalitarian right. We waited almost
too long before reading Hitler's *Mein Kampf*. We must not
make that mistake today. Like Hitler, the Communists have
given us their plans. Before it is too late, we must read and
understand the works of Joseph Stalin—such books as *The October Revolution, The Problems of Leninism, Foundations of
Leninism*.

Many people who have not read these books profess to find
great idealism in communism. There is always appeal in slogans
of equality and freedom. Liberation of the oppressed and exploited strikes a deep chord. The summons to cast off the yoke
of those who suffer is a call to strong humanitarian instincts.

The Communist Manifesto takes these subjects as its theme.
It was published in 1848 by Marx and Engels who saw the factory system at its worst. Men, women and children were crushed
in its wheels, broken by long hours, enslaved by low wages. A
caste system held grandfather, father and son in the same social
and economic group, unable to escape. The power of kings, the
power of economic monopoly and the power of finance united
to crush and exploit the common man.

The Manifesto undertook to answer these problems. "The
proletarians," it stated, "have nothing to lose but their chains.

They have a world to win. Workingmen of all countries, unite"
—those were ringing words. The Manifesto was, indeed, one of
the most powerful political documents of all time. Some professed to find in it the flavor of Thomas Paine and Thomas Jefferson. Exploitation of men was to cease. The people were at
last to become their own masters.

These expressions of idealism attracted men of good will.
Others saw in the Communist program of nationalization a cure
for the evils of monopoly. Others saw in the Soviet scheme
work for all, starvation for none. Seeing these aims, they
thought they were good. But they overlooked the terrible price
in life and moral values which the Communists exacted.

It is time that we were no longer misled by those high-sounding slogans, by the Communist mirage of freedom, equality, and
opportunity. As realists, we must look at communism as it is
practiced by Communists today. For communism in actual operation on the world scene is as destructive of democratic values
as the tsarism that preceded it or the fascism whose mad march
we stopped only recently.

We can put to one side the problems of communism in
Russia. We the democrats will be the first to defend the right
of any people to live under the government of their choice. When
they confine their totalitarian regime within their borders, they
are entitled to tolerance in working out their own experiments.
But the Russian borders do not mark the orbit of communism.
Stalin announced in his book, *The October Revolution*, that the
Russian Revolution constituted "the beginning and premise of
the world revolution." We have seen much of that prophecy
come true. The plan is to undermine all the democracies. The
aim is to win by default, if possible, but to win under any and
all circumstances and at any price. That is what the current
Communist propaganda means when it says, "There is no power
in the world that can prevent the death of capitalism, the growth
of the indignation and struggle of the working people against
the reactionary bourgeoise. . . . This is what Leninism, the
Marxism of our epoch, teaches us."

The techniques whereby the Communists plan their domination of the world reveal at least three *basic* and *irreconcilable*
differences between their philosophy and ours.

First. Marx and Engels wrote that "the proletariat must first of all acquire political supremacy, must rise to be the leading class of the nation, must constitute itself *the* nation." That has often been taken to mean that the political power of the state was at last to be transferred to the people. The common man was to come into his own. All the people were to have a new charter of liberty. Indeed the current Communist propaganda in this country is that communism is "a society in which the people themselves are the master and determine the fate of their country."

Lenin made clear that "the proletariat" and "the people" were not synonymous. He announced that the dictatorship of the proletariat "has meaning only when one class knows that it alone takes political power into its own hands, and does not deceive itself or others by talk about popular, elected government, sanctified by the whole people." By Lenin's dictum the political power of the state was to go into the hands of one class and one class only. Everyone else would be disenfranchised.

Today's Communists have gone Lenin one better. They have not placed the political power in the hands of even one class. They have given it all to a central bureau—one select political clique. It is that small group that declares war, makes peace, and establishes the party line that dictates the conduct of their agents in all the countries of the world.

Here we have the first deep and fundamental difference between Communists and democrats. It is the very antithesis of democracy to have the political power of a nation vested in one group—whether it be a man, a corporation, or a class. The struggle of the democracies of western Europe through the years has been to get rid of that kind of dictatorship. We followed that course in this country. We experienced life under a monarchy; and mild as it was compared with Communist totalitarianism, our fathers expended lives and treasure to be rid of it.

Those who designed our charter of government knew that other oppressions would come—perhaps even the old ones in new garb—if the dictatorship of a king were to be replaced by the dictatorship of one group. Tyranny is the same whatever mask it wears. The men who composed the Philadelphia Con-

vention in 1787 knew that. They worked from the premises that
Madison advanced: (1) that the function of government was to
keep the various groups of society in balance by preventing one
from exploiting or overriding another, and (2) that government
itself might become adverse to the society over which it presided
and hence must be kept in bounds. And so we, like the other
democracies, designed a system of government to keep any one
group—whether it be social, economic, religious, or political—
from being the repository of political power.

We disperse political power among all groups. By doing so
we have some guarantee that no one group will permanently
acquire the upper hand over others, that no one group will use
the sanctions of the law and the power of government for the
exploitation of others. When one group acquires all the powers
of government, freedom can be had only through revolution.
That is, I think, the head and font of all the revolutions the
world has seen.

But when political power is dispersed among all the people,
the tyranny of any one group need be temporary only. For the
people can have their revolution at the polls without the sacrifice
of life or the destruction of property. They can be rid in peaceful ways of the hold which any group has on their national life.
That is a great virtue of the democratic way.

That has happened again and again in the history of this
country. Political power has not long been concentrated in the
hands of a few. One example will illustrate my point.

The last century saw us develop a huge industrial plant, cal-
lous in its attitude towards the rights both of the men who oper-
ated it and the public that it was designed to serve. An industrial oligarchy grew up around it and controlled governors, legislatures and even courts. The men and women whose blood and
sweat went into the plants were the expendables. Long hours,
unsanitary and unsafe conditions of work, low wages were the
rule not the exception. Property rights were supreme, human
rights were forgotten.

This is the chapter in American history that the Communist
propaganda has exploited to this day. Their propaganda would
have the world believe that these conditions persist. It pur-

posely overlooks the great exertions of democratic government that were used to rectify those conditions. Though we are far from perfect, we have in this country evolved an advanced form of industrial democracy. Human rights are in the ascendency. Men are no longer owned by machines.

It took time to do these things. But the important fact is that they were done. Moreover, they were achieved not by revolution but by the peaceful route. Bryan pleaded with the nation's conscience. From Altgeld of Illinois to Al Smith of New York came a militant band of public figures to proclaim against the evils of our industrial system. Theodore Roosevelt, Woodrow Wilson, Franklin D. Roosevelt headed the national reforms that gradually restored the balance of power. Labor unions emerged, acquired strength of character, and grew in power equal to the might of the industrial giants with whom they had to deal.

Society by definition is the aggregation of many, diverse pressure groups. The secret of wise government is to leave room for each group to live and express itself. The democratic way, by wide dispersion of ultimate political power among all the people, makes it impossible for any one interest to get and keep, at least for long, the authority to exploit the others.

The Communists defy this principle and by putting all political power in the hands of a few repudiate the basis of free government as we know it.

The premise on which the Communists build this theory is also hostile to our traditions. The Communists assume that the basic problem in society is class warfare. But the idea of class or caste has not taken hold here. The only real aristocracy we know is the aristocracy of individual initiative and achievement. Men who work in overalls today can become corporation executives tomorrow. There is no station in private or public life closed to any man or woman, no matter how lowly his start. The lists are open to all; and the ribbons go to the fleet.

We would not be true to our genius if we embraced the class warfare theory. Class warfare and the American character are foreign to each other.

Moreover, the Communists miss the mark by concluding that the basic conflict in modern industrial society is between labor and management. There is conflict between those groups. But that is not significant, for life is full of conflict and tension. The process of living is indeed adjustment between competing forces. The conflict between labor and management continues but it has evolved into manageable form both in this country and in the democracies of Western Europe. Collective bargaining has been the foundation on which industrial relations can be stabilized. Strikes will continue. But labor's right to a fair wage, to a just share of the earnings of industry is recognized more and more. The right to work is a part of our economic bill of rights. Guaranteed annual wages are increasing. Labor is becoming a working partner with management in factories that were hostile to the idea only a decade ago. In these and in a myriad of other ways mediation, negotiation, peaceful adjustment and law are taking the place of strife and warfare in industry. The Communists, who preach the other doctrine, choose not to know the truth of American industry.

While the most important single problem of our economy lies in the industrial field, it is not the conflict between labor and management. It is the conflict between the industrial plant (composed of both labor and management) on the one hand and society on the other. Our standard of living turns in large measure on the productivity of both the men and machines that comprise industry. Our industrial plant is a great source of our national income. Property depends on an economy of abundance. An expanding economy demands increased productivity. Decreased production means depression. These are joint problems of labor and management.

That is the central problem of the complex industrial society in which we live. The Communists offer no answer to it and indeed communism was not conceived as an answer to it. Communism was launched in a land of poverty where industrialization was still far distant. It has yet to master the problems of an industrial society. The Communists do not come to us with any scientific blueprint for a machine age. They therefore do not offer us the key to the problem that both here and in the other democracies is most pregnant with potential conflict. Yet even if we could be sure that they offered us an economy of abundance, we could not accept the offer. As we have seen, they substitute rule by one select political clique for Lincoln's concept of government of the people, by the people, and for the people. They trade our political heritage—our right to franchise —for a police state.

This is a matter on which we the democrats can never compromise. The difference between us and the Communists at this point is *fundamental* and *irreconcilable*.

Second. We come to the second basic difference between the two philosophies. The Communists need a police state because they try to pour man into one mould. It's been tried before—by all the tsars, and kings and Hitlers that have tramped the earth. It has never succeeded for long. And it never will. For man was born for freedom, not for slavery. Man cannot be standardized like automobiles, or screws, or nails. God gave man the same amazing diversity that He gave the flowers in the mountain meadows.

The Communists with their police state defy that fact. News is a standardized product issued by a central government bureau. There is no room for a crusading journalist to expose the failings of those in office. Art, music, and literature are weapons of political warfare. They are called subversive if they depict the sad side of the Communist society or raise doubt concerning the wisdom, or virtue, either of the system or the officials who manage it. Like the press they must follow the party line. Defections from it entail severe penalties. There is no "free trade in ideas" such as Holmes talked about. The solution to every social and economic problem, the answer to every question must meet the approval of the ruling clique. No other answers are tolerated. There is only one road to salvation. All other roads lead to concentration camps.

The matter was rather humorously summarized the other day by Winston Churchill when he compared the totalitarianism of the Left and the Right to the North and South Poles. He said, "If you woke up tomorrow morning at one or the other you would not know which it was. There might be more penguins at one end of the world and more polar bears at the other, but all around you would be ice and snow and the blast of freezing winds over dreary spaces."

There are few dreary spaces in the democracies, imperfect as they are. We have great diversity—from art to politics. Some democrats are socialists, some are capitalists. We are committed to no single panacea for all our problems. We can have a TVA in Tennessee or on the Columbia without nationalizing all the enterprises along Main Street. We can proceed by trial and error and undo four years from now what we do today. We can let man express himself in art and the letters. He is restrained only by the laws of libel and obscenity. We can let man give vent to his views, however noxious they may seem to those in power. We can experiment with new techniques unrestrained by commitments to any one political faith.

The Communists have no such freedom or flexibility. Their religion is dialectical materialism which permits of no compromise. All must conform or perish.

We the democrats of the world cannot compromise with that philosophy. To do so would be to discard our Bill of Rights and to place ourselves again in the chains that we struggled for centuries to remove.

Third. A third *basic* and *irreconcilable* difference between the Communists and the democrats is in their political techniques. Ours is a civic genius described by William James as the tolerance of one political party for the other. The party in power is on probation only. It has its innings; and it stands or falls on the record of its performance. No police or army suppresses an opposition or keeps the winner of the last election in office.

The Communists have no such tolerance for the opposition. Up to the time the Communists win an election, they talk and even act like democrats. They adopt the tactics of parliamentary government. The words and slogans they use are familiar and appealing to democrats. They believe in "free elections." They plead the cause of justice. They are against the exploiters of human beings. They pose as champions of every oppressed person or group. But once they take office, it is for keeps. Once that happens, the liquidation of all opposition parties commences.

Surely the Communists must be on the side of the angels, it is said. For they are identified with every cause that seems to champion human rights. But the Communists plead the liberal causes for quite a different purpose than do the liberals. Their purpose is to seduce the liberals, mislead the conservatives, and confuse everyone. A truly liberal government is an anathema to them and their aim is to destroy it. They do not want reform for others. They want power for themselves. That is why they speak in favor of socialism but against the socialist regime in England. Their chance of getting power disappears if democratic government is strong and reliant. Their real hope lies in fostering conditions that breed discontent.

It is important that this technique be understood. Stalin makes it clear in his *Foundations of Leninism* and *The Problems of Leninism*. The Communists plan two revolutions. First the bourgeois revolution and second the proletarian revolution. With the bourgeois revolution the Communists take over existing democratic institutions. That's what happened recently in Czechoslovakia. That's what they have been trying to do in Italy and France. To gain control of existing democratic governments they use democratic tactics. They talk and behave like democrats and proclaim the democratic virtues perhaps even more loudly than the democrats themselves. But they take control of a democratic government for only one purpose—to destroy it. Its destruction and the appropriation of its powers by the central body in Moscow constitute the second, the proletarian revolution. Both revolutions take place without moving an army or dropping a bomb. They have indeed the outward appearance of constitutional government in the democratic sense.

Between these revolutions the Communists bring into play two ancient political techniques designed to eliminate all political opposition—techniques borrowed from the tsars—techniques that have been the political tools of tyrants from time immemorial: murder and terror.

The use of murder and terror make fear the dominant, overriding influence in public affairs. Once fear grips the hearts of the people the Communist ranks become swollen.

The political techniques of the Communists stand condemned by the standards of the democrats. We refuse to accept fraud and deceit as standards of public conduct. We reject murder and terror as political weapons.

These then are three of the basic and irreconcilable differences between the philosophy of the Communists and that of the democrats.

In the area of ideological conflict, foreign policy and domestic policy must necessarily be integrated into a total *national* policy—a policy which practices at home what we preach abroad.

We can best urge the democratic way on the peoples of the world if our conduct at home sets an inspiring example of democracy in action.

If we are truly to be an arsenal of democratic faith, we must first inspire and justify that faith by our own performance. We must manage our own affairs in such a fashion that our domestic achievements will kindle in the hearts of people throughout the world an unshakeable faith in the validity of the democratic system.

On the *domestic front* the course is easy if we have the faith and honesty to take it.

1. We must not make bogy-man of the Communists in this country. It is not the Communists themselves that we in this country should fear, for they are no more than 100,000 in number. All we need fear is our susceptibility to their propaganda. Our first duty then is to understand their purposes and methods. If we do that, their influence will be no greater than their numbers. It is only when we do not understand, that the Communists exert an influence far out of proportion to their strength. It is important to remember that the Communist influence in the democratic state is essentially divisive. Their aim is to pit one liberal against another, conservatives against liberals, race against race, labor against management. We the democrats must not fall victim of that strategy.

2. We must restore integrity to our own political tactics by putting an end to the shameful practice of branding as a Communist everyone who espouses a liberal reform or promotes a program for the underprivileged. If the late George

Norris were alive today, promoting his beloved TVA, some would label him a Communist by showing that in Russia power projects are nationalized. By that reasoning the great Labor Party in England would also be communistic. Yet we know that a socialist democratic regime is an anathema to the Communists.

When liberals are pilloried as Communists, the Communists influence grows and spreads. For then the liberals and Communists are driven closer and closer together. Thus do conservatives play the Communist game of breaking the ranks of the democrats, dividing a nation into camps that become more and more hostile.

We must keep our country a place where men are not afraid to think and read and speak freely and without restraint.

3. We must become politically more conscious. The Communists through the use of their principle of democratic centralism confine their differences within their ranks. Once the party line is fixed, they present a united front to the world. In that way they make the most effective use possible of their minority position. They also are the most active political agents of all time. While the rest of us relax, the Communist workers are busy ringing doorbells, writing literature, and spreading their faith. We cannot throw away our political independence and intellectual integrity by fixing our own party line and compelling allegiance to it. But we must take our politics more seriously. If we throw our full energies into political organization and activity, the Communists will be impotent in our affairs. They could not then win by default; and it is only by default that they can gain a strategic hold on important groups in this country. Labor unions have taken the lead in showing how the result can be avoided.

4. Effective democratic government is the political antidote to communism. Reactionary governments nurture the conditions on which communism feeds. The kind of democratic government that will submerge the Communist influence is a liberal, progressive government that recognizes the human rights of all citizens, raises the standard of living at all levels of society, eliminates the insecurity of this industrial age, and wipes out

the poverty that has plagued man from the dawn of history. Nothing short of this kind of political program will defeat the aims of the Communists.

On the *foreign front* the problem is more difficult but the choice is not between war and appeasement. Neither will solve the problem which confronts us. A war would produce a world in ruins with poverty and illness on every hand and suffering and dislocations of life unequalled in history. That is the environment in which virulent ideas flourish. That is when the Communists come into ascendency. On the other hand appeasement means that the Communists are encouraged by our default to undermine flourishing democracies. Both of these alternatives we reject as unnecessary and improvident.

1. The answer to the Communists on the foreign front, as on the domestic front, is a political program. We must be equipped and prepared to meet the political program of the Communists at whatever point in the world they may select for action. We must ourselves regain the initiative by promoting in our own areas of influence tried-and-true political antidotes to communism.

Our greatest error would be to fashion our foreign policy merely in terms of anti-communism. We will fail miserably if we do more than that. For then we will end by railing at the Communists, taking no steps to eliminate the conditions on which Communists thrive. If we follow that course, war will soon appear as the only alternative.

2. We must design a foreign policy which will espouse and promote liberal, humanitarian programs for the masses of people of the world. It must strengthen the democratic forces in other nations and not entrench reactionary interests that thirst for power.

Most of the areas of the world are bleak and desolate when measured by the living conditions of the people. At times the people live under a serfdom of poverty and disease. At other times it is an industrial or political serfdom. The Communists are artists in exploiting these conditions. They can promise pie-in-the-sky—in fact the whole world—to those who will enlist in their political army. Revolution may indeed seem a welcome relief to those who have been exploited. It may to desperate men have the appeal of a swift and cleansing purgative that sweeps before it all the rot and filth of the old tyranny that has oppressed them.

Those impulses cannot be controlled by talk and promise of vague and remote democratic ideals. America's voice, if it is to be powerful among the masses of people, must do more than talk of the glories of democracy. If we want the hundreds of millions of the peoples of the world in the democratic ranks, we must show them the way with practical programs of social reconstruction. The European Recovery Program serves that end; and so does the China Aid Act, at least in part.

3. We cannot force such programs on other nations. But we must stand ready to suggest them and help to work them out. We must stand ready to support *with sanctions* the liberals of any country who have programs of social reconstruction for their people. There are in many countries men both in and out of government who have the inner strength and vitality to formulate programs for their own people. . . .

The real victory over communism will be won in the factories and rice fields of the world rather than on the battle fields. The fight against communism depends for its ultimate success on the people of the various nations, not on their governments. Thus we must support those who represent democratic values and who have practical programs for political action. When we prop up governments that are self-seeking, corrupt, or fascist, we lose ground in the worldwide struggle against communism. When we stand behind the liberal and progressive forces in other countries, we become identified with their interests in the eyes of the peoples of the world. Then the democratic cause gains strength and character. Then the flood tide of communism will begin to recede.

4. This course requires the backing of a strong, alert and mobile military machine. For weaklings have never yet won a campaign—political or otherwise—against dictators.

These should be our articles of faith. . . . If we adhere to them, we will be true to our character and ideals. If we fail, we will fail proudly, not miserably as men do when they compromise with principle. If these be our articles of faith, we will keep alive the ideals of freedom and decency even in defeat. Even if disaster overtakes us, we will have left a heritage from which men can draw strength and inspiration when the day for revolution against the new political bondage comes.

But there need be no failure. Success is assured if we are true to ourselves. We have a system which, though far from perfect, is strong with idealism. It gives elbow room for men of all races and all beliefs. It is vital and dynamic. And it works. We have the means of shaping the world in our pattern. If we do, freedom will be assured for all men. The decision is in the hands of this generation. It is a challenge to our political competence. For western civilization it is the greatest challenge of all time.

THE AMERICAN COMMUNIST PARTY [4]

1. No discussion of the future relations between the United States and the Soviet Union can be complete if it fails to examine the status and role of the American Communist party. This party, not a political party in the ordinary sense, is the Communist International operating in the United States. In our judgment the American Communist party is an unqualified liability from the standpoint of effecting mutual understanding and genuine collaboration between the Soviet Union and the United States. We therefore cannot agree with those who contend that this organization on account of its small membership can be regarded as a factor of little or no consequence in the situation. To be sure, this party has not the slightest chance to achieve its revolutionary purposes in any foreseeable future, but because of its character, its patterns of behavior, and its historical association with the Soviet Union, it nevertheless exercises a negative influence out of all proportion to the numbers officially enrolled as members. The experience of a quarter of a century demonstrates that both

[4] From "America, Russia, and the Communist Party in the Postwar World," written by John L. Childs and George S. Counts, Teachers College, Columbia University, for the Commission on Education and the Postwar World of the American Federation of Teachers. p. 62-75. John Day Company. New York. 1943. Reprinted by permission of the American Federation of Teachers.

the people of the Soviet Union and the people of the United States have a common stake in the dissolution of this party. A candid account of this experience is particularly important at this time as American Communists are trying to capitalize the Soviet Union's great deeds in the war for their own ends.

2. The first essential to an understanding of the American Communist party is to grasp the fact that it is an arm of the Communist International. This international organization has headquarters in Moscow, and is controlled by Moscow. In spite of its alleged international character, history has demonstrated that it does not and cannot operate independently of the policies formulated by the All-Union Communist Party of Soviet Russia. The fact that the Soviet Government disclaims all responsibility for the Third International and represents each national Communist party as sovereign in its own country has long since failed to deceive any informed person respecting the realities of the situation. The behavior of the various official Communist parties of the world before, during, and after the Soviet-Nazi Pact establishes irrefutably this organic connection with Moscow. *Before* the pact the American Communist party advocated collective security against all aggressors, and characterized France, Britain, and the United States as great democratic countries; *during* the pact it proclaimed the war an imperialistic struggle for colonies and markets, denounced these very same countries for betraying the interests of the working class by participating in the war, and sabotaged the effort of the United States to give aid to those who were resisting the aggressions of fascism; and, finally *after* the pact was destroyed by Hitler's invasion of Russia, it proclaimed the war a holy crusade for the liberation of mankind from the Fascist "cannibals," revived the policy of a United Front with the capitalist democracies, urged all-out prosecution of the war on both the home and the fighting fronts, and demanded the ruthless suppression of all critics and isolationists. This is but one illustration of many that might be given to prove the subservience of the American Communist party to a foreign power. Its supreme loyalty is not to the American people, but to the Soviet Fatherland. No organization thus convicted of disloyalty can serve as an instrument for improving the relations of the United States with the Soviet Union.

3. The second essential to an understanding of the American Communist party is a recognition of its commitment to the philosophy of a proletarian world revolution. It was created originally for this purpose, and it is so constituted that it can serve effectively no other purpose. Having been designed to promote this revolutionary end, it now finds itself in an anomalous position, because, presumably, this world revolutionary objective is no longer a primary concern of the Soviet Union. Moreover, this revolutionary philosophy, as we have shown, was a product of men whose minds were conditioned by economic and social conditions different in many respects from those which prevail in the United States, a country which long ago got rid of the last vestiges of feudal society, and also a country which has had a long and promising experience with democratic processes and institutions. Consequently, even if the American Communist party had no organic connection with Moscow, it would remain a distinctly alien influence in American society. Both its thought and its practices are forced into the molds of this system of nineteenth-century European revolutionary dogma. Even its language is cluttered with terms and phrases that have little meaning to people reared on the North American Continent. The first and supreme loyalty of American communism is to the Soviet Union; the second is to this revolutionary idea and mission. It ever operates to build the party which it believes is destined to play this great historical role in the overthrow of capitalism. Whenever circumstances compel a choice between the interests of the party and the welfare of any group or organization with which its members are identified, it never hesitates to put the party first.

4. In striving to attain these two essential objectives, the American Communist party follows a pattern of organization and procedure as alien as its purposes. This pattern was developed for the most part in tsarist Russia and was designed to enable a small group of deeply devoted reactionaries to operate amid conditions of blackest tyranny and oppression, where secrecy and absolute solidarity were essential to survival. This pattern concentrated authority and power of decision in a central bureau or committee, which acted as the directing head, formulated all important policies, developed the conception of a "party line," and imposed obedience and military discipline upon all members.

When the original Russian party came into power and sought to build an international organization, this pattern was adopted not only by the Third International but also by all national branches of the Communist party. This was easily accomplished because of the great authority and prestige which the Russian revolutionists enjoyed owing to the successes they had won. Even as the Russian party was organized into numerous cells controlled from the center, the Third International was also organized so that the national branches of the Communist party were reduced to the status of cells, likewise controlled from Moscow. Experience has shown that whenever leaders in the American Communist party have attempted to break this control, they have been forced either to surrender abjectly or to suffer expulsion from the party.

5. Crucial to the understanding of the operations of the American Communist party is the so-called "party line." By this "line" is meant the position taken by the Communist leadership on whatever subject. Thus the line covers many areas of life not ordinarily associated with political activity. Indeed it permeates the entire life of a member of the party, involving questions of art, morals, philosophy, relationships with groups and organizations, attitudes toward persons, and responsibilities to be discharged in one's occupation, including positions in government, education, and all voluntary organizations. Moreover, it should be understood that the broad outlines of this policy are made, not by the leadership of the American Communist party, but by the International leadership in Moscow. One of the errors of the ordinary American citizen, whether liberal or conservative, is to assume that an individual can be a member of this party and at the same time exercise the right of private judgment in any area in which the "line" has been defined. For an individual member to violate the "party line," unless he is instructed to do so for purposes of intrigue and conspiracy, is sure to result, first in censure and, if carried further, in expulsion from the party with all the attendant dangers of exposure. In this connection it should always be remembered that the American Communist party has two categories of members: one, those who are publicly known as enrolled members; two, those whose membership is

concealed—by far the larger group. These latter will under practically all circumstances deny membership, not even stopping short of perjury, and in view of the conspiratorial nature of the organization, live in constant dread of exposure. The secret character of their connection with the party subjects them to many subtle but powerful controls. In addition to the enrolled members there is a third group known as fellow travelers who in all crucial matters follow the party line and seek to advance the interests of the party. In some cases interested persons of considerable prestige are advised not to enroll as members because it is supposed that they will be more useful to the party in the role of independent liberals. The power of the discipline of the party was recently revealed in the behavior of party members and even party travelers in connection with the Soviet-Nazi Pact.

6. The power of a disciplined, conspiratorial group, operating on the principle that the end justifies the means and having its objectives and its strategy authoritatively determined by centralized leadership, is not to be measured by the number of its members, nor by the number who vote for its candidates at public elections. The power of small numbers operating according to this pattern has been known to military commanders from the earliest times. This principle has also been found to be potent in the field of politics, particularly in a democratic society whose institutions are organized to give the widest freedom to individuals and groups. The American Communist party has devised a great variety of procedures and agencies by which it can take advantage of this freedom so essential to the life and health of American democracy. It sends its members into all organizations through which public opinion is made and expressed in order to advance the two supreme purposes outlined above. It penetrates particularly the labor unions, because of its analysis of social forces and its philosophy of proletarian revolution. For similar reasons it strives to acquire leadership of all underprivileged and exploited groups, races, and classes, such as the unemployed, people on relief, Negroes, and share-croppers. It also seeks to penetrate middle-class groups and organizations in the leadership of public opinion such as newspaper workers, artists, teachers, writers, social workers, government employees, and even

religious bodies. In those fields where suitable organizations do not exist to advance its ends, it sets up under its own concealed control new agencies of propaganda and social action, which, though made to appear to the public as genuine philanthropic and social improvement organizations led by disinterested people, are in reality what Communist leaders designate as "transmission belts" of the party. The League for Peace and Democracy was for a time the most successful of all their agencies of this type. Whenever the Communist control of such agencies is exposed, or the non-Communist sponsors assume the actual direction, the party seeks either to dissolve or disrupt them.

7. In its effort to capture for its purposes both governmental and voluntary agencies and organizations, the American Communist party has developed an amazingly detailed pattern of action. It deliberately schools its members in the techniques of capture, and requires them to allot a large portion of their time and energies to this kind of work. They are trained in the art of public speaking, in the mastery of the tricks of parliamentary tactics, in the ways of delaying and speeding up action in public meetings, in the methods of wearing down opponents and of confusing issues, in the techniques of creating division, particularly by the introduction of resolutions cunningly devised for the purpose, and generally in an ever developing variety of means by which the procedures of democratic group deliberation and decision can be manipulated by a minority in order to attain predetermined ends. Prior to any important meeting or convention they hold a caucus of the members who are to attend in order to outline both the strategy and tactics to be followed in gaining whatever results are deemed important for the party. By circulating rumors, or by direct attack, they misrepresent both persons and measures; in similar fashion they seek to build up the reputations of those who are subject to their control and whom they would elevate to positions of leadership. They will go to almost any length to discredit leaders who refuse to cooperate with them in those organizations whose work they consider vital to their own program. Believing as they do that the end justifies the means, they have developed into a fine art both the defamation and vilification of character, and the enhancement and build-

ing-up of reputations. In fine, the use of these techniques of capture, manipulation, and control, possible only in a regime of liberty, constitutes an attack on the moral foundations of American democracy.

8. It should be clear from the foregoing description of the purposes, control, organization, and patterns of behavior of the American Communist party that it is a movement whose leaders do not consider themselves bound by either the principles of American democracy or the standards of ordinary group morality. The American people have been slow to recognize that the conflict with this revolutionary and conspiratorial group is, in the last analysis, a conflict of two moralities. This failure to grasp the nature of the issue presented by this party is rooted in two virtues of the American people. The one is their devotion to the freedoms defined by the civil liberties and the rights of minorities. The other is their devotion to the democratic conception of social justice and equality. Being aware of the serious inequalities of our society, and also uneasy in conscience about our failure to overcome them, many have tended to respond with sympathy to this Communist movement which professes to be the militant and uncompromising champion of all exploited and underprivileged groups. Because of their faith in the ideals of liberty and the social aims of democracy, they have been unwilling to conclude that any movement would deliberately exploit both these liberties and the real distress of certain groups in our society in order to achieve its own long-run power purposes.

9. The actual record of the objectives of the American Communist party during the past twenty-five years, however, shows that it has produced consequences exactly as evil as its purposes and methods of behavior would have led one to anticipate. The path of this party is strewn with the wreckage of persons and movements. Experience has demonstrated that it adds not one ounce of strength to any liberal, democratic, or humane cause; on the contrary, it weakens, degrades, or destroys every cause that it touches. For example:

a. It has betrayed the social idealism of many of the finest youth of our country. These young men and women, sensing and profoundly disturbed by the deep injustices of our society

and the contradiction of want in the midst of potential plenty,
have sought to identify themselves with a movement which would
deal fearlessly with the underlying causes of these maladjust-
ments in our country. Inspired to action by these ideals, they
have gone into the Communist party only to become demoralized
and rendered unfit for the really important and difficult tasks of
democracy in this critical period of social transition. From a
wide acquaintance with many of these disillusioned and broken
young people, we know how long and painful is the process of
recovery from this experience.

b. It has spread confusion and created division in the ranks
of organized labor and of all liberal, social, and political movements. It has set labor union against labor union, liberal against
liberal, worker against worker, race against race, and thus dis-
sipated the resources of democracy. The experienced leaders of
these workers' organizations and liberal political movements were
the first to discern the true character and tendency of the American Communist party. Many of these organizations have excluded Communists from their controlling membership—even
the American Civil Liberties Union.

c. It has driven men and women, distinguished in the sciences, the arts, and humanitarian movements, from active participation in the public affairs of our society. It has also caused
many to shun worthy and necessary public activities because they
have learned from bitter experience to suspect that their work
in these movements is being used for hidden and ulterior purposes of the Communists.

d. It has fed through the years reactionary and Fascist tend-
encies in our society. The irresponsible and flippant manner in
which this party has entered into revolutionary agitation and
activity, while at the same time seeking to maintain a respectable
position in the United States and be granted full public support
and defense, has made it easier for the obscurantist and reactionary factions in our country to identify every popular, liberal, and
democratic movement with communism. The Communist party
has lightly aroused revolutionary activity and temper without
ever having prepared itself to bear the consequences of such
action. By thus playing into the hands of the nascent Fascist

elements in our country, it has handicapped all movements struggling to achieve fundamental social changes by rational and
peaceful means. Friends of democracy can respect and support
honest, radical movements that are making a sincere effort to
deal with institutionalized injustice; they can have only contempt
for a party that tries to be both legal and conspiratorial, above-
ground and underground, at one and the same time. This
duplicity is inherent in the status and program of the present
American Communist party.

e. It has built up in the mind of the American people a
great heritage of ill-will toward the Soviet Union. It has produced this effect for two main reasons. First, as a matter of
historical fact, it has sustained an organic connection through
the Communist International with the Soviet Union. As this
fact has become generally known, the American people have
deeply resented the intrusion of a foreign power in this manner
into the domestic life of our country. Second, it has increasingly
proclaimed itself the authentic champion, spokesman, and interpreter of the new Soviet state to the American people. As a
consequence, the antagonisms generated by its unprincipled
methods of operation described above have been transferred to
the Soviet Union. Many Americans have come to think of the
Soviet Union as a country whose people follow in all their behavior the patterns followed by the members of the American
Communist party. No other foreign state faces so grievous a
handicap in its effort to establish relations of mutual confidence
with the American people and government. This obstacle must
be removed, if the Soviet Union and the United States are to
collaborate effectively in the postwar world.

10. The American Communist party, an organic part of the
Communist International, is thus a primary problem for both the
United States and the Soviet Union at the present time. So far
as our domestic affairs are concerned, American democratic
forces will undoubtedly, in time, develop adequate means for
dealing with this disloyal and conspiratorial organization. To do
this will require a more mature conception of what can and cannot be embraced by the democratic process. It will also require
a further definition of the democratic theory of civil liberties,

for the present theory was not elaborated to take account of behaviors such as are the rule and not the exception in the practices of the Communist party. Once the moral foundations of
democracy are clearly understood, it will be perceived that the
behaviors of the Communist party are in conflict with those
foundations and must be treated accordingly. We have every
confidence that American democratic forces will find means to
preserve all the essential guarantees of the civil liberties, while
at the same time they take the steps necessary to get rid of the
abuses inherent in the practices of these totalitarian political
movements, whether Fascist or Communist in origin, control, and
purpose.

So far as our relations with the Soviet Union are concerned,
the problem of the Communist party cannot be resolved from
the American side alone. We have pointed out that it is an
official branch of the Communist International and that the
maintenance of this agency is a survival from an earlier policy
of the Soviet Union. Unfortunately that policy has never been
repudiated completely, nor has the political apparatus of this
Third International ever been finally rejected. On the contrary,
the Soviet Union still utilizes it whenever she believes that her
national interest can thereby be served. . . . Before concluding
our discussion of the American Communist party, however, we
want to define the ultimate source of its strength.

11. We believe that the responsibility for the dissolution of
the Communist party rests, in the first instance, with the American people. We believe also that this dissolution is to be best
achieved not through the proscription of the party, but rather
through the removal of those conditions on which the party
feeds. The ultimate source of its strength derives, not from the
connection with the Soviet Union through the Third International, but from the weaknesses, injustices, and failures of contemporary American society. Its strength stems from chronic
unemployment, from widespread insecurity bred by the recurring
crises in our economy, from want in the midst of potential plenty,

from inequalities suffered by various cultural and racial minorities, particularly the Negroes, and from the refusal of our society resolutely to mobilize its resources to overcome these deficits, and reenact under changed conditions its democratic purposes. The supporters and sympathizers of this party are drawn from adults who want to work but are forced to subsist on a dole; from young people trained in our schools and colleges for socially useful activity, but unable to find it after the completion of their training; from members of professional groups such as artists, writers, health workers, and engineers who, in spite of the great public need for their services, are denied a chance to work in their chosen professions; from minority groups and races who are nurtured in the democratic ideal of equality, but fail to experience it in the daily practices of our society; and, finally, from ardent idealists who believe in the democratic conception, but see it denied in so many aspects of our national life. These are the deeper sources from which the strength of the American Communist party derives; its threat will not be removed until these unnecessary and unjust conditions are removed from American society. It is because of the existence of these depressed and discontented groups in our country that an agency like the Communist International has a chance to manipulate our internal affairs for its own ulterior purposes.

CIVIL LIBERTIES AND THE COMMUNISTS [5]

The comparatively low ebb at which the Communists now find their fortunes in the United States—largely as a result of [their] blatant devotion to a foreign state—is no measure of the indirect influence they still exert over some liberal minds. The era of the Popular Front has left a legacy of concepts that are clearly still at work in the field of civil rights. . . . It is a tribute to the skill, persistence, and truculence of Communist propaganda that many Americans have come to uphold certain "rights" that are not rights at all, and some of which make no sense in this or any other kind of political society. For example:

[5] From article by Robert Bendiner, Associate Editor of the *Nation*. *Commentary*. 5:423-30. May 1948. Reprinted by permission.

1. *The right of anonymity.* The idea here appears to be that to ask a man in public whether he is a Communist is a violation of the secret ballot, a breach of his constitutional rights, and, generally speaking, a blasphemy against the democratic faith. The reverse, of course, is true. Secretiveness and conspiracy are the essence of the tyrannical state, but are incompatible with the practice of democracy, whose life blood is the free and open interchange of ideas. To quote from Morris Ernst, a veteran champion of civil rights who now finds himself in conflict with his absolutist colleagues: "The marketplace of thought is no longer free when competitors may enter it anonymously and *fight* democracy while they hide under the cloak of democracy." Technically, the right of anonymity, so far from having a legal existence, is expressly denied in the whole system of enrollment involved in party primaries. To have a hand in the nomination of a Republican or Democratic candidate, a voter must declare himself an enrolled member of one of those parties, which he does by signing, in the polling booth, a declaration that he intends to vote the appropriate ticket in the ensuing election. Lists of these enrolled party voters are compiled, by district, and may be had for the asking, or for a small fee, at any Board of Elections. This does not prejudice the right to a secret vote, since no one is obliged to register by party. It merely assures that people who wish to identify themselves with a party to the extent of helping to choose its candidates will do so without concealment. (From none of these facts, however, is it to be inferred that a Congressional committee has the right to question citizens publicly about their politics in the absence of a clear and legitimate purpose. Such a purpose might be the intention to propose germane legislation, but surely not to bring about a man's dismissal from private employment.)

2. *The right to belong to any and all organizations.* Not even the Communists have the effrontery to claim this on legal grounds, but they have so thoroughly intimidated and befogged the more vulnerable type of liberal mind that in certain progressive circles it is considered treason to democracy to exclude Communists from organizations avowedly dedicated to democratic causes. The argument is, first, that this is a form of red-baiting,

the arch sin; second, that it divides the forces of "light"; and third, that once an individual or organization embraces the belief that you can't work with the Communists, he or it is headed straight for damnation and a spiritual affinity with the Reverend Gerald L. K. Smith. From its founding a year ago, the liberal Americans for Democratic Action has been determined to keep out Communists for the simple and normally persuasive reason that their entire philosophy, not to mention their current political line, is utterly at variance with the organization's; and it is for this very reason that the ADA is damned by those liberals who are so steeped in the psychology of the Popular Front that such essential discrimination appears only as a kind of persecution. I once asked a confirmed fellow traveler just how the Communist party would feel about admitting an ADA member in the impossibly hypothetical case that one would care to join. "That's entirely different," she said. "The Communist party has its own philosophy and long-range objectives"—a privilege evidently not to be credited to the rest of us.

Akin to this particular Communist claim is the insistence not merely on the right of free speech, which is certainly not contested here, but on the highly questionable "right" of an individual to speak at private gatherings of his choice, however unwilling they may be to hear him. New Yorkers may recall the recent instance of a Congressional candidate who had been invited to address a community house forum only to find the invitation canceled when the sponsors learned more of the nature of his political history and affiliations. The matter appears to have been bungled, and the organization would doubtless have done better to let its invitation stand. But the clamor that the candidate's right of free speech had been violated was typical of the specious approach made even to this most fundamental of all rights.

3. *The right to a government job.* That a person can be dismissed from government service in such a way as to prejudice his chances for making a living in private life is beyond denial. However, the manifest importance of establishing fair dismissal procedure—fair to the individual and fair to the government— should not be clouded by any question as to an individual's

"right" to hold government office. Seth W. Richardson cleared the air on this point when he took over the chairmanship of the newly created Loyalty Review Board. "Legally," he said, "the government is entitled to discharge any employee for reasons which seem sufficient to the government, and without extending to such employee any hearing whatsoever. . . . We believe that the rights of the government in that respect are at least equal to those possessed by private employers." In this view, as has been pointed out by Arthur Krock, Mr. Richardson had behind him the force of a classic decision by the late Oliver Wendell Holmes, certainly no laggard in the protection of civil rights. Deciding the case of a policeman dismissed for political activity, Justice Holmes wrote:

> The petitioner may have a constitutional right to talk politics, but he has no constitutional right to be a policeman. . . . There are few employments for hire in which the servant does not agree to suspend his constitutional right of free speech, as well as idleness, by the implied terms of his contract. The servant cannot complain, as he takes the employment on the terms which are offered him. On the same principle the city may impose any reasonable condition upon holding offices within its control.

4. *The right of revolution.* In support of this concept, advanced only in lofty theoretical circles, reference is commonly made to the Declaration of Independence, the works of English political philosophers going back to 1688, and a few key passages from Jefferson and Lincoln. In particular, it is recalled that Jefferson once remarked that "the tree of liberty must be refreshed from time to time with the blood of patriots and tyrants"; and that on another occasion he invoked the Lord to "forbid that we should ever be twenty years without . . . a rebellion." I have no wish to question the self-evident truth, set forth in the Declaration, that "whenever any form of government becomes destructive of these ends [the rights to life, liberty, and the pursuit of happiness] it is the right of the people to alter or to abolish it, and institute new government." But while the Constitution provides the means of altering the government, it most assuredly provides no right to abolish it. No instrument of government does that, because no government can

at any time contemplate itself in the role of a destroyer of men's "unalienable rights." Revolution is a right that men will of necessity assume if long enough subjected to tyranny, but it is a natural right stemming from the concept that government derives its power from the consent of the governed, and not a right specifically conferred by the state.

It is fatuous, therefore, and paradoxical for revolutionists to argue, in effect, that in order to prove itself democratic a government must share their view that it has become tyrannical and must conspire with them in its own destruction by facilitating their activity. The destruction of the government is an end they will have to accomplish strictly on their own power, if they are intent on doing so, and at the risk that failure in such enterprises generally entails. Washington, fresh from a revolution of his own, effectively nullified the right of Daniel Shays and his men to resort to armed rebellion, though they could have made out a good case for it. And Lincoln, for all his statements that whenever a people "shall grow weary of the existing government, they can exercise . . . their revolutionary right to dismember or overthrow it," nevertheless fought a bloody war to prevent just such dismemberment. It need hardly be pointed out, perhaps, that those who invoke the "right of revolution" here will often defend any degree of tyranny in other countries as a legitimate protection of the state against those conspiring to overthrow it.

Recognizing the spuriousness of some of the Communist claims, sincere liberals nevertheless find themselves in a dilemma. They must steer a course between the hysteria whipped up by the Communists themselves, for purposes having little to do with civil liberties, and a repressive spirit in high places that can all too easily get out of hand. . . . Liberals must understand that the absolutist civil rights position presents a double danger: it fosters the growth of totalitarianism by a self-defeating tolerance and by virtue of that very growth it stimulates repressive measures from the Right, which, in turn, endanger the whole structure of civil liberties.

Freed of the self-imposed burden of opposing any and every restraint on the Communists, however unofficial, liberals might reexamine the "rights" claimed by Communists, separating the real from the factitious.

Conceding then, as many already do, that Communists not only have no "right" to government jobs but are in fact incongruous in the role of trusted workers for a government they have every desire to undermine and supplant, liberals might concentrate their attention on how to eliminate them without doing injustice either to the Communists in their capacity as private citizens or to innocent suspects. Denying the "right" of Communists to belong to other political organizations, liberals might the more readily defend the genuine right of Communists to maintain their own party openly and to speak freely in its name. Denying the "right" of the Communists to foment violence, liberals would be in that much better a position to defend the rights of all to advocate peaceable social change, however far reaching. And finally, denying the "right" of anyone to propagandize without responsibility, they would be able to sponsor effective governmental curbs on extremist groups without injuring the fabric of democracy.

FREE SPEECH AND ITS RELATION TO SELF-GOVERNMENT [6]

[The] Constitution derives whatever validity, whatever meaning, it has, not from its acceptance by our forefathers one hundred and sixty years ago, but from its acceptance by us, now. Clearly, however, we cannot, in any valid sense, "accept" the Constitution unless we know what it says. And, for that reason, every loyal citizen of the nation must join with his fellows in the attempt to interpret, in principle and in action, that provision of the Constitution which is rightly regarded as its most vital assertion, its most significant contribution to political wisdom. What do We, the People of the United States, mean when we provide for the freedom of belief and of the expression of belief?

[6] By Alexander Meiklejohn, philosopher and educator. From his book *Free Speech and Its Relation to Government*, p.ix-xiv. Harper & Brothers. New York. 1948. Reprinted by permission.

The First Amendment to the Constitution, as we all know, forbids the Federal Congress to make any law which shall abridge the freedom of speech. In recent years, however, the government of the United States has in many ways limited the freedom of public discussion. For example, the Federal Bureau of Investigation has built up, throughout the country, a system of espionage, of secret police, by which hundreds of thousands of our people have been listed as holding this or that set of opinions. The only conceivable justification of that listing by a government agency is to provide a basis for action by the government in dealing with those persons. And that procedure reveals an attitude toward freedom of speech which is widely held in the United States. Many of us are now convinced that, under the Constitution, the government is justified in bringing pressure to bear against the holding or expressing of beliefs which are labeled "dangerous." Congress, we think, may rightly abridge the freedom of such beliefs.

Again, the legislative committees, federal and state, which have been appointed to investigate un-American activities, express the same interpretation of the Constitution. All the inquirings and questionings of those committees are based upon the assumption that certain forms of political opinion and advocacy should be, and legitimately may be, suppressed. And, further, the Department of Justice, acting on the same assumption, has recently listed some sixty or more organizations, association with which may be taken by the government to raise the question of "disloyalty" to the United States. And finally, the President's Loyalty Order, moving with somewhat uncertain steps, follows the same road. We are officially engaged in the suppression of "dangerous" speech.

Now, these practices would seem to be flatly contradictory of the First Amendment. Are they? What do we mean when we say that "Congress shall make no law . . . abridging the freedom of speech"? What is this "freedom of speech" which we guard against invasion by our chosen and authorized agents? Why may not a man be prevented from speaking if, in the judgment of Congress, his ideas are hostile and harmful to the general welfare of the nation? Are we, for example, required by the First Amendment to give men freedom to advocate the abolition of the First Amendment? Are we bound to grant freedom of speech to those who, if they had the power, would refuse it to us? The First Amendment, taken literally, seems to answer "Yes" to those questions. It seems to say that no speech, however dangerous, may, for that reason, be suppressed. But the Federal Bureau of Investigation, the un-American activities committees, the Department of Justice, the President, are, at the same time, answering "No" to the same question. What is the valid American doctrine concerning the freedom of speech?

Throughout our history the need of clear and reasonable answering of that question has been very urgent. In fact, under our system of dealing with problems of domestic policy by "party" discussion and "party" action, the demand for such clarity and reasonableness is basic to our "democratic" way of life. But, with the ending of World War II, that demand has taken on a new, and even greater, urgency. Our nation has now assumed, or has had thrust upon it by Fate, a new role. We have taken leadership in the advocating of freedom of expression and of communication, not only at home, but also throughout the world. In the waging of that campaign we Americans have made many accusations against our enemies in war, hot or cold. But our most furious and righteous charge has been that they have suppressed, and are suppressing, the free exchange of information and of ideas. That evil drawing of a smoke curtain, we have declared, we will not tolerate. We will not submit to it within our own borders. We will not allow it abroad if, by legitimate means, we can prevent it. We are determined that, with respect to the freedom of its communications, the human world shall be a single community.

Now, the assuming of that high and heavy responsibility for a political principle requires of us, first of all, that we understand what the principle is. We must think for it as well as fight for it. No fighting, however successful, will help to establish freedom unless the winners know what freedom is. What, then—we citizens under the Constitution must ask—what do we mean when we utter the flaming proclamation of the First Amendment? Do we mean that speaking may be suppressed or that it may not be suppressed? And, in either case, on what grounds has the decision been made?

The issue here presented has been dramatically, though perhaps not very effectively, thrust upon the attention of the citizens of the United States by a recent order of the Attorney General. That order restricts the freedom of speech of temporary foreign visitors to our shores. It declares that certain classes of visitors are forbidden, except by special permission, to engage in public discussion of public policy while they are among us. Why may we not hear what these men from other countries, other systems of government, have to say? For what purpose does the Attorney General impose limits upon their speaking, upon our hearing? The plain truth is that he is seeking to protect the minds of the citizens of this free nation of ours from the influence of assertions, of doubts, of questions, of plans, of principles which the government judges to be too "dangerous" for us to hear. He is afraid that we, whose agent he is, will be led astray by opinions which are alien and subversive. Do We, the People of the United States, wish to be thus mentally "protected"? To say that would seem to be an admission that we are intellectually and morally unfit to play our part in what Justice Holmes has called the "experiment" of self-government. Have we, on that ground, abandoned or qualified the great experiment?

Here, then, is the question which we must try to answer as we interpret the First Amendment to the Constitution. In our discussions of public policy at home, do we intend that "dangerous" ideas shall be suppressed? Or are they, under the Constitution, guaranteed freedom from such suppression? And, correspondingly, in our dealings with other nations, are we saying to them, "The general welfare of the world requires that you and we shall not, in any way, abridge the freedom of expression and communication?" Or are we saying, "Every nation may, of course, forbid and punish the expression of ideas which are dangerous to the form of government or of industrial organization which it has established and is attempting to maintain"?

No one, of course, may prescribe that citizens of the United States shall interpret the Constitution in this way or that. It is not even required that the meaning of the Constitution shall be in the future what it has been in the past. We are free to change that meaning both by interpretation and by explicit amendment. But what is required of us by every consideration of honesty and self-respect is that we practice what we preach, that we preach only what we practice. What, then, as we deal with the present, as we plan for the future, do we intend that the principle of the freedom of speech shall mean?

COMMUNISM VS. THE CONSTITUTION [7]

We are now engaged in defending our country and ourselves against Russian aggression, which has created, supported and used Communist parties and "front" organizations in other lands to assist and spearhead its efforts to undermine and seize governments through other means than the free electoral choice of the peoples concerned. Although "sedition" is an ancient evil, the Soviet-Communist use of seditious organizations as a "fifth column" against governments in other countries is of comparatively recent origin. "Sedition" is used in this paper to describe advocacy of the overthrow of our federal or state governments by force and violence if need be. It is intended to mean what is sometimes called "peacetime treason"; the use of the word "treason" does not convey what is meant in view of its restricted constitutional definition and requirements. "Sedition," as thus used here, does not include mere criticism or libels of government or public officials, which were forbidden by the obnoxious Sedition Act of 1798. The terms used in this paper have to be taken in their modern connotations, in the light of the revelations as to Communist organizations, methods, and objectives.

Marx and Engels began teaching communism in 1848, a hundred years ago. The objectives of this seditious philosophy, as consistently stated by all of its interpreters from Marx to Stalin, have been the overthrow of capitalism throughout the world by violence, the establishment of the dictatorship of the proletariat; and by the extinction of the bourgeoisie, the attainment of a so-

[7] From article by Frank B. Ober, of the Maryland Bar (Baltimore). *American Bar Association Journal.* 34:645-8+. August 1948. Reprinted by permission.

called "classless society," in which the state will eventually wither away.

This sinister, corroding doctrine makes its chief appeal to those in such poverty that they have nothing to lose by a change. Revolution inevitably feeds on distress. It also attracts political opportunists, gullible mystics or so-called intelligentsia, whose theories have never been tested by the hard facts of reality.

Although the doctrine of communism has been taught for a century, it achieved its first *practical* success in the bloody Russian revolution of thirty years ago. It thus changed from an abstract international philosophy to a weapon of nationalist aggression. The Comintern was then formed in Moscow, with sections in each country, to further Russian aims.

The American Communist party was formed as a section of the Comintern in 1919, in response to the directions of its president Zinoviev. Absolute obedience to the Comintern was required of its branch parties in other countries. Leaders of the American party, such as Browder and Foster, have been members of the Executive Committee of the Comintern, making frequent trips to Moscow for instructions, and the Executive Committee itself is under the complete domination of the Kremlin.

This so-called dictatorship of the proletariat really means a one-man control of a political oligarchy that rules, through an active Communist party of 6,000,000, a great nation of some 200,000,000. Such a government can only be maintained through a ruthless police state, which is the complete antithesis of our constitutional form of government. Such a state tolerates but one party and liquidates or enslaves its political opponents, and rules its own people, through a secret police, by terroristic methods; it denies freedom of speech and assembly and makes a mockery of the administration of justice. Today, ten to twenty million political prisoners are held in slave camps in Russia, in addition to millions of war captives.

Considered from the standpoint of true liberalism, or human freedom, it is the most reactionary of all forms of government that have been known in the recorded history of the world.

While the formation of Communist parties in other countries under the domination of the Comintern manifested her ultimate aggressive intent against other nations, Russia was for more than twenty years too occupied with her own revolutions, famine and experiments, to constitute any imminent threat to the rest of the world. This long period of inactivity lulled the rest of the world into a false feeling of security.

Meanwhile, as pointed out by Mr. Churchill, communism had begotten fascism and the more murderously efficient nazism through which Hitler came to power. It was Hitler who perfected and improved the weapon which the Communists had forged, the seditious fifth column, to aid him in his conquests of other countries. In Austria, in the critical year 1938, and in Czechoslovakia and Norway later, Nazi parties and local Quislings aided his armies. The Communists, then temporarily allied with Hitler, also contributed largely to the fall of France. Russian communism commenced its expansion, successfully using seditious fifth columns in conquering, between 1939 and 1948, ten Eastern European nations, with a population of 93,000,000 and an area of some 629,000 square miles. The pattern of the Communist method is clear: (1) organization of a strongly disciplined Communist party with members who are individually pledged to carry out the mandates of their leaders, who, as history abundantly shows, slavishly follow the party line, irrespective of their own national interests—the opposition to war during the temporary Russian alliance with Hitler and subsequent support thereof is perhaps the most dramatic example out of a multitude of instances of goose-stepping to Kremlin music; (2) infiltration of labor unions to stir up industrial strife for political ends; (3) espionage and sabotage; (4) planting of Communists in key government positions; particularly in police and army posts; (5) forcible overthrow of the existing government by the minority Communist party at some psychological moment of political or economic crisis, and usually with the presence or threat of the Red army; (6) elimination of all opposition parties and the liquidation of their leaders; and (7) finally, the formalization of the conquest through so-called democratic elections, at which 100 per cent of the electors are frightened into voting for the Communist party and the local Quislings selected by Moscow.

The "cold war" in other countries is in full swing, Finland is in process of absorption, and a third or more of the voters in France and Italy vote the Communist ticket, though their recent bids for power were unsuccessful. In China, the Communists, with Russian support, control a large part of the country.

There are likewise strong Communist parties in most of the countries in the Western Hemisphere, as the Canadian spy trials and recent violent events in Chile, Brazil, Colombia and Costa Rica have warned. In our country the party is credited with less than 100,000 members, yet, as pointed out by J. Edgar Hoover, we should not be lulled into a false complacency, because, as the Communist boast, for every one who is an active member there are ten ready to follow the Communist line. They have so cleverly maneuvered themselves into strategic positions that never in history did so few control the thoughts and actions of so many.

We have but recently been reminded by Mr. Churchill of the almost incredible mistake of the democratic countries in permitting Germany to rearm after World War I, which led inevitably to World War II. Warfare is no longer preceded by formal declarations. "Cold" warfare is waged during intervals of peace, or the armed truce which is so often blindly mistaken for peace. We have just proved again that, under our Constitution and given sufficient time and protection by allies to prepare, a war can be magnificently won. But once again we see the danger signals of another war and the establishment of beachheads in the form of seditious parties.

When the actual shooting starts, statutes giving necessary power to protect the nation and prosecute the war, such as the War Powers, Espionage and Trading with Enemy Acts, are upheld by the Courts under the war power. However, it is becoming increasingly apparent that we must have the power to prevent sedition before the shooting starts, if we are to keep out of war, or be in a position to successfully defend ourselves again. It is of particular importance, therefore, to examine how the efforts of Congress, the Executive and the states to prevent sedition in peacetime have fared under the Constitution as interpreted by the new Supreme Court.

Taking Congress first—four of its more important efforts have been (1) to prevent naturalization of, or to deport seditious aliens; (2) to legislate directly against sedition; (3) to hinder and control sedition through alien and other registration statutes; and (4) to purge the government and labor unions of Communist or other seditious persons.

1. It is manifestly impossible to screen aliens properly when naturalized, and hence the statute provides for the deportation of seditious aliens. The importance of the alien problem lies not in the threat from a few seditious aliens considered as separate individuals. But there is danger, inherent in having 5,000,-000 aliens in our midst, that there will be built up seditious organizations on a large scale, even though most aliens are loyal. Even before the 1938 rape of Austria, when the danger of seditious organizations was first clearly demonstrated by current history, the Supreme Court, as then constituted, seven times, without a dissenting voice, had upheld Congressional efforts to prevent infiltration by seditious citizens, upon evidence that the applicant had not satisfied the conditions Congress had made prerequisite to citizenship.

But in 1943 the new Court, by a five-to-three decision, in the *Schneiderman* case, reversed the findings of both lower Courts, which had held that a Communist organizer and leader should be deported for having been naturalized by mistake, because he had plainly spent his life, before and after his naturalization in 1927, in *attacking* the Constitution, and could therefore scarcely be considered "attached" to its principles, as required by the statute then in force. To protect this Communist the majority of the new Court refused to apply the usual rule giving finality to concurrent findings of fact by two lower Courts where supported by substantial evidence. Next, while conceding there was evidence on which a reasonable man could find the Communist party urged the overthrow of government by violence, it held that the opposite finding would be a "tenable conclusion." Chief Justice Stone, in a strong dissenting opinion concurred in by Justices Roberts and Frankfurter, from a wealth of documentary evidence, pointed out (1) the American Communist party was a section of the Comintern; (2) it repeatedly and systematically

advocated illegal acts and the forcible overthrow of government;
(3) it was instructed "to join systematically lawful and unlawful
work" under penalty of expulsion, and "create everywhere a
parallel illegal apparatus which at the decisive moment should
do its duty by the party and in every way possible assist the
revolution"; and (4) its refusal to assist the efforts to undermine and destroy the army was held treason to the Third International. He concluded by saying:

> It would be little short of preposterous to assert that vigorous aid,
> knowingly given by a pledged party member in disseminating the party
> teachings to which reference has been made, is compatible with attach-
> ment to the principles of the Constitution.

Congress attempted in the Act of June 28, 1940, to tighten
the deportation laws by providing for the deportation of any
person who had at any time within five years after entry been
a member of or affiliated with a party advocating the forcible
overthrow of government. Nevertheless, in 1945, the Supreme
Court refused, in a habeas corpus proceeding, to sustain the
deportation of Bridges. The administrative officers had found
sufficient evidence that Bridges had been a Communist. But the
majority of the Court thought the government had not proved
the case. They reversed the finding of the hearing officers,
Judge Sears and Attorney General Biddle. As was pointed out
in the dissent of Chief Justice Stone, Justices Roberts and Frankfurter, the Court thus ignored the rule, consistently followed in
all other types of cases, that the Court will not disturb an administrative finding if there is substantial evidence to sustain it.

The *Girouard* case in 1946, which overruled three earlier cases
denying naturalization to applicants who qualified their allegiance
by refusal to bear arms for their new country, though less directly
pertinent, follows the same pattern.

2. Congress has legislated directly against sedition in such
statutes as the Civil War Seditious Conspiracy Act, making it a
crime to conspire to overthrow the government, and this Act
was applied in 1937 by the First Circuit Court of Appeals to a
conspiracy to overthrow the Porto Rican Government.

The Subversive Activities Act of June 28, 1940, in addition
to proscribing incitement to mutiny in the armed forces, makes
it unlawful for individuals to willfully advocate or circulate

printed matter advocating the forcible overthrow of government, or to organize any group for that purpose, "or to be or become a member of . . . such . . . group . . . *knowing the purposes thereof.*" This latter part has been upheld by the Circuit Court of Appeals of the Eighth Circuit in 1943 in the *Dunne* case, but mere denial by the Supreme Court of certiorari leaves doubt as to whether it will be ultimately upheld.

3. A third class of statutes, aimed at indirectly controlling sedition by registration, includes:

The Alien Registration Act of 1940, under which almost 5,000,000 aliens have been registered; the Foreign Agents Registration Act, requiring the registration of all foreign agents, and under which there are currently registered some 252 agents of foreign governments; the Voorhis Act, requiring registration of subversive organizations.

The first two acts have been held constitutional. But the Voorhis Act, requiring registration of subversive organizations, has apparently not been passed upon, and only five organizations have registered under this Act.

4. The fourth class of congressional statutes seeks to purge the government of disloyal employees.

The Hatch Act, for example, makes it unlawful for a federal employee to advocate or to have membership in a political organization advocating the forcible overthrow of the government. All recent appropriation acts, in addition, make it a felony for such disloyal employees to receive money from any appropriation.

This part of the Hatch Act has not been specifically ruled upon by the Supreme Court. Doubt is cast on its constitutionality by the broad language in the *Lovett* case in 1946, where a rider to an appropriation bill, directed at withholding the salaries of three named individuals whom Congress deemed subversive, was held unconstitutional as a bill of attainder.

A somewhat similar effort has been made by Congress in the Taft-Hartley Act to purge labor unions of Communist leadership, in recognition of the fact that control of labor unions is the most powerful weapon of the Communists, as indicated by current events in Europe. This statute has been sustained in lower court decisions.

The Mundt-Nixon Bill passed the House by a vote of 385 to 58 in May, but was not acted on by the Senate. After finding that Communist political organizations are part of a worldwide conspiracy directed by a foreign power against the United States, it, among other things, makes unlawful attempts to establish a totalitarian dictatorship under foreign control; denies employment and passports to members of such organizations knowing them to be of that type; and requires registration of such organizations as the Attorney General, subject to judicial review, determines to be Communist political or Communist front organizations.

The American Bar Association's House of Delegates passed a strong resolution supporting this type of legislation. The bill does not, in terms, outlaw membership in the Communist party, as the overwhelming majority of our people would like, as evidenced by a three to one vote in a recent Gallup poll. It is submitted that the direct prosecution in *Court* of seditious organizations and their leaders and, on conviction, the confiscation of their funds and papers, would be more just and effective than mere registration with the Attorney General—which would seem to involve both penalties under the proposed statute, and a confession of guilt under other statutes.

To recapitulate, Congress has met successive defeats by the Supreme Court in a series of efforts to tighten naturalization laws; has passed many laws aimed at purging the executive departments of Communists; and the Subversive Activities Act of June 28, 1940, to supplement the Civil War Conspiracy Act, which laws still have to run the gauntlet of the Supreme Court; and has passed registration acts aimed at indirectly controlling sedition, which have been upheld. In response to a widespread public demand, the House has passed the Mundt-Nixon Bill, designed to implement the fight against sedition, but its future in the Senate and Supreme Court remains in doubt. [The bill never passed the Senate.] Congress has not, however, outlawed the party or prevented Communists from having seats in Congress, itself. A Communist, while a felon, if he accepts pay from the executive department and is subject to prosecution also under anti-sedition statutes, may apparently run on the Communist ticket and be elected to Congress.

IDEOLOGY FOR DEMOCRACY [8]

The very first thing we need to do is to acquire all the knowledge we can about communism. That first step is basic to all others. In any kind of contest, there is great advantage in knowing all one can about one's competitor, his strong points and his weak points. That is true as between individuals; it is true as between nations, and it is even more emphatically true as between conflicting ideologies.

You in education know better than most of us how true that is. When you go at a problem, you hunt for all the facts, line them up, add them up, strain them through the colander of candor. You don't let facts truckle to preconceptions or pet prejudices. And you don't let blind emotionalism obscure them.

We know so little about communism, and we need to know so much. We need to know how communism is planted and how it takes root in the minds of men—why men turn to communism.

We have been inclined to lump Communists in one all-embracing category and blind ourselves to the clear evidence on every hand that there are many reasons why men turn Communist.

The Communist strategist knows this well, and trades upon the susceptibilities of different kinds of people with widely varying appeals. We must recognize that fact before we can get answers to questions such as these:

Why, for instance, should any Swiss be a Communist, when Switzerland's democracy has been a vigorous, going force for three hundred years, and the Swiss have lived in economic and political order, in peace and in relative prosperity? But there are Communists in Switzerland.

Why should a Swede—a citizen of the great "middleway" nation—turn Communist? But there are Swedish Communists.

And above all else, why should an American—living in the most favored, prosperous country in the world—become a Communist? But we have American Communists.

[8] From address by Eric Johnston, President, Motion Picture Association, before the Iowa State Education Association, November 5, 1948. Motion Picture Association of America, Washington, D.C. p. 4-7. Reprinted by permission.

The very existence of Communists in these countries tells us that communism is no longer just an appeal to the *workers* of the world to unite because they have nothing to lose but their chains.

It has outgrown such swaddling siren songs. It still uses all its old appeals, but today it bids boldly for the intellectual, the disgruntled, the credulous and the cultured—as well as the hungry, the poor and the miserable.

Broadly speaking, there are at least five types of Communists, and perhaps each type could have various subdivisions.

First, there is the Lenin type of Communist. These are the doctrinaires, the revolutionists, the fanatics. They are willing to take any risk—any chance—to gain their ends. Such are the men who rule Russia—the members of the Politburo, their commissars and lesser party leaders—their camp followers. They are cold cynical realists, unswayed by emotion.

Second, there is the intellectual Communist. He may be utterly sincere in a faith that communism is all it claims to be. He may, in fact, believe completely that communism is the sheltering arm for the hopeless and the despairing. He is infatuated with the theoretical utopia he calls communism.

Third, there is the man-against-the-world Communist. He may have a personal grievance against the old order; racial discrimination or the childhood memory of injustice to himself or to his family may prompt his conversion. Or, again, he may be merely frustrated by his own inability to move ahead in a democratic world. He may believe that communism will give him the miracle of rebirth.

Fourth, there is the emotionally immature Communist. He may be snared by the Communist appeal for a brotherhood of man. He may see it as the only way for him to help reform the world. It is possible he revels in the conspiratorial aspect of communism. Or he may simply have gulped the story that communism will inevitably rule the world, and he wants to be on the winning side. Caught young, this type of Communist often falls away from the faith as he matures, learns to think for himself and understands that he was duped by false slogans and false promises.

Fifth, there is the stomach Communist. He turns to communism in sheer desperation. The fine points of Communist ideology mean little or nothing to him. Saving the world means little or nothing to him either. He wants to save himself. He is hungry. The democracy he has known seems to have failed him, and the new and more resounding promises of communism ring loud in ears which belong to a starving body.

Communism dangles before the man who has nothing at all, the promise of a plot of land—a share in a factory—any material inducement he may want. It was with such glittering and gaudy pledges for the future that communism made marked headway in Italy. In Italy there are more than two million card-carrying Communists today—more than in any other country outside of Russia itself—and eight million persons, one out of every three Italian voters, cast Communist ballots in the last election.

The great rank and file of Communists and Communist sympathizers in the non-Communist world today come in this fifth type—the stomach Communist. The worker level is the arena where the main event of Democracy vs. Communism is being fought.

Russia cannot create the conditions in which communism takes root. She can aggravate them and take advantage of them. She does. She exploits them to the utmost through her ideological warfare with democracy. Everywhere you look, Communist techniques twist and turn and back and fill in the hunt for the best chances to stab at the existing order and needle it for its failures and inequities.

It's important to keep in mind that basic Communist dogma remains fixed, and so do its objectives. But its methods and approaches are as shifty as the footwork of a skilled boxer.

Just as communism plays on the varying susceptibilities of different kinds of individuals, its approach may vary from country to country.

Collectivization of the land is a fundamental dogma of Communist ideology, but look at the different tactical approaches on this problem in Italy and France.

In Italy where farm land is held in huge estates, the Communists promise to break up and distribute the holdings among the people.

In France, where there is wide diffusion of land ownership, the Communists have submerged propaganda about land division and have concentrated on the injustices and hardships of industrial workers.

Capitalizing on the injustices of established systems is the negative side of the Communist technique. On the more positive side, Russia is trying to buy people with the promise of a better tomorrow for themselves and their children. Communism offers a mixed bouquet of blandishments and beguilements. It has something for everybody in its promises of a materialistic utopia. It is going to end war, it says; and all depressions, all want, all injustice, all inequalities. It will cure every ill of the world—down to and including rheumatism, dandruff and the common cold.

But her propaganda salesmen skillfully whitewash the hardships, sufferings and injustices in Russia in the last thirty years and in the satellite countries in the last few years.

We may laugh at the Communist promises and call them absurd and preposterous, but there are millions of people who don't laugh at them. They accept them and believe them.

Let's quit laughing, and start thinking and acting wisely. The ability of communism to use the grievances of the masses as ladders to power is a deadly serious thing. It converts its ideology to power, then entrenches that power irreversibly by police state methods. No country thus far has thrown off communism once it has come into power, because the secret ballot goes out when the secret police come in.

Ideological warfare is a high-falutin' phrase in American ears, but call it what we will, we must meet it head-on. We must meet it with a positive ideology of our own. Communism is selling our weaknesses: we should be able to sell some of our strengths. And the sooner we overcome our weaknesses the more powerful story we'll have to tell.

COMMUNISM IN THE UNITED STATES [9]

The Communist movement in the United States began to manifest itself in 1919. Since then it has changed its name and its party line whenever expedient. But always it comes back to fundamentals and bills itself as the party of "Marxism-Leninism." As such, it stands for the destruction of our American form of government; it stands for the destruction of American democracy; it stands for the destruction of free enterprise; and it stands for the creation of a "Soviet of the United States" and ultimate *world* revolution.

The preamble of the latest constitution of the Communist party of the United States proclaims that the party "educates the working class, in the course of its day-to-day struggles, for its historic mission, the establishment of socialism."

The phrase "historic mission" means to the Communist, using his own words, "achieving the dictatorship of the proletariat; . . . to raise these revolutionary forces to the surface and hurl them like a devastating avalanche upon the united forces of bourgeois reaction, frenzied at the presentiment of their rapidly approaching doom."

In recent years the Communists have been very cautious about using such phrases as "force and violence." Nevertheless, it is the subject of much discussion in their schools and in party caucus where they readily admit that the only way in which they can defeat the present ruling class is by world revolution.

The Communist realizes that he can create his order in the United States only by "bloody revolution." *The History of the Communist Party of the Soviet Union* is used as a basis for planning their revolution. Their tactics require that to be successful they must have:

1. The will and sympathy of the people.
2. Military aid and assistance.

[9] By J. Edgar Hoover, Director, Federal Bureau of Investigation; Member of the Board of Trustees, George Washington University. Based on statement made before House Committee on Un-American Activities, March 26, 1947. *Confidential —from Washington*. No. 47. George Washington University. Washington, D.C. June 1948. Reprinted by permission.

3. Plenty of guns and ammunition.

4. A program of extermination of the police, as they are the most important enemy and are termed trained Fascists.

5. Seizure of all communications including radio stations; busses, railroads, and other forms of transportation.

They evade the question of force and violence, publicly. They hold that when Marxists speak of force and violence they will not be responsible—that force and violence will be the responsibility of their enemies. They adopt the novel premise that they do not advocate force and violence publicly but that when their class resists to defend themselves then they are thus accused of using force and violence.

Anyone who opposes the American Communist, the Communist party of the United States, is branded as a "disrupter," a "Fascist," a "Red baiter" or a "Hitlerite," and becomes the object of a systematic campaign of character assassination. This is easily understood because the basic tactics of the Communist party are deceit and trickery.

The great god of the American Communists, Comrade Lenin, in various speeches and writings urged the use of deceit and trickery and his converts live by his injunction: "The strictest loyalty to the ideas of communism must be combined with the ability to make all necessary practical compromises, to maneuver, to make agreements, zig-zags, retreats and so on, so as to accelerate the coming to power."

Lenin's views were incorporated in the *Thesis on the Fundamental Tasks of the Second Congress of the Communist International*. The following provision is familiar to all American Communists:

> In all countries, even the freest, "legal and peaceful" in the sense that the class struggle is less acute in them, the time has fully matured when it is absolutely necessary for every Communist party systematically to combine legal with illegal work, legal with illegal organization. ... It is necessary, immediately for all legal Communist parties to form illegal organizations . . . Illegal work is particularly necessary in the Army, the Navy, and police . . . .

Continuing, the Thesis states:

The absolute necessity in principle of combining illegal with legal work is determined, not only by the sum total of the specific features of the present period, the period of the eve of the proletarian dictatorship, but also by the necessity of proving to the bourgeoise that there is not, nor can there be, a sphere or field of work that cannot be won by the Communists.

On May 28, 1942, Hon. Francis Biddle, then Attorney General, in reviewing the deportation proceedings of Harry Bridges, found that the Communist party from the time of its inception in 1919 believes in, advises, advocates, and teaches the overthrow by force and violence of the Government of the United States.

Since then much has happened to the Communist movement. In 1944 the party dissolved and became the Communist Political Association. The constitution of the new CPA in 1944 omitted references to "Leninism" and the "Historic Mission." That was the era when they were advocating a second front and all-out production for victory in the war. But, even then, they secretly held to their historic mission. In an injunction to party members, Eugene Dennis, now general secretary of the party, said, "Irrespective of name, we are and shall continue to be an American working class political organization, guided by the science of Marxism-Leninism."

But that era was short-lived. Immediately after Jacques Duclos, the French Communist leader, blasted the American Communists as deserting the Marxian cause, the CPA was relegated to oblivion and the present Communist party of the United States was reborn. A new constitution adopted in July 1945, referred to the party as basing itself "upon the principles of scientific socialism, Marxism-Leninism" and reincorporated the reference to the party's "historic mission."

In establishing the party's illegal character in 1942, the then Attorney General Biddle based his findings on the contents of the same Communist publications which today are being sold and circulated in party circles. The American Communist, like the leopard, cannot change his spots.

The Communist party line changes from day to day. The one cardinal rule that can always be applied to what the party line is or will be is found in the fundamental principle that the support of Soviet Russia is the duty of Communists of all countries.

One thing is certain. The progress which all good citizens seek, such as old-age security, houses for veterans, and a host of others, is being adopted as window dressing by the Communists to conceal their true aims and entrap gullible followers.

The record of the American Communists conclusively proves their true feelings. In the prewar days, when they were allied with Hitler, they marched on Washington protesting selective service, lend-lease, and shouted "The Yanks are not coming." The American Peace Mobilization picketed the White House until the day before the Nazis marched into Russia. Then within less than a month, it reconverted into the American People's Mobilization, demanded all-out production, and started the chant for the second front.

The march of Red fascism is a cause for concern in America. But the deceit, the trickery, and the lies of the American Communists are catching up with them. Whenever the spotlight of truth is focused upon them they cry, "Red baiting."

The numerical strength of the party's enrolled membership is insignificant. But it is well known that there are many actual members who because of their position are not carried on party rolls.

The Communists claim that for every party member there are ten others ready, willing, and able to do the party's work. Herein lies the greatest menace of communism. These are the people who infiltrate and corrupt various spheres of American life. So rather than the size of the Communist party the way to weigh its true importance is by testing its influence, its ability to infiltrate.

The size of the party is relatively unimportant because of the enthusiasm and iron-clad discipline under which they operate. It might be of interest to observe that in 1917 when the Communists overthrew the Russian Government there was one Communist for every 2,277 persons in Russia. In the United

States there is one Communist for every 1,814 persons in the country.

One who accepts the aims, principles, and program of the party, who attends meetings, who reads the party press and literature, who pays dues and who is active on behalf of the party "shall be considered a member." The open, avowed Communist who carries a card and pays dues is no different from a security standpoint than the person who does the party's work but pays no dues, carries no cards, and is not on the party rolls. In fact, the latter is a greater menace because of his opportunity to work in stealth.

The burden of proof should be placed upon those who consistently follow the ever-changing party line. Fellow travelers and sympathizers can deny party membership but they can never escape the fact that they have played into the Communist hands, thus furthering the Communist cause by playing the role of innocent, gullible, or wilful allies.

The Communists have developed one of the greatest propaganda machines the world has ever known. They have been able to penetrate and infiltrate many respectable and reputable public-opinion mediums.

They capitalize upon ill-founded charges, associating known honest progressive liberals with left-wing causes. There are few appellations more degrading than "Communist." It should be reserved for those justly deserving the degradation.

The Communist propaganda technique is designed to promote emotional response with the hope that the victim will be attracted by what he is told the Communist way of life holds in store for him. The objective is to develop discontent and hasten the day when the Communists can gather sufficient support and following to overthrow the American way of life.

Communist propaganda is slanted in the hope that the Communist may be aligned with liberal progressive causes. The honest liberal and progressive should be alert to this. The Communists' most effective foe can be the real liberals and progressives who understand their devious machinations.

Communists and their followers are prolific letter writers. Some of the more energetic ones direct numerous letters of protest to editors, signing a different name to each. Members of Congress are well aware of Communists starting their pressure campaigns by an avalanche of mail which follows the party line.

The party has departed from depending upon the printed word as its medium of propaganda and has taken to the air. Its members and sympathizers have not only infiltrated the airways but they are now persistently seeking radio channels.

The American Communists launched a furtive attack on the motion picture industry in 1935 by the issuance of a directive calling for a concentration in Hollywood. The orders called for action on two fronts: (1) an effort to infiltrate the labor unions; (2) to infiltrate the so-called intellectual and creative fields.

In movie circles, Communists developed an effective defense a few years ago in meeting criticism. They would counter with the question, "After all, what is the matter with communism?" It was effective because many persons did not possess adequate knowledge of the subject to give an intelligent answer.

The party is content if it is possible to have inserted in a picture a line, a scene, a sequence, conveying the Communist lesson and, more particularly, if they can keep out anti-Communist lessons.

The Communist tactic of infiltrating labor unions stems from the earliest teachings of Marx, which have been reiterated by party spokesmen down through the years. They often succeed in penetrating and literally taking over labor unions before the rank and file of members are aware of what has occurred.

The great masses of union men and women are patriotic American citizens interested chiefly in security for their families and themselves. In those instances where Communists have taken control of unions, it has been because too many union men and women have been outwitted, outmaneuvered, and outwaited by Communists.

The Communists have never relied on numerical strength to dominate a labor organization. Through infiltration tactics they have in many instances captured positions of authority. Communists have boasted that with 5 per cent of the membership the Communists, with their militancy, superior organizational ability and discipline, could control the union.

If more union members took a more active role and asserted themselves it would become increasingly difficult for Communists to gain control. Patriotic union members can easily spot sympathizers and party members in conventions and union meetings because invariably the latter strive to establish the party line instead of serving the best interests of the union and the country.

The recent Canadian spy trials revealed the necessity of alertness in keeping Communists and sympathizers out of government services. The high command of the Communist party regards such assignments of sufficient importance to demand that party members not contact fellow members in the government. If such government employees are carried on party rolls at all they are assigned an alias. Instructions were issued that all party membership cards of government employees be destroyed and that party organizational meetings in government circles be discontinued. Informal social or union gatherings which could not be identified as Communist meetings were to be continued. The dangers of permitting Communists or sympathizers to work in government circles are obvious.

There has developed, however, as a result of Communist propaganda, some fanciful feeling that no distinction should be drawn and that Communists have a right to government jobs.

From July 1, 1941 to March 26, 1947, the FBI investigated 6,193 cases under the Hatch Act, which forbids membership upon the part of any government employee in any organization advocating the overthrow of the Government of the United States.

For the purposes of investigation the Attorney General has ruled that a number of organizations in addition to the Communist party are subversive under the Hatch Act because of Communist influence.

The FBI does not make recommendations. It merely reports facts and it is up to the interested government departments to make a decision. Almost invariably, of course, subjects of investigations deny affiliation with subversive groups, often despite strong evidence to the contrary.

The united-front program of the Communist party was launched at the Seventh World Congress of the Communist International in 1935. The Communist party in the United States immediately took up the program and a systematic plan was worked out of infiltrating existing organizations with Communists.

For the most part, front organizations assumed the character of either a mass or membership organization or a paper organization. Both solicited and used names of prominent persons. Hundreds of groups and organizations have either been infiltrated or organized primarily to accomplish the purposes of promoting the interests of the Soviet Union in the United States, the promotion of Soviet war and peace aims, the exploitation of Negroes in the United States, work among foreign-language groups, and to secure a favorable viewpoint toward the Communists in domestic, political, social, and economic issues.

The first requisite for a front organization is an idealistic title. Hundreds of such organizations have come into being and have gone out of existence when their true purposes have become known or exposed while others are continually springing up.

The Communist party of the United States is a fifth column. It is far better organized than were the Nazis in occupied countries prior to their capitulation. They are seeking to weaken America just as they did in their era of obstruction when they were aligned with the Nazis. Their goal is the overthrow of our government.

There is no doubt as to where a real Communist's loyalty rests. Their allegiance is to Russia, not the United States.

A Communist leader made the following statement: "I believe that everyone should know that we are for Russia and if need be we will die for the cause. I don't mean that war with Russia is coming soon. I hope not, so that Russia will be better prepared."

What can we do? And what should be our course of action? The best antidote to communism is vigorous, intelligent, old-fashioned Americanism with eternal vigilance. I do not favor any course of action which would give the Communists cause to portray themselves as martyrs. I do favor unrelenting prosecution wherever they are found to be violating our country's laws.

As Americans, our most effective defense is a workable democracy that guarantees and preserves our cherished freedoms.

I would have no fears if more Americans possessed the zeal, the fervor, the persistence, and the industry to learn about this menace of red fascism.

Once public opinion is thoroughly aroused as it is today, the fight against communism is well on its way. Victory will be assured once Communists are identified and exposed, because the public will take the first step of quarantining them so they can do no harm. Communism, in reality, is not a political party. It is a way of life—an evil and malignant way of life. It reveals a condition akin to disease that spreads like an epidemic and like an epidemic a quarantine is necessary to keep it from infecting the nation.

THE TEST OF A FRONT ORGANIZATION

These are easy tests to establish the real character of front organizations:

1. Does the group espouse the cause of Americanism or the cause of Soviet Russia?

2. Does the organization feature as speakers at its meetings known Communists, sympathizers or fellow travellers?

3. Does the organization shift when the party line shifts?

4. Does the organization sponsor causes, campaigns, literature, petitions, or other activities sponsored by the party or other front organizations?

5. Is the organization used as a sounding board by or is it endorsed by Communist-controlled labor unions?

6. Does its literature follow the Communist line or is it printed by the Communist press?

7. Does the organization receive consistent favorable mention in Communist publications?

8. Does the organization represent itself to be non-partisan yet engaged in political activities and consistently advocate causes favored by the Communists?

9. Does the organization denounce American and British foreign policy while always lauding Soviet policy?

10. Does the organization utilize Communist "double talk" by referring to Soviet-dominated countries as democracies, complaining that the United States is imperialistic and constantly denouncing monopoly capital?

11. Have outstanding leaders in public life openly renounced affiliation with the organization?

12. Does the organization, if espousing liberal progressive causes, attract well-known honest patriotic liberals or does it denounce well-known liberals?

13. Does the organization have a consistent record of supporting the American viewpoint over the years?

14. Does the organization consider matters not directly related to its avowed purposes and objectives?

THE RED WEB IN U.S. LABOR [10]

Everyone knows that the Communists have infiltrated a considerable number of labor unions in the United States, to wield power far out of proportion to their numbers. But the average American has only a foggy idea of how this has been accomplished. The Communists don't just get up in a union meeting and say, forthrightly, "We're moving in." Their ways are dark and devious. They are masters of the smear, adept at worming into key offices and committees, unsurpassed at spreading dissension and confusion, and extraordinarily clever at manipulating stupid, gullible and power-hungry labor leaders.

The technique of gaining control of a labor union is the same, on a smaller scale and with slight modifications, as that used by the Soviet Union in taking over the governments of neighbors in eastern Europe.

During the years in which I was a Communist party member, organizer and editor, I helped develop this technique. I have seen it operate many times, under direct orders from Moscow, to bring a labor union under the domination of Communists whose

[10] From article by Louis Francis Budenz, Professor of Economics, Fordham University. *Collier's.* 122:13-14+. October 23, 1948. Reprinted by permission.

every act was motivated by a fanatical devotion to the interests of Soviet Russia alone. I know of no union in which the Communists comprise more than a small minority, but a minority that often is able to control thousands. For example, about 90 per cent of the *officers* of the United Electrical, Radio and Machine Workers Union are either Communists or under Communist discipline, while the *membership* is probably 95 per cent non-Communist.

Joseph Curran, president of the National Maritime Union, last year reported that out of a total membership of some 70,000, not more than 500 were Communists. Yet this comparatively small group of comrades at one time filled 107 of the Maritime Union's 150 national offices!

An even smaller proportion of Communists kept the huge United Automobile Workers Union in constant turmoil, and for all practical purposes dominated it, until they were finally defeated by Walter Reuther.

Successes like these, and the official actions of some of the Communist-controlled unions, well illustrate what the Communists mean when they say, "One party member should be able to move at least 1,000 persons in support of the party line."

The infiltration technique and boring from within involve the use of fraud, trickery, falsehood, treachery and double dealing without parallel. The Communists literally stop at nothing, and they keep everlastingly at it. They cloak their activities under slogans like "trade-union democracy" and "unity," and loudly profess to work on behalf of "the masses." What they actually mean by the masses, as I have seen clearly brought out more than once in party caucuses and conventions, is a small and closely knit group which shouts in the name of the majority but represents only a Communistic minority.

When the Communists set out to infiltrate a labor union they join the organization in pairs, or, in larger numbers if possible. All of them have been carefully trained in special schools for the work. In a variety of ways they try to make themselves indispensable. If a thankless office is unfilled, they volunteer for it; if a difficult or distasteful job is undone, they do it. They run for office constantly, and are frequently successful because they build up reputations as hard workers for the union.

They try particularly to get into such posts as executive secretary and legislative agent. Both of these offices are extremely important. An executive secretary can frequently commit his organization to action widely at variance with the actual desires of the membership; while many a Communist legislative agent, supposedly working in Washington and elsewhere for his union, is in reality busily spreading Communist propaganda and working in Russia's behalf.

Once the Communists have established themselves as important members of a union, they begin to test their strength, trying to uncover potential party members or fellow travelers. At a union meeting one of the comrades will introduce a resolution embodying a part of the current Communist line. In the debate which follows he and his fellow Reds note carefully who supports the Communist viewpoint. Then another resolution, a little stronger in its advocacy of Russian policies, is introduced and the same procedure is followed. A third resolution, which may denounce the "imperialistic foreign policy" of the United States, is offered. Union members who appeared to favor all three resolutions are then asked secretly to join the Communist "fraction."

If enough members join, still another party-line resolution is introduced, and the Communists force it through by a very simple method. By bickering and arguing they delay adjournment until most of the non-Red union members have tired and gone home. Then, usually without even a quorum present, the resolution is passed and the party line becomes an official pronouncement of the union.

If a union member or official refuses to have anything to do with the Communist fraction, and divulges whatever Red offer has been made to him, the comrades immediately smear him without mercy. Scandalous rumors are circulated about his private life. If he is an official, demands are made that he be investigated. He is denounced as a Red-baiter, a labor spy and a gangster. Sometimes the Reds even accuse him of being a Communist.

William Z. Foster, head of the American branch of the Communist party, once fired this last accusation at Reuther. In June of 1941, when Reuther was fighting the Communists who were trying to prolong the strike at the plant of the North American Aviation Company in California, Foster asserted that Reuther had "even tried for membership in the Communist party, and was rejected on the grounds of his obvious opportunism." I know Reuther made no such attempt, because only a short time before, I had been sent to Detroit by the Communist Political Committee to try to persuade him to join the Red "top fraction" in the U.A.W. He flatly refused to do so.

Communists who have infiltrated a labor union make careful studies of the union's officials and other principal figures. Elaborate reports describe each man's habits, list his likes and dislikes, and in particular assess his weaknesses and note his attitude toward other officers. Evidences of jealousy or dissatisfaction are used to create discord.

Many times I have sat in Communist caucuses and other meetings where quarrels between anti-Communists were engineered, and then watched non-Red union leaders lose strength this way under the sly and skillful prodding of the Reds. From innumerable reports of the workers in the field I learned that the fostering of quarrels and the encouragement of interunion bickering was one of the Communists' most effective weapons.

If a union official indicates a willingness to play ball, the Communists immediately make a great to-do about "cooperating with the leadership." For a while they enthusiastically support everything their prospective victim proposes. But it is a cooperation that has led to destruction, with the exception of a few instances in which a strong man like Reuther has succeeded in beating the Communists at their own game. However, even a strong man will sometimes lose to them. . . .

To make certain that there is no deviation from the party line by Communists and to see that Reds take advantage of every break, a high-ranking Communist . . . attends every labor convention held in the United States. These functionaries usually take rooms in an obscure hotel, and from there direct the activities of the comrades. I have . . . seen them, with the aid of a small minority of comrades, throw a labor convention into a turmoil which required days to settle. I have also seen them call in a labor leader who had displeased them and give him a severe dressing down.

Three of the chief agencies for union infiltration in this country are the subversive office worker, the labor lawyer who is under Communist control, and the International Workers Order. The last-named is a "fraternal insurance agency." . . . The IWO is so important it might be called the first front of the Communist conspiracy. It helps the party in many ways; its local officers throughout the country are used for secret Communist conferences, and its representatives (most of them are not known to be Communists) push the party line with great industry. The IWO also provides money for the work of the party. . . .

Communist office workers, particularly young women secretaries, have been of great assistance to the party throughout its existence and especially so since the organization of the Office and Professional Workers Union, which has been Communist controlled since its inception and has a large Red membership. The party makes strenuous efforts to install at least one faithful member of this union in the office of every labor leader, particularly those who hold national, or important local posts.

A Communist secretary, if the party can trust her, is under strict orders to make carbon copies of all important letters dictated by her employer, especially those that deal with political or union affairs. She reports confidential conversations overheard in her employer's office, and notes the names of his visitors. All information she can pick up is sent to . . . headquarters of the American Communist party, where so many plots inimical to American interests have been hatched. There it is carefully read and classified. It gives the party an immense advantage when dealing with a labor union or its leadership. . . .

During the half-dozen years that followed [1929], the Communists, for the first and only time in the history of their conspiracy, worked openly toward their objectives. Not only did they boast of receiving orders direct from Moscow but, convinced that the proletarian revolution and Communist domination of the world were just around the corner, they filled their newspapers and magazines, and the manifestoes and resolutions adopted at party conventions, with undisguised calls for an uprising and the seizure of power in the United States.

Most of these calls to revolution, in all of which the advocacy of violence is clear, appeared in the *Daily Worker*, most important of American Communist newspapers, every issue of which is carefully searched by the comrades for directives. In everything printed by the Communists during this period their allegiance to Soviet Russia was clearly shown. . . .

Strikebreaking, accompanied by elements of labor spy activity, became a regular Communist tactic. But if it looked as if the Reds' strike-stopping tactics were winning, they promptly would do a switch to prolong the trouble. During the Allen-A lockout in Kenosha, Wisconsin, in 1929, when a settlement seemed in prospect, the Communists published a pamphlet flatly accusing the AF of L of violence. The struck corporation promptly reprinted the pamphlet, distributed huge numbers and there was more trouble than ever. This is still part of the Communist technique. When employers and labor leaders have agreed upon a settlement, and the dispute suddenly flares up again with impossible demands being put forward by the union, it is a pretty good sign that the Communist membership has been busy.

THE REDS ARE AFTER YOUR CHILD [11]

The man with whom I had lunch recently was angry. It was about his daughter, who had just come home from college.

"Education has turned her into a Red," he said. "She used to be a sensible kid, but now she's up in arms against everything I've ever stood for. I wouldn't mind if education had merely converted her to democratic socialism—or any American kind of ism—but when it switches a youngster's allegiance from the United States to Soviet Russia, something ought to be done about it."

That parent's story was one I had heard before. Thousands of boys and girls are being exposed to communism every year in our schools and colleges, and a good many of them are catching the virus. This is not because youth today is any more gullible or radical than in the past, but because the Communist leadership is shrewd enough to direct its best efforts toward our young people, and clever and unscrupulous Communists have infiltrated our educational system and are using every instrument at their

[11] By Harry D. Gideonse, President, Brooklyn College. *American Magazine.* 146:19+. July 1948. Reprinted by permission.

command to win and convert the minds of students to the doctrines of Marx and Lenin.

While we are spending billions to wage the cold war abroad and to help build a world in which there is a reasonable chance to live in peace as well as in self-respect, our young people are under unremitting attack here at home. As my luncheon companion said, we must do something about it.

The danger is a very real one. During the past few years the Communists have lost ground on several fronts in this country. Russia's international policy of ruthless aggression has alienated many former sympathizers and fellow travelers. The labor unions have shown an increasing tendency to expose Red conspirators and expel them from positions of power. But in spite of setbacks on these sectors, the directors of Communist strategy are still concentrating an enormous effort on the youth front. They are throwing everything they have into a drive to convert our young people to their doctrines because they know, as Hitler did, that if they can get our youth of today, they will have the nation tomorrow.

Nobody can tell you exactly how many Red teachers and students there are in our educational institutions. Because of their false fronts, their conspiratorial methods, and their invariable willingness to lie and commit perjury, it is often difficult to detect a Communist professor, student, or student organization. It can be stated with assurance, however, that there are thousands of them in our educational system. In almost all colleges of any size, and in many secondary schools as well, Communists are working actively to undermine the students' faith in American foreign policy, to intensify racial and religious friction among Americans of diverse cultural backgrounds, and to promote the general attitude that "Moscow is always right."

As president of Brooklyn College for the last nine years, and before that as a member of the faculty of the University of Chicago and of Columbia University. I have had the opportunity to obtain a close-up view of Communist operations on the youth front. I have seen how they recruit new members, how they manipulate innocent organizations for their purposes, how they attempt to penetrate every field of student activity and student thought. But when I speak of their operations on a national scale I am not relying upon my own observations alone.

Attorney General Tom C. Clark recently named a lengthy list of civic and educational organizations which he described as hotbeds of communism, and reported that the Reds are not confining their efforts to college students. "The Federal Bureau of Investigation," he said, " has learned that the Communists have started a campaign to recruit our children to their ideology—the younger they are, the better."

The United States Office of Education has also frankly acknowledged the growing menace. Admitting the grave challenge of communism in our schools, this federal agency recently announced plans to foster the teaching of democratic concepts and values on a nationwide scale, and to inaugurate studies which will show how undemocratic forces are trying to infiltrate our institutions.

At the same time, the House Un-American Activities Committee has issued a report describing the widespread activities of a Communist youth organization which masquerades under the fine-sounding name of American Youth for Democracy. This organization, which was formed in 1943 as a direct successor to the former Young Communist League, now has chapters in sixty colleges in fourteen states and a total membership of more than 16,000.

The AYD is manipulated by shrewd and specially trained organizers operating behind the scenes, according to the House Committee's report, and behind a veil of high-sounding slogans it follows the Trojan Horse policy of the Communist International with all of its characteristic underhanded and devious ability to exploit the idealism and inexperience of young people. While it insists that it is American and democratic, I do not know of a single occasion on which its policies were not in strict accord with the "party line" laid down by Moscow.

But the AYD is only one of the national student organizations through which communism is stalking the campuses. The Young Progressive Citizens of America, which is an offshoot of the Communist-dominated Progressive Citizens of America, claims members at sixty-five colleges scattered from Connecticut to California. During the past year we have witnessed the unfolding of a concerted international and national plan to capture control of the nation's largest student group, the National Student Association.

The effort failed miserably. The spotlight was put on the comrades and on their false whiskers, everyone was alert and informed, and in the light of a really intelligent majority which did not allow itself to be shaken by disruptive tactics, the National Student Association was established as a genuinely national and representative group.

In the high schools and elementary schools organized subversive activity is also widespread, although the intensity of the effort varies enormously from one area to another. In a number of states public investigations have revealed disturbing piecemeal evidence, but it is too frequently true that the methods of investigation are amateurish and un-American in the sense that the true evidence for the charges is not revealed, or that no opportunity is given for a reply by the teachers who are accused.

It is too easy to accuse a teacher or a textbook of "communism" because, say, a federal control of money and banking is urged. By such a standard Abraham Lincoln and Woodrow Wilson were both Communists, and the preservation of the American system means the preservation of the opportunity for continuous public criticism and modification of our institutions. The difference between constitutional democracy and totalitarianism is precisely the provision in the former for orderly legal methods of criticism and change which are protected by the government itself.

Our objection to the Stalinists is not an objection to social change, but an objection to conspiratorial and camouflaged activity in which lies and perjured testimony are regarded as acceptable methods of achieving Moscow's purposes.

The danger is real, but our methods should be in accordance with our own rules of the game. A good model was set up by the New York State Legislature Investigation (the so-called Rapp-Coudert Committee), although it was active for only a limited period of time. Its reports are full of well-substantiated data and incidents. They tell—one example among many—of a woman teacher in one New York school who testified she was subjected to a virtual reign of terror by students and faculty members alike when she refused to subscribe to Communist views. Among other things, she found the Soviet emblem of hammer and sickle drawn on the blackboard in every classroom.

At another high school where the former YCL had fomented riotous disorders, a teen-age Red told the principal he might find it necessary to kill him in the event violence was necessary to overthrow the government. The statement was flamboyant and puerile, of course, but it illustrates the sort of ideas with which youngsters are being indoctrinated in some schools.

Now, the great question is: Why do so many American students fall for the Red line? They enjoy under our system greater advantages than were ever offered to any previous generation of youth. How can they swallow the totalitarian philosophy which would deprive them of most of these advantages?

I have been asked that question many times, and there is no one simple answer. It lies partly in the nature of youth itself, which is eternally in revolt against adult authority, but mostly in the ingenious and often brilliant techniques which are employed by Red organizers and Red fronters. Communists have no ethics in our sense of the word; they subordinate morality to the interests of what they call "the class struggle," and there is no device they will not use to take advantage of the idealism, inexperience, and desire-to-join which characterizes most boys and girls during and immediately after adolescence. They have a thorough understanding of young people and know just how to go about winning their sympathies, and they know how to exploit the weaknesses of our educational organization.

I have observed this often during the first days of a college term. Our high schools and colleges have grown with unprecedented speed in the last decades. The public complains about the cost, but the facts are that we are almost everywhere engaged in a diluted mass education in which principals and presidents preside over gigantic institutions, and classes are so large that individual contact becomes accidental and impersonal. The majority of new students feel a bit lonely and insecure after they matriculate. They want desperately to make friends and really "belong" in their new environment. Many older students ignore them in a somewhat superior manner, but not the Commuists. Since they have a line of goods to sell, they are right on hand to extend their friendship.

This is true not only in huge metropolitan institutions like Brooklyn College, but throughout the country. At dozens of colleges last year the Young Progressive Citizens of America set up reception desks at registration time where they warmly welcomed freshmen on their first day at school. They do not preach political propaganda in their first contacts, but they offer the new students advice on the best places to eat and to get their laundry done; they invite them to meetings or social affairs, and make each newcomer feel that he has at last found a group which is warmly interested in his individual and social welfare.

At some schools where Red groups are not chartered or where the school itself has little or no recreational space, the Red organizers rent halls or empty stores off the campus for meeting places or hangouts and invite prospective members there. In every case they flatter the new student's ego, make him feel that he is an intellectual among intellectuals, and that he ought to join their fine liberal group. When he does join he doesn't realize, in one case out of a hundred, that he is getting into an organization which is actually directed by the Kremlin. Indoctrination comes later, when personal contacts have been established and a relationship of confidence has been built up.

As a part of the social approach, popular jazz bands and big-name speakers are often used by the Communists to attract students to their parties or mass meetings. In New York colleges, "name bands" and popular authors have been used several times as such bait.

Nor do the Reds hesitate to use sex appeal to win recruits. If a boy is wavering about joining one of their groups and is worth some special effort because of qualities of leadership, a pretty girl member may be assigned to help him make up his mind. Or a handsome youth may suddenly take an emotional interest in a girl the Communists want to convince. This may sound a bit lurid to some people who are not familiar with the facts, but I have seen such tactics used many times in different places.

For example, a Communist group at an Ohio college recently tried very hard to bring into its ranks a young liberal who was a Phi Beta Kappa and an officer of the student council. When ideological arguments failed, he was invited to a house off the campus where drinks were served lavishly. He was then told he could bring a girl to the house any time he wished to, provided he joined the group. If he didn't happen to know any girls without bourgeois notions of morality, he could be introduced to one. After the lad has yielded to the temptation, they have a scandal story to scare him into conformity if he should prove to be obstreperous on some subsequent occasion. I cite this case only because it indicates the lengths to which Communists will go to enlist the bright youngsters they want.

Perhaps the most effective tactic they employ, however, is their practice of espousing popular campus causes and protesting militantly against anything which they can make appear as unfair practice, student exploitation, or discrimination. Since no school is perfect—and the morale of teaching staffs is not so high as it might be, because of inadequate salaries—they not infrequently hit upon conditions which really should be remedied and, when their cause has any merit, many high-minded students invariably join hands with them.

This policy fits in perfectly, of course, with the general Communist strategy of creating discontent in the masses and fomenting constant revolt against the *status quo*. Revolution can only be accomplished through class struggle, they are taught, and if there is no class struggle on a campus they start one by finding some grievance, real or imagined, to agitate about.

I have seen them do this over and over again. If the sandwiches at a college cafeteria are a bit thinner than those sold elsewhere, if the price of milk includes a service charge, if the college bookstore seems to be making a profit, if a student, teacher, or janitor appears to be the victim of an unfair deal, the Reds can be counted on to stir up the whole school about it, call mass meetings, circulate pamphlets, and form picket lines.

Another basic tactic which Red student organizers pursue everywhere is that of penetrating non-Communist campus organizations which they feel they can manipulate or use as a "front of innocents." These may include student councils, Greek-letter societies, local YMCA and YWCA groups, and even church clubs. Communists scorn religion, of course, as "opium for the masses," but since deceit and subterfuge are their principal tools, they do not hesitate to profess belief in God if it will serve their ends.

Sometimes special Red fronts are organized to attract a whole new group of innocent recruits for subsequent intensive cultivation. Within the last year I have personally observed a song-and-mandolin and a folk-and-square-dance group which were set up by ardent fellow travelers as devices with which to secure intimate contact with promising new human material. . . .

The great majority of young people who are drawn into Communist organizations or front groups by various subterfuges never become actual members of the Communist party. Most of them drop out eventually when they are required to study and embrace the tenets of Marxism-Leninism, but there is always a certain percentage who develop into dyed-in-the-wool Reds.

I have noticed that most of these come from either underprivileged or overprivileged homes. It is easier to understand why a child of the slums might rebel against society than it is to understand why one from a wealthy family should turn to communism. But many do, including boys and girls in exclusive private colleges, and I believe the answer lies in the fact that the rich student often suffers from a sense of guilt because he has everything, or seeks to attract attention to himself because he has been either neglected or overly dominated at home by his successful parents.

Whatever the reason, the underprivileged and the wealthy produce most of the red-hot Reds on the campus, and while they comprise but a small minority at most colleges, they can create disturbances out of all proportion to their numbers. I have seen this demonstrated frequently. . . .

Communist professors and teachers play an important part, of course, in the broad-scale campaign to convert our youth to

Stalinism. In some cases, they subtly disseminate propaganda in their classrooms. In others, they cooperate closely with student organizers. If a Red teacher discovers that one of his students has somewhat radical leanings, for example, he may suggest that he attend some meeting of the local AYD chapter. At the same time, he may quietly tip off the officers of the chapter that the boy appears to be ripe for serious Communist indoctrination.

Soon after I took my present post at Brooklyn College, a legislative investigation was initiated to determine whether there were subversive activities in the public school system of New York City. Since there is always a fear that such an inquiry will curb or punish the legitimate desire of any teacher to exercise his normal political rights as a citizen of this country, I wanted to establish clearly for our own faculty that I would personally cooperate vigorously with the state's effort to curb genuinely subversive or unprofessional activities, but that I had no sympathy whatsoever with the view that a teacher is in some way deprived of some of the political and civil rights which every American enjoys as part of his birthright under our Constitution.

I called a staff meeting to invite any teacher who was willing to admit open and aboveboard membership in the Communist party to consult me, and I promised that I would use the full force of my position to protect his rights as a citizen to exercise any political option that was open to any other citizen. I made it very clear that I would not myself knowlingly endorse the appointment of a Stalinist or a Bundist, but that the legitimate civil rights of any present member of the staff would be protected. No one spoke up, although three gentlemen later resigned under charges of conspiratorial and subversive conduct without even taking advantage of their legal right to a public trial in which they could have been represented by their own attorney.

The reason is, of course, obvious. The Communists and their fellow travelers always discuss these cases as if they involved an infringement of civil or intellectual liberties. In fact, these folks are in trouble because they lie and perjure themselves, and they engage in underhanded methods which cannot be tolerated in any member of a professional group. To a good Stalinist, "truth" and "honor" are—as Marx taught—mere "bourgeois prejudices" or—as Lenin said—"morality is subordinated to the interests of the class struggle" but, to a good American, anyone who regards "truth" as dispensable in the pursuit of his political or professional purposes is *unfit to teach.*

Open Communist propaganda in the classroom is exceedingly rare. The real hazards are far more subtle and indirect. But in our large and impersonal modern schools and colleges possibilities exist, and until we have more liberal budgets to staff our educational institutions more adequately the comrades will seek to exploit them. The New York State Legislative Investigation reports a book called, *Education and the Social Conflict,* in which its author . . . tells English teachers how to use students' book reviews "as vehicles for clarifying the issues between the workers and the ruling classes as reflected in the books reviewed." He slyly advises science teachers not to put as much emphasis on the design and operation of the dynamo, telephone, airplane, and radio as he does on the "roles these instruments have played in uniting workers within each country and throughout the world."

Even geography can be given a Red slant. When discussing the products of various countries, the teacher is counseled to talk about "the grinding poverty of millions—the peasants planting rice in China, Cubans living on next to nothing amid endless fields of sugar cane, Alabama share croppers, Pennsylvania coal miners, makers of cheap garments in New York sweatshops." . . .

What can we do about this clever, versatile, and well-organized Communist program which is threatening youth on so many fronts? Well, there is one thing we must not do: We must not give way to the hysteria which characterizes those conservative and reactionary elements who would combat the totalitarian left by suspending civil rights or curtailing liberal thought in this country. The essential characteristic of the free institutions which we must defend is that they protect the right to differ from the majority, if the minority views are honestly and openly defended. Totalitarians repress all deviations from party orthodoxy, and we should, above all, be careful not to become totalitarians ourselves in our efforts to defend our system against totalitarianism.

There are, I think, two methods of approach which will effectively protect our interests. First of all, we should remember

that Woodrow Wilson's "pitiless publicity" is an old and tried
device in a free society's tool chest. No one need fear the conclusions of our young people if the argument is "out in the
open," with the true labels and the real supporters visible for
all observers. Secondly, we should remember that Communist
infiltration is often successful because there are weaknesses in
our treatment of young people which are cleverly exploited by
the Communist and fellow-traveler fronts. If we find effective
remedies for these soft spots, the most attractive and insidious
propaganda will fall on barren ground. . . .

REPORT ON U.S. COMMUNIST PARTY [12]

Hostility toward American Communists is based less on their
stated program than on the belief that they are agents of the
Soviet Union, that they are working toward violent overthrow
of our form of government and that the system they would put
in its place is essentially totalitarian.

What follows are the opposing points of view on these theses
—comments on five charges that are frequently made against
the party.

The Communist view is stated by Eugene Dennis, general
secretary of the party. The opposite point of view is expressed
by Matthew Woll, vice president of the American Federation of
Labor. Both comments on the charges were made in longer form
and have been condensed with the approval of the authors.

1. *The first loyalty of the Communist party is to the Soviet
Union and it is only secondarily concerned with the American
welfare.*

MR. DENNIS SAYS: The first and second loyalty of American
Communists is to our working class, our people and our coun-
try, of which we are an integral part. As I stated in Madison
Square Garden on September 19, 1946:

We American Communists give allegiance to only one power: to
the sovereign power that resides in the American people. We are

    [12] From article by A. H. Raskin, writer on labor problems for the *New York
Times* since 1931. *New York Times Magazine.* p. 72-6. March 30, 1947. Reprinted by permission.

American workers, Marxists and patriots. Today and on the morrow, as in the past, in war or in peace, we will loyally defend the genuine national interests of our people, of our country.

Some 15,000 Communists sealed this sacred pledge with loyal and exemplary service in the war against Hitlerism and Japanese militarism; and, years before that, some 4,000 American Communists likewise honored this principle by fighting and dying in freedom's cause and our country's interests against Franco fascism.

What is really at the bottom of the unfounded charge that we are "disloyal" is the fact that we have worked tirelessly for American-Soviet cooperation. Because of our resolute position in favor of American-Soviet friendship the anti-Sovieteers, the warmongers, who are intensely anti-American, try to brand us as "foreign agents." But this slanderous charge will not deter us from continuing to advocate and consistently fight for Franklin D. Roosevelt's program for USA-USSR amity and collaboration which is so vital to our country's national security and the cause of world peace.

It is not the Communists but the trusts—the DuPonts, Westinghouses, U. S. Steel, General Electric, etc.—who have a loyalty other than to the United States and the American people. They —the trusts—are the ones who put their monopoly and cartel interests above the interests of the nation. They are the ones who are ready at all times to betray the nation.

MR. WOLL SAYS: The Communist party and its subdivisions in the United States have only one loyalty. This loyalty is to the Russian Communist party machine which dominates the Soviet Government. The Communists in our country are not really interested in improving the conditions of the American workers. When Communists do fight for such improvements it is only a means to an end—to enable them to win influence over workers so as to snare them into the Communist party or its myriad of satellite organizations.

Let me illustrate: Before June 22, 1941, the Communists were for strikes in American industry in order to cripple its war potential, as shown by the North American aviation strike. Then they were against the Selective Service Law and against all measures for adequate national defense. The heads of various CIO unions who follow the Communist party line organized a telegram drive on Congress against the enactment of the Selective Service Law.

However, the moment Hitler attacked Russia, the Communists—without any explanation as to any change of conditions in the United States—suddenly switched tactics completely. Overnight, in response to the changed conditions in which Russia found itself, they became super-patriots. They were now for clamping down on every effort of the labor movement to better the conditions of the workers. Higher wages and shorter hours no longer concerned them in the least.

These Communist party line followers forgot about the needs and interests of their members—in order to insure continued production for Russia. It was not American but Russian patriotism that explained the Communist party anti-strike policy after June 22, 1941, and during the rest of the war period. It was solely in the interest of their Russian masters and not out of concern for the safety of America that the Communists then resisted and denounced every attempt by American labor to preserve their rights and promote their basic interests.

The trade unions have always been considered by the Communists as their central and most vital field of operations. By capturing trade unions, the Communist minority hopes to be able to control or paralyze the economic life of whole nations. Domination of the trade unions is particularly important for the Communists at this critical international moment, since the world is grappling with the central problem of postwar reconstruction. This is especially true for war-ravaged countries in Europe and Asia. It is through their control of the French trade union movement that the French Communists have been able to score huge successes in elections and to have a paralyzing hold and veto power on the economic life of France.

2. *The party is part of a worldwide fifth column serving the interests of the USSR.*

MR. DENNIS SAYS: The Communist party is an American working-class party. It bases itself on the needs and aspirations of the American people and utilizes the universally applicable principles of the social science of the working class, Marxism. The CPUS unmasks and combats all native and imported fifth columnists—the reactionary and Fascist elements, the agents of monopoly capital. That is why, over the years, we have waged political warfare against the Gerald L. K. Smiths, the Father Coughlins, the KKK, the Silver Shirts, the Hearsts and McCormicks, and now also against American Action, Inc.

Far from being a "worldwide fifth column," Communist parties throughout the world, as in France, Yugoslavia, China, Brazil, etc., have already won the respect of their people as being the best patriots, the best defenders of the national interests of their countries. That is the role to which the Communists in the United States are equally and ardently committed.

What is true of the allegation that we Communists are part of a "worldwide movement" is a fact that we are not only American patriots but also working-class internationalists. This, in fact, makes us better Americans devoted to the genuine interests of our country. In this—in our solidarity with all freedom-loving peoples—we are true to the tradition of Paine, Jefferson and Lincoln. We subscribe fully to Lincoln's declaration that "the strongest bond of human sympathy, outside of the family relation, should be one uniting all working people, of all nations and tongues, and kindreds."

MR. WOLL SAYS: No one can show a single instance where a Communist party organization in any country took a position on any question differing from the stand taken by the Russian Government. No Communist anywhere can show a single line of criticism of any Russian policy or difference with any Russian pronouncement. No matter how important a leader or group of leaders in any Communist party may be, if he or they should show the slightest sign of independence of opinion or intention to differ with the line handed down from Moscow, he or they are quickly removed, dropped, exiled or liquidated.

This is what makes a Communist party monolithic—one loyalty, one inspiration, one source of instructions, one aim—to serve the interests of their Russian Communist masters. Hence the Communist parties of all countries, at all times, carry out all orders as part of an international machine for a common purpose

—to weaken all governments that are not in accord with, that
do not lend support to, and that do not yield to, Russian pressure and purposes.

For instance, the Communists denounced Roosevelt as a
Fascist when he was for the NRA and against the Stalin-Hitler
part. But the same Roosevelt was perfect at Teheran and Yalta.

When Russia was against Perón the Communists in the
United States were against Perón. But when Perón and Russia
signed a commercial pact and established close diplomatic relations, the Communists in the United States, the Argentine and
throughout the world stopped their attacks on Perón and began
to seek increasing collaboration with him. Prior to Russia's getting together with Perón the WFTU [World Federation of
Trade Unions] publications denounced the Argentine government. But the moment Russia changed its line toward Perón
the WFTU publications stopped questioning, criticizing and denouncing Perón.

This is fifth-column work and performing the work of an
agency of an alien government. There is no doubt that these
operations are directed from an international center. The moves,
maneuvers and shifts of all Communist parties in all parts of
the world are made simultaneously upon a central signal and for
a common objective.

Of course, formally the Communist International may be
dissolved. Actually it is working on all eight cylinders and using
a high-octane gas.

Today Paris is formally the central headquarters of the actively functioning, but officially nonexistent, Comintern. The
American Communist party leader Foster and all Communist
leaders and agents visit Paris as correspondents and authors to
our State Department, but really for getting instructions and new
lines from Moscow. Often there may even be a Pravda correspondent on hand to serve simultaneously in three capacities—
Comintern agent, NKVD or MVD listening post, and correspondent for his Moscow paper.

Whenever possible, such "3-in-1" agents in Paris are individuals with experience particularly in Anglo-Saxon countries—
like the United States. Of course, these Russian fifth colum-

nists operate under different names at different times. Shingle or no shingle, new name or old name, it's the same nefarious conspiracy of totalitarian communism against human dignity, democracy and free trade unionism.

3. *The party receives instructions and financial support from Russia.*

MR DENNIS SAYS: The Communist party has never received "instructions and financial support from Russia." If by "Russia" is meant, repeating a deliberate confusion, the former Communist International whose headquarters were at Moscow, then the statement is in place that before 1940 we were affiliated with the Communist International, and occasionally exchanged fraternal opinions with Communist parties of other countries.

In 1940, however, upon passage of the Voorhis Act—which we then denounced as destructive of the democratic rights of the people and designed to destroy the Communist party as an open, legal political party—we severed all ties with the Communist International. In 1943 the Communist International itself was dissolved.

Any identity of views reflected then or now in the positions taken by our party and other Communist parties did not nor does not result from "international ties" or "instructions" from the Soviet Union. The identity of views which does exist on one question or another results solely from an independent interpretation of our universal science of Marxism, of problems common to the working class of the world, and in promoting world peace and democracy.

This does not mean that the views of all Communist parties are identical on all matters. In the independent development of views it often happens that differences of opinion develop on specific questions. Such differences develop because each party works out its policy independently, in accord with national needs. They are ultimately resolved because Communists everywhere work on the basis of a science whose principles are internationally valid.

It is notorious that British and American imperialism have given and are giving instructions and financial support to every backward and reactionary force throughout the world, as in

Kuomintang China, Spain and Greece, to stem the advancing tide of the world's democratic forces. However, our party's only financial support comes from the advanced sections of the American working class and people. Our only "instructions" come from the dictates of the historic and immediate needs of the American working class and people.

MR. WOLL SAYS: When Communist officials in the United States deny that they receive instructions or financial support from Russia they are torturing the truth and overworking their imagination. A perusal of the Communist press in the United States or in any other non-Russian country will prove beyond a shadow of doubt that these sheets regularly and religiously reflect Russian state policy. Among Communists, Moscow is often spoken of as "Mecca."

Being conspiratorial organizations, the Communist parties do not operate according to the rules of normal democratic procedure, which we commonly associate with American political life. In fact, communism today is nothing else but a conspiracy operating in the sole interest of Russia. Hence, it would indeed be very hard to find receipts in the United States to prove financial support from some banks, Kolhoz in Russia, or the Soviet publishing house. Underground business is never conducted with overground methods. Funds need not be transmitted openly or directly.

The Communist conspirators are not that careless these days. Funds might be transmitted through business institutions which make a profit in commercial relations with friendly trusts in friendly countries. Sometimes, when collections are made at public meetings, big sums might be announced as donations by American "angels" but they might well have come on the wings of Moscow.

4. *The party's aim is the violent overthrow of the American system.*

MR. DENNIS SAYS: The position of the Communist party on this question is definitively embodied in the constitution of the Communist party, which states:

> Adherence to or participation in the activities of any clique, group or circle, faction or party which conspires or acts to subvert, undermine,

weaken or overthrow any or all institutions of American democracy, whereby the majority of the American people can maintain their right to determine their destinies in any degree, shall be punished by immediate expulsion.

Force and violence—resistance to the process of basic social change—have always been initiated and exercised by reactionary classes bent on maintaining their power and privileges against the will of the overwhelming majority. The counter-revolution of the Southern slavocracy in our own Civil War—1861-65—is proof of this historic truth.

And at this very moment, throughout the world, Communist parties, as in Poland, Czechoslovakia, Yugoslavia, Bulgaria, etc., are contributing all their energies to helping insure a peaceful course of social development for their countries. At the same time, American and British imperialists are giving aid and comfort to the pro-Fascists in these countries, as well as in France, who seek to foment disorder and bloodshed calculated to bring the reactionaries into power.

However, in the interests of democracy and peace, we American Communists place as the central task of the coming period the need of rallying the broadest labor and democratic coalition for the defeat of the forces of pro-Fascist reaction at home and abroad. And this is the only way to orderly social advancement.

We have made abundantly clear the character of our immediate and long-range aims. Our immediate objective is to protect the living standards and democratic rights of the American people and to prevent fascism from coming to power. We work to defeat the anti-labor legislation of the GOP and the Southern Bourbons; to promote the economic security of the people; to help win equal rights for the Negro people and full civil liberties for all; and to safeguard and implement the cause of peace and Big Three unity, particularly through the fulfillment of the Potsdam, Moscow and Teheran agreements.

Our ultimate objective is socialism, that is, the common ownership and operation of the national economy under a government of the people, led by the working class.

MR. WOLL SAYS: When Communist party officials deny that they are for the violent overthrow of the American democratic system, they know they are telling anything but the truth. The lie is an old and oft-used weapon of the Lenin-Stalin arsenal. The "A B C of Communism" preaches it. Lenin's manual of Communist strategy and tactics—"The Infantile Sickness of Left Communism"—proudly proclaims the lie as a keystone of Communist action, especially in the trade unions.

The program of the Communist International, which has never been revised or replaced, categorically states that the struggle for power is not a peaceful one and that the revolutionary overthrow of the capitalist system will be and must be a violent one. Oh, yes! When Communists in any country talk patriotic at any time, they are only maneuvering and camouflaging their basic aim. These tactical maneuvers are not changes in purpose or principle. The Communists will use any means to justify and attain their ends. To Communists, the end justifies all means. What's a little lie as a means to achieve their big end? Flexibility of tactics and rigidity of purpose are the inseparable twins of world communism. It is this dual feature which explains the ease with which Communist parties adapt themselves to sudden shifts of line ordered from Moscow.

5. *There is no difference between communism and fascism insofar as totalitarian disregard for personal rights and freedom is concerned.*

MR. DENNIS SAYS: Communism and fascism are as different as day is from night. As I stated on September 19 at the Madison Square Garden:

We say to American labor: the criminal falsehood that communism and fascism are Siamese twins, this pro-Fascist attempt to identify opposites, is an old trick. . . . Not only the Communists but also millions of non-party anti-Fascists know fascism is the open, ruthless dictatorship of the most reactionary monopolies, of the sixty families; socialism is the rule of the workers in alliance with the working farmers and all common people. Fascism is race hatred, pogroms and lynching; socialism is the equality and friendship of peoples and nations. Fascism is the debasement and destruction of all cultural values, of human decency; socialism means the flourishing of culture, the achievement of the dignity of man. Fascism organizes war; socialism champions peace. These are facts, proved by life, by history.

This is not just a question of theory. In the great anti-Fascist war which was for our country as well as for others, as President Roosevelt said, a war of survival, the Socialist Soviet Union was our stanchest ally and bore the brunt of the war; and in every country the Communists were among the best and most self-sacrificing fighters for the preservation of the democratic achievements of their peoples and for liberation of their countries.

This was not an accident. It followed from the position of the Communists of all lands as great patriots, as the most resolute fighters for democracy and social progress, and the most uncompromising foes of fascism, which is the mortal enemy of all democracy. One does not have to be a Communist to recognize that the greatest issue of our time is the conflict between democracy and fascism, and that communism and fascism are diametrically opposite and the struggle between them is to the death. The history of the anti-Axis war, including the role of the Communists in all national resistance movements, makes this crystal clear.

As to personal rights, under capitalism, the personal freedom and "dignity" of the individual is determined, in the last analysis, by how much money one has. It is only under socialism that the masses of the people can come into their own, and that the full flowering of the individual will be possible. The truth of this is attested from time to time even by some of the correspondents of *The New York Times* when reporting objectively on the USSR.

MR. WOLL SAYS: Of course there are differences between communism and fascism. Yet, though there is no total *identity,* there is enormous *affinity* between them. They are totalitarian in theory and practice. Communism, fascism, nazism, falangism are based on the one-party system—on a monopoly of power in the hands of a single party—without any other organization having the right to have an office, publish a leaflet or paper or get any radio time.

Communism, nazism, fascism and falangism rely on terror as the last court of justice and decision. This system of terror is used against dissidents within the Communist party as well as against the people in Communist Russia at least as much as it was in Nazi Germany.

These four "isms" strive not only to have complete political power in the hands of their ruling bureaucracy, but to gather up in the hands of their chiefs all other instruments of social, economic and even moral power. In this respect, communism as practiced in Russia represents the most totalitarian of all totalitarian systems. In Russia there are no capitalist corporations or church institutions to share power, in the least, with the monolithic party dictator. Here poets and politicians are purged alike.

In Russia, even the church is now an organic part of the state apparatus. Thus the Russian Greek Orthodox patriarchs have recently been given clean and new uniforms to replace the old soiled ones described by Willkie. Today, the Russian patriarchs are harnessed as agents of Russian foreign policy in the Middle East and in the struggle to extirpate Catholic influence in the Balkans. Stalin has learned more than a lesson from the Czars of old, from the imperial Kremlin of yesterday.

In the last three weeks the party has been engaged in a fight for its life. The fight began with President Truman's message on foreign policy, the Communist party and President Truman's order that no Communist could enter or remain in the Federal Government. It continued last week in hearings before the House Labor Committee.

Many anti-Communists have voiced opposition to outlawing the party. Such suppression, they contend, would be a denial of democratic rights and would have the effect of driving the party underground, rather than destroying it.

The party is not tearing up its long-range plans. Looking beyond its current difficulties, it is already thinking about the next depression, which it expects to arrive late this year or early next year. If millions are thrown out of work, it believes the nation will turn toward Communist solutions.

THE TECHNIQUES OF COMMUNISM [13]

The technique of seizing countries and subjecting their people has made enormous strides in ten years. As an artist in the destruction of nations, Stalin is way ahead of Hitler. . . .

[13] By Bertrand de Jouvenel, distinguished French Journalist. *Human Events*, 5, no. 13: 1-4. March 31, 1948. (1710 Rhode Island Ave., Washington, D.C.) Reprinted by permission.

Recalling Hitler's conquest of Czechoslovakia or his earlier conquest of Austria, one remembers the tramping troops, the churning tanks, and the big parades which underlined the achievement. Hitler relied on visible military means.

That was necessary in the case of Czechoslovakia because Hitler had no fifth column there. It is a legend, nourished by the Communists, that Hitler possessed fifth columns in every country. In fact Hitlerism was primarily Pan-Germanism and appealed only to German nationalism. Stalinism, on the other hand, is primarily a world enterprise. Soviet imperialism is unlimited in the range of countries it can subvert. . . .

There should be more emphasis on the fact that there has been no sign of the Russian army in the second conquest of Czechoslovakia. The whole job has been accomplished from the inside. There is nothing to show any intervention except Zorine's arrival from Moscow in mid-February, an easily overlooked crudity which can surely be avoided in the next operation. On the whole, therefore, the Stalin technique has been as smooth as that of Hitler was clumsy. A wit defines the Kremlin slogan: "The subjection of the people must be the work of the people themselves."

How is it done? Every school of strategy has its favorite maneuver, used in every instance with the slight variations demanded by circumstances. Let us analyze the Communist strategy for the seizure of individual nations. It has several subtle operations.

The first of these may be termed Operation "National Anthem." It consists in identifying the Communist party with patriotism, not, as formerly, with internationalism and antimilitarism. All the national idols which were formerly an object of mockery are now ostentatiously revered. In the United States, Jefferson and Lincoln are now patronized by the Communists. In France, the Joan of Arc anniversary used to be an occasion for Catholic celebrations. Now the Communists demand to be the first in honoring this "admirable daughter of the people." The party is bringing out a series of popular booklets, celebrating the great Frenchmen. Our kings are not forgotten in this series.

Operation "National Anthem" makes possible Operation "Unanimity," which we in France call Operation "Lamourette" from the name of a famous kiss exchanged by political enemies. Operation "Unanimity" leads to the formation of a "popular front" against "reaction," realized in France after the liberation but happily dissolved by M. Ramadier. In Czechoslovakia the "popular front" paved the way for the February *putsch*.

Operation "National Anthem" and Operation "Unanimity" are immensely profitable to the Communists. First, the appeal to the masses is enormously enhanced. A discovery the Marxists made rather late in the day is that the common man is a patriot, very sensitive to national glory. For years the progress of communism was blocked merely by its open contempt for national feeling. It was most important to wash off this blot and very useful to have General de Gaulle, or a writer like François Mauriac, testify that no better patriots could be found than the Communists. Operation "Unanimity" further gives a tone of respectability to Communists. Another discovery for Marxists is that the common man likes respectability.

In addition, Operation "Unanimity" places Communists— while still a minority—in control of governmental machinery. The use to which Nosek put his possession of the Ministry of the Interior appeared plainly during the crisis at Prague.   He made the police a party weapon.

For the conquest of key positions, however, another operation is essential.   This, in our crude French manner, we call Operation "Cuckold."   It is directed against the Social Democrats, or those whom, in America, you strangely call "Liberals."

In all European countries the Social Democrats have built up any number of powerful workers' organizations, unions, youth movements, women's movements and so forth.   Now, in a movement of brotherly love, the Communists propose to share their all with the Socialists.   In fact they leave the chairmanships to the Socialists and take the less impressive secretarial jobs. Stalin has shown what can be done from a secretary's office.   The work of organization centers there, and within a little time the unions are "colonized" by Communists.

Thus it was with the French CGT [Confédération Générale de Travail].   Thus it was with the Czech labor federation. . . .

And a "conference" of eight thousand union delegates was
scheduled in Prague for Sunday, February 22. These hand-
picked men were on the spot at the decisive hour.

I have left for the last an operation which is of capital importance in the whole procedure of conquest. It is Operation
"Smear," which we call Operation "Basile" from the famous
praise of calumny which all opera-goers know. Operation
"Smear" is designed to cripple resistance to the Communist seizure of power, and to do this well in advance.

During the period of Operation "Unanimity," the Communists show a most generous disposition to get on well with
all and sundry. But gradually it begins to be noised about that
So-and-So is a Fascist sympathizer, or anti-Semitic, or pro-
German, or "Isolationist"—or something. The rumor never
openly originates with the Communists, but their accomplices,
carefully dispersed in shadow newspapers and shadow societies,
take it up. And, in the absence of any serious restraint upon
libel, the smear proceeds gaily on its way. It is aimed at anyone who, while he may not even be an enemy of the Communists,
is regarded by them as a possible element of strong resistance.
So he must be purged, not by the Communists but by his own
friends and associates, who may be themselves a little susceptible
to this refinement of blackmail.

The whole point of Operation "Smear" is that if you can
taint a few courageous people, then the taint can be easily
extended to their less courageous friends, and to the friends of
their friends. Thus Operation "Smear" eats up the bones of
the resistance to communism.

Then the time comes for Operation "Reichstag," thus termed
in honor of Goering. Operation "Reichstag" consists in the
discovery of a plot. But it must be a really bad plot, with
capitalists and financiers and foreign powers involved. If the
Nazis can be dragged in even at this late date, let us not despise
their horror value. The accusations brought in Prague add up
to a most fantastic story. But then the Communists are endowed
with a surrealist sense of humor. The more unlikely the conspiracy, the more people are shown doing things out of character,
the more they like it. It illustrates the character of the bourgeois
society which, as students of Marx know, is a mystification. So

if the priest can be depicted as hiding dollars in the sacred vessels, the old-fashioned radical serving as agent for the Nazis, all the better.

Such are, in brief, the methods by which communism seizes power. I have described the technique in France. But it is similar everywhere.

EXCERPTS

As Nathaniel Peffer has pointed out, the basic motivation of the Soviet policy is almost immaterial at this stage. For whether the Russians have desired to "liberate" the Asiatics in the interests of Soviet communism or of a new Russian imperialism, the struggle has been directed against the Western powers. Lenin's dictum, that the capitalistic states could be most effectively attacked by undermining their empires, has obviously been adopted as Soviet strategy.

There is no doubt that the Oriental peoples have no desire to replace Western overlordship with Russian rule. However, the antagonism toward the colonial powers is so intense that native movements have been willing to work with any power which promised aid. Moreover, some Soviet tactics have been well conceived. The Oriental Institute in Moscow has trained hundreds of "activists"—natives of Korea, Japan, China, Indo-China, the Dutch East Indies, Malaya, Burma, India, etc.—who have gone back to their home bases and, without broadcasting their Communist affiliations, have established extensive Communist networks. A process of "education" through personal contacts between the Soviet "experts" and native leaders has apparently been in progress for many years. Sedulous efforts have been made to settle Soviet-inspired groups in areas where their influence could be felt most effectively. And large Soviet embassy staffs have been stationed in strategic spots to promote Soviet objectives in East Asia.—*"Current Readings on International Relations," edited by Norman J. Padelford and F. Pauline Tompkins. p. 300. Massachusetts Institute of Technology. Department of Economic and Social Science. International Division. Publication no. 5. 1949.*

Justice Oliver Wendell Holmes, sustaining the Espionage Act of 1917, as a wartime measure, said: "The question in every case is whether the words used are used in such circumstances and are of such a nature as to create a clear and present danger that they will bring about the substantive evils that Congress has a right to prevent." The reader may apply this rule of "clear and present danger" to current heresy hunting:

Mundt-Nixon bill, requiring Communists to register as foreign agents, was passed by the House, 319 to 38. Its sponsors have announced that it will be reintroduced in the next regular session of Congress.

President Truman's blanket order initiating a "loyalty check" of all federal employees in all departments except State, Army, Navy, and the Atomic Energy Commission.

Publication of the Attorney General's blacklists of subversive organizations.

The Condon case. Director of the Bureau of Standards, branded by Chairman Thomas of the House Un-American Activities Committee as "one of the weakest links in our atomic security" and an associate of "alleged Soviet espionage agents." Although denied a hearing by the committee, Dr. Condon was exonerated completely by the Commerce Department's Loyalty Board and by the Atomic Energy Commission.

Ouster from Hollywood jobs of ten film writers and executives after their refusal to answer whether they were or were not Communists at hearing before the House Un-American Activities Committee.

Mme. Joliot-Curie, wife of a French Communist, detained at Ellis Island.

Passports denied to a reporter for the Daily Worker and to an American Labor party congressman.

Hearings of disloyalty charges against Oak Ridge atomic laboratory scientists, two of whom were suspended. The charges were based on anonymous accusations, not made under oath.— *Survey Graphic. Ag. '48. p. 367.*

A quarter-century ago . . . the believer in Russian communism and utopian communism might be identical. Any optimistic young reformer might fancy that he embraced Lenin and Sir Thomas More together; he might believe that the communism of Plato and that of Trotsky had much in common. A multitude of people all over the world, including laborers, students, intellectuals and social workers, did to some extent confound the two faiths.

In our time, however, a clear line can be drawn between the disciple of Russian communism and the disciple of utopian communism. Anyone who admires the iron regime of Stalin has bidden farewell to the dreams of Robert Owen and William Morris, and to the moderate Marxianism of Kautsky and the Fabians. Russian communism is at the opposite pole from all true liberalism.

It is vital in the present situation for us to understand this. And to understand it we must have a clear perception of the great difference between the theories held by the liberal on the one side, and the Communist on the other.

True liberals of all shades of opinion, including orthodox Socialists, agree to the fundamental principle that majority rule shall be loyally accepted so long as it respects the basic rights of minorities. No matter how much the Wilsonian liberal detested Harding's type of reaction, no matter how deeply Norman Thomas' followers abhorred Coolidge's policies, they yielded full obedience to the government.

The Communist, however, rejects this principle. His party doctrine is Communist rule or general ruin. To him an opposition victory at the polls is simply the signal for conspiracy, sabotage and secret subversion. As a minority, the Communists give no deference to any majority; they reject all the rules of the democratic game; they concoct plots, infiltrate at all weak points, cripple every machine they can touch and stand ready at any moment to seize power by force.

The problem of coping with such elements is therefore simplified. We are not concerned with a movement; we are concerned with a militant minority, alien in allegiance.—*Allan Nevins, Professor of American History, Columbia University; Editor, Yale University Press "Pageant of America" series. In "What is a Communist?" New York Times Magazine. My. 2, '48. p. 64.*

The steps by which totalitarian and fascist minds wage psychological warfare on democracy are simple and few. First, they create suspicion, distrust, fear, confusion, and bewilderment. They let markets collapse, depressions set in, unemployment zoom high. They undermine confidence in interdependent groups: management, labor, government. Wherever possible, they paralyze the processes of life. Next, they promise a remedy: security and certainty to the hungry, the confused, the bewildered, in return for all their rights and their liberties. Granted that, they then move in for the kill. The "masses"—their term—they herd while the "elite" feast. Democracy is then dead. A totalitarian oligarchy rules. Thus exploited and controlled, the people themselves are immobilized and enslaved. Atrophy or revolutionary violence follow. Under such circumstances, neither peace nor growth exists among men. . . .

All activities which restrict the freedom of the individual conscience in matters of religious worship are thoroughly un-American activities.

What un-American activities today threaten our freedom of speech and of inquiry and thought? All efforts to discredit, defame, or silence opposition: to treat citizens with whom one disagrees, as Jefferson said, as if they were criminals. To guard against emotional slogans and mass delusions, the people of the United States give all the right to test their ideas openly. The totalitarian rigidity of censorship, of thought-control, forbidden books and the burning of books, are not a part of our national life. The present efforts of some business and religious groups, in an unholy alliance, to whip public opinion into a frenzy allegedly to save the nation from communism rather than to present facts which will enable the people actually to understand Russia before they fight it—these efforts are, in kind, the Fascist inquisitional scare technique which Hitler directed against Communists, Freemasons, and Jews. Such Fascist incitation to hatred is no part of democracy. Fascism, both secular and clerical, is no friend to free, democratic societies. Fascism feeds not only on fears, suspicions, emotions, and poverty. It feeds also on ignorance. Who will save a free democratic society from all totalitarianism, from the police state of all varieties?

Free men must think for themselves. To do so, they need facts. They need to learn to think. They need thorough schools and a free press. . . .

In the present psychological aspect of the total war for control over all aspects of life, we, as a democratic people, entrench freedom against all forms of irresponsible centralized authority. We cannot find the strength which we so greatly need in mass submission to dictatorial domination, in ignorance, nor, least of all, in fear. Our strength, our only hope lies in that unrestricted give-and-take which keeps all forever mindful of both the individual's rights and the people's general welfare.—*Warren Taylor, Assistant Professor of English, Oberlin College. "American and Un-American Activities." My.* 20, '47. *p.* 1+.

The Czechoslovak crisis in February 1948 brought the United States Government up against two of the toughest peacetime questions ever to face a democracy in the field of foreign affairs. These questions are: (1) How can a nation based on legal procedures successfully wage a political power struggle against a nation that constantly uses illegal means? (2) How can a democracy, based on the right of all men to organize political parties of any persuasion, declare that it will oppose the right of the Communists to take power by legal means in another country? These questions are not part of an academic exercise indulged in by Washington; they represent the most difficult problems facing the average American in these difficult times. . . .

It is easier to define the problem, however, than to solve it. First of all, in any preelection campaign, the Communists always get outside aid to buy newspapers and all the support necessary to convince the voters to go to the polls—and vote Communist. The United States, however, does not have any "secret funds," especially for such purposes. It did have them during World War II—we called them "unvouched funds," for which the President did not have to account to Congress—but it has no such funds today. Hence the United States authorities cannot quietly match the Communist election funds; it cannot provide assistance to the trade unionists who are working, some of them unwillingly, with the pro-Communist Socialists; in a word, the

United States cannot act in this effective but admittedly illegal preelection game, being divided as to the use of "illegal measures" and Congressional appropriations for such purposes.

Hence, the legal tradition of the United States strengthens our moral case but weakens our efforts to block the illegal election tactics of the Communists. The Government cannot even proclaim publicly that aggression by Communist trickery inside a key European country would be considered aggression against the vital interests of the United States. Such a statement would, for a democracy that has in the past so scrupulously defended the rights of minorities, involve questions of the most fundamental nature.

The problem after World War I was how to defend the rights of minorities; the problem now in many countries is how to protect the rights of the unorganized majorities against the techniques of the Communist minority. The trouble with a power struggle like the present one is that unless the people in the country concerned will respond openly and courageously to moral arguments and legal efforts to help them, the opposition has enormous illegal advantages at critical points.—*Joseph S. Roucek, Department of Political Science and Sociology, University of Bridgeport. Annals of the American Academy of Political and Social Science. Jl. '48. p. 63-4.*

[Communism's] greatest strength lies clearly in the fanaticism of its adherents and in their willingness to use any means which they feel will conduce to the end they have in mind. In spite of their insistence that Communist tactics always dictate the espousal of every cause involving the direct interests of the working class, the Communists are clearly not committed to seeking the improvement of world conditions for its own sake. Nor do they have to weigh policies by their contribution to any end other than the triumph of the Revolution and the aggrandizement of the USSR, with which that triumph is held to be bound up.

They have been willing in the past to see reactionary dictatorships replace relatively benign and progressive republics in the hope that the next step would be a turn of the wheel in their favor, as the logic of their philosophy leads them to expect. Such was the policy of the Communists in the last years of the Weimar Republic.

Similarly we now find them, as in the United States today, deliberately splitting the progressive forces and trying to insure the election of reactionaries to Congress in order that the discontent which they expect to ensue should assist their own cause. However much it may conceal itself at times, there can be no doubt that the whole purpose of Communist strategy is to accentuate the divisions in Western society and to discredit any approach to its problems other than their own. There has never been a single case—and under the Communist doctrine there could not be a single case—in which a coalition between Communists and Socialist or liberal groups has been genuine on the Communist side.

For this reason, the presence of communism as an active factor in any political situation puts an almost intolerable strain upon the conscience of anyone sincerely devoted to the traditional liberal method of settling political issues by discussion and compromise. With the Communists, there can be, as we have seen, no discussion, no compromise and in the ordinary sense of the word, no good faith, since for Communists, the keeping of one's word is secondary as a moral duty to the promotion of the Revolution.

The problem for the liberal is whether in spite of all these things to allow the Communists to enjoy (and consequently to abuse) the civil rights which have been built up over a long period in liberal societies or whether to regard the Communists (and other exponents of closed systems such as fascism) as *ipso facto* disentitled to enjoy privileges based upon moral concepts which they repudiate.

The events of the years since the end of World War II have suggested that this is one of the most important as well as one of the most agonizing problems of our age.—*Max Beloff, Reader in the Comparative Study of Institutions, University of Oxford, and Faculty Fellow, Nuffield College. Behind the Headlines. Vol. 8, no. 4. S. '48. p. 22-3.—Canadian Institute of International Affairs. Toronto.*

In keeping with their belief that although intellectual and cultural activity arises out of the social system it can and must be used to influence social development, the Soviet leaders have created a vast propaganda machine to spread their ideas and theories both at home and abroad. There is no Soviet Ministry of Propaganda. But the Communist party has a widely ramified network of propaganda bodies ranging from the administration of propaganda and agitation to individual propagandists and agitators in primary party organizations. Their function is to explain and interpret Soviet and party policy to the general public and particularly to ordinary party members who are called on to serve as a leaven among the non-party masses. Mainly through them and the party groups which are expected to act as the leading force on all state and public institutions, organizations and bodies, the Soviet leaders are able to insure that the press and wireless and all other visual and oral means of spreading the written and spoken word will be preaching the same views about the same things from Brest Litovsk to Vladivostok and from Murmansk to Alma-Ata. The Chief Administration for Literary and Publishing Affairs and the use of a single Soviet news agency to collect and distribute news, particularly foreign news, provide further powerful aids to uniformity.

The Communist party also has an elaborate system of party schools and courses giving instruction in Marxism-Leninism. Marxism-Leninism is even made a compulsory subject for study and examination in all Soviet universities and higher education institutions. For example, in spite of the war and although not published until 1938, *The Short History of the Communist Party of the Soviet Union* has already been issued in thirty-one million copies in every conceivable language. Writers, scholars and all other members of the Soviet intelligentsia are expected to use their talents and energies not only to pursue their own particular specialties but to pursue them in a way which will conform to and promote Marxist-Leninist ideas and help the Soviet leaders to make the Soviet people more ideologically aware of and therefore more intent on fulfilling the tasks before them. "In Soviet society," we are told in *Bolshevik*, No. 21, November 1946, "science and the arts collaborate with the policy of the

party and state and under the guidance of this policy . . . serve
. . . the cause of building communism. . . . Only if guided by
this policy can literature, the arts, science and philosophy fully
achieve their real purpose, . . . and play an active role in the
creation of new forms of life." As the Central Committee of the
Communist party made brutally clear in August and September
1946 in its decrees on literature, drama and the cinema, etc.,
all forms of intellectual activity in the Soviet Union must serve
political ends and there can be no art or science for its own
sake or for the sake of beauty or truth.

Soviet propaganda to the outside world is naturally on a
somewhat less massive scale than propaganda at home. But it
pours out in a broad and steady stream through the press, the
wireless, the Soviet news agency and various less obvious channels, giving maximum currency to Soviet views and theories
and inspiring maximum criticism of everything and everybody
thought to stand in their way.—*George H. Bolsover, on staff of
the British Embassy at Moscow*, 1943-1947. *International Affairs. Ap. '48. p.* 176-7.

It is perfectly true that the Communist way of life is immoral in the light of Christian principles. Paradoxically, however, some of the most truthful characters of our times have
passed through a Communist phase. From 1918 to 1938 the
young of the Western, Christian world were attracted to communism for highly moral reasons. They had been through
devastating war; they were born into disorienting depressions.
Freedom in the traditionally free society was often honored in
the breach. Looking about them at unemployment, at a decadent
literature and at an apparently moribund church, the young who
came of age after 1918 often jumped into the arms of Lenin
for reasons of eminently Christian emotion. It was all too easy
to discredit the actual life of capitalism when one had an un-
tested vision of utopia shining in the mind.

To call the role of sensitive spirits who displayed sympathy
with Marxism for moral reasons in the '20's and the '30's is
virtually to recite a *Who's Who* of the arts and letters. Novelists like Ernest Hemingway and John Dos Passos, philosophers

like John Dewey and James Burnham, journalists like Eugene
Lyons and Louis Fischer, poets like Archibald MacLeish and W.
H. Auden, even ambassadors like William C. Bullitt—the names
still decorate the collectivist manifestoes of the '20's and '30's.
In France there were André Gide, Nobel prize-winning novelist,
and André Malraux, who broke with communism to become a
French patriot and advisor to De Gaulle.   In other parts of
Europe there were novelists Ignazio Silone and Arthur Koestler,
whose *Darkness at Noon* is the best fictional representation of
Russian purge psychology.   One by one these people went marching forth to look at—or for—the collectivist utopia, and one by
one they came marching back.

An early convert to Soviet collectivism, the United States
journalist Lincoln Steffens returned from a Moscow pilgrimage
with the news that he had "seen the future, and it works."   But
those who returned after Steffens reported they had made grisly
forays into hell.   Those who had become Communists in Germany, France, Spain and the United States often backtracked to
say they had touched pitch without ever going to Russia.   Out of
the depths of their tragically human experience they gave warnings that a dark conspiracy against all the moral values of the
West was gaining momentum.

But who was there to listen?   Before 1939, when Communists were preaching the "Popular Front" against fascism in
Spain and elsewhere, those who had no experience of the secret
life of communism were afraid of annoying a seemingly friendly
ally.   After August of 1939, the date of the Nazi-Soviet pact,
the Western world was more disposed to listen.   But this period
lasted only until Hitler attacked Russia in June 1941.   Before
August 1939 and after June 1941 the sensitives who had come
back from hell were forced to publish their evidence in such
struggling organs as New York's Social Democratic *The New
Leader*.   In the columns of *The New Leader* one could learn
why more respectably capitalist journals frequently refused to
print the works of the voyagers from hell.   It was because the
fellow travelers of the Communists had throughout the '30's
infiltrated strategic journalist positions, from which they could
direct the new literary trends.   For a time in New York the

Communist and fellow traveler transmission belts overlapped liberal circles so effectively that practically all opinion was distorted by social pressures arising far on the Left. It was smart in those days to be Red.—*Editorial "How Red a Herring?" Life. S. 6, '48. p. 24.*

I have been reading a good deal about Russia as a slave state, but the beginnings of slave-statism are now obvious in this country, and I hate the signs. Freedom of speech and freedom of religion are becoming merely theoretical. The right to be agnostic or atheist if one pleased, the right to hold any political doctrine one earnestly felt was the most rational, the right to develop one's intellect according to one's own taste, to be a mature and reasoning individual, to be independent—not one of a cowed and frightened herd—these used to be *sine qua nons* for any American. But if we are now going to become a regimented, militaristic, police state; if we are now going to adopt the totalitarian features of the countries we have just conquered in the great names of liberty and democracy, then let us know about it at once and realize what we are in for! If an American may not ponder Karl Marx, Nietzsche, Schopenhauer, Bertrand Russell, H. G. Wells, Thoreau, Tom Paine, Robert Ingersoll, Henry George, or Mark Twain's "The Mysterious Stranger," without being hauled up before the Committee on Un-American Activities and clapped into jail, let us know that now. Let Congress compile an Index Expurgatorius of what we shall read or not read. Let them devise a catechism for loyal Americans which shall include kneeling toward the United States Chamber of Commerce and the National Association of Manufacturers every morning; let all our actions and affiliations be supervised by the FBI.

I used to think that America was a land where one could breathe deep, indulge in plenty of criticism, stretch one's arms and one's mind with plenty of elbow-room, go one's way without warnings from narrow-minded bigots, or thug-minded politicians. Well, it seems to me that we can keep it that way, if we still forcibly object to being forced to subscribe to some petty legislator's moronic creed. All the star-spangled flapdoodle in the

world isn't worth one sage, enlightened sentence in the writings
of Justice Holmes, in the speeches of the late Franklin Delano
Roosevelt or Senator Norris.   If we wish to make this country
great, it lies in our own spirits, in our own consciences so to
do.   It won't be done through big newspaper spreads paid for
by our enormous corporations blatting of a free enterprise of
which they know nothing and which they do everything in their
power to suppress.   It won't be done by the biggest Washington
lobbying in our history on the part of the vested interests.   It
won't be done through the blatant power of money, the greed of
industrialists, or the venality of public servants.   It *will* be done
by "speaking out in meeting," speaking the faith that is in us,
speaking even harsh criticism of the sins and blunders of those
who rule our country, a country where—as my brother thought—
every one's dream has a right to grow, every crazy notion has a
right to be heard, every man can stand up on his hind legs
and speak his piece.   May our country always be like that.   May
it always rise triumphant over its shabby politics, its corrupt
misleaders, its moral cowards, and its mental degenerates!   May
honest Americans always be able to walk abroad like free men!—
*William Rose Benét, Associate Editor, Saturday Review of Litera-
ture.   Saturday Review of Literature.   S.* 20, '47.   *p.* 36.

It is fitting . . . that we take this occasion to proclaim to the
world the essential principles of faith by which we live, and to
declare our aims to all peoples.

The American people stand firm in the faith which has inspired this nation from the beginning.   We believe that all men
have a right to equal justice under law and equal opportunity to
share in the common good.   We believe that all men have the
right to freedom of thought and expression.   We believe that
all men are created equal because they are created in the image
of God.

From this faith we will not be moved.

The American people desire, and are determined to work for,
a world in which all nations and all peoples are free to govern
themselves as they see fit and to achieve a decent and satisfying
life.   Above all else, our people desire, and are determined to

work for, peace on earth—a just and lasting peace—based on genuine agreement freely arrived at by equals.

In the pursuit of these aims, the United States and other like-minded nations find themselves directly opposed by a regime with contrary aims and a totally different concept of life.

That regime adheres to a false philosophy which purports to offer freedom, security, and greater opportunity to mankind. Misled by that philosophy, many peoples have sacrificed their liberties only to learn to their sorrow that deceit and mockery, poverty and tyranny, are their reward.

That false philosophy is communism.

Communism is based on the belief that man is so weak and inadequate that he is unable to govern himself, and therefore requires the rule of strong masters.

Democracy is based on the conviction that man has the moral and intellectual capacity, as well as the inalienable right, to govern himself with reason and justice.

Communism subjects the individual to arrest without lawful cause, punishment without trial, and forced labor as a chattel of the state. It decrees what information he shall receive, what art he shall produce, what leaders he shall follow, and what thoughts he shall think.

Democracy maintains that government is established for the benefit of the individual, and is charged with the responsibility of protecting the rights of the individual and his freedom in the exercise of those abilities of his.

Communism maintains that social wrongs can be corrected only by violence.

Democracy has proved that social justice can be achieved through peaceful change.

Communism holds that the world is so widely divided into opposing classes that war is inevitable.

Democracy holds that free nations can settle differences justly and maintain a lasting peace.

These differences between communism and democracy do not concern the United States alone. People everywhere are coming to realize that what is involved is material well-being, human dignity, and the right to believe in and worship God.

I state these differences, not to draw issues of belief as such, but because the actions resulting from the Communist philosophy are a threat to the efforts of free nations to bring about world recovery and lasting peace.—*Inaugural address, President Harry S. Truman, January 20, 1949. Congressional Record. Ja. 20, '49.*

Communism has been in this world a long, long time. Plato expounded it in *The Republic*; ancient Jews, like the Essenes, practiced it; early Christianity appealed especially to the under-privileged who were easily convinced that communal living was an essential part of the Gospel of Jesus.

Through all the ages, men have sought economic equality and security, and they have often preferred them to political freedom. During the first half of the nineteenth century, a host of pre-Marxian Socialists or Communists (for the terms were often used interchangeably) agitated for a planned economy which should liberate the masses from exploitation, establish a cooperative commonwealth, based on the solidarity of the whole human race, and enable mankind to live in comfort, peace and happiness.

In the writings of Saint Simon, Lamennais, Fourier and Proudhon in France; in the worker's movement of Wilhelm Weitling, the philosophical tailor of Germany; in the "Com-munity of Equality" of Robert Owen, the successful British capitalist who became "the father of English socialism"; in our own Brook Farm experiment by the New England elite; and in the scores of Communist colonies that once flowered on the soil of frontier America, we see sincere expression of a humani-tarianism that is practically synonymous with applied Christianity.

Under the impact of the revolutionary propaganda of Karl Marx, these utopian Communists have been almost forgotten. Marx espoused a "scientific socialism" that had no place for sentiment or religion, and championed the class struggle, but even Marx's economic determinism assumes that under proper circum-stances human nature can be remolded so as to rid the world of the competitive struggle and the private profit motive, and that men can become so kind and just and cooperative that the state eventually will "wither away."

Today, we are told, there is one state where the proletarian revolution, a la Marx, has been accomplished. Debatable as that may be in view of the many reforms that are still in process, certain features of the present day Russian experiment in communism must be recalled to mind, for though they are historical facts, many of the American champions of Marxism would like to overlook them.

Totalitarianism had its origin in Soviet Russia. Mussolini and Hitler merely copied the pattern, and molded it to their hearts' desire. Russia is ruled by a small party dictatorship. A well-disciplined minority seized the government thirty years ago, and a minority continue to control it. Troublesome opponents —whether industrialists, generals, intellectuals, or recalcitrant laborers and peasants—were liquidated in blood purges as indiscriminate, extensive and violent as those of Hitler and Himmler. When trials were held at all, they were often a mockery of justice, as we understand the term, and the victims were charged with crimes so fantastic as to seem little short of ridiculous. Thousands were condemned to Siberia and the labor camps which became the prototype for the later concentration camps of Central Europe.

Soviet Russia, though technically a federal state, and tolerant of many non-Russian languages, is really dominated by one state which covers about three fourths of the area of all Russia, and contains about two thirds of its population. A rigid censorship controls press and radio. Elections are held after the fashion of Hitler's famous plebiscites. There are no opposition candidates in the Russian system of elections. The Supreme Council of the Soviets is essentially a mass meeting of party henchmen somewhat like the great Nazi party festivals at Nuremberg. The Council is a legislative body only in the sense that it approves what Stalin and his bureaucracy propose. The Russian secret police were the model for the notorious Nazi Gestapo. The methods of these two organizations were similar, the brutal techniques of terrorism, without regard for law. Religion described as "the opiate of the people" was displaced by a new orthodoxy of atheism and materialism, and the educational program, unquestionably successful in many of its purposes, nevertheless has as its main objective the indoctrination of the young, to support the existing dictatorship. —*Carl Wittke, Dean, College of Arts and Sciences, Oberlin College. "What Shall We Do with the Communist Party?" Ap. 16, '47. p. 1-2.*

On grounds of national security, the government has concluded that the only prudent course to adopt is to insure that no one who is known to be a member of the Communist party, or to be associated with it in such a way as to raise legitimate doubts about his or her reliability, is employed in connection with work the nature of which is vital to the security of the state.

No reasonable exception can be taken to the terms of the Prime Minister's statement. The state, he said, is not concerned with the political views as such of its servants, and so far as possible alternative employment on the wide range of nonsecret government work will be found for those who are deemed to be unsuitable for secret work. Experience both in Great Britain and elsewhere has shown that membership of, and other forms of continuing association with, the Communist party, may involve the acceptance by the individual of a loyalty which in certain circumstances can be inimical to the state.

However regrettable this decision may be—and there are consequences that involve some further consideration—no government could pretend that there are not certain duties of such secrecy that the state ought not to employ in connection with them anyone whose political discretion is in doubt. It shows a misconception of the Prime Minister's statement and purpose to urge that such action should only be taken after the individual concerned had had opportunity of appeal to some form of tribunal, or after weighing evidence by a judicial process. The point is that there is no specific charge brought against the individuals affected. As Mr. Attlee said, it is not suggested that in matters affecting the security of the state all civil servants who adhere to the Communist party would allow themselves to forget their primary loyalty to the state; but there is no way of distinguishing such people from those who might endanger the security of the state.

The government in this precautionary measure has manifestly stopped well short of the point at which liberty and conscience are imperilled or economic sanctions raised against particular political creeds. Western democracy works by toleration and governs by consent, and the government's moderation is in startling contrast to the methods pursued by Eastern communism—its rigid intolerance, intransigience and persistent attempts to overrun the frontiers of sincere democratic patriotism, and to crush freedom wherever it exists. To survey the plight of freedom in the satellite countries of the USSR is to realize the enormous contrast, and also the moderation and realism of the British government's action. . . .

In dealing with the danger to the state of Communist activities, a profound saying of Burke may be recalled: "It is no inconsiderable part of statesmanship to know how much of an evil ought to be tolerated." The government has rightly decided that democratic principles do not call for the toleration of treason and terror, and it has wisely left it to the community to decide on the larger and fundamental issue, whether, in a democratic society, free scope should be given to those who seek to destroy democracy and to set up an intolerant regime.

If, therefore, the government, in administering the decision, makes sure that impartial justice is done where the person concerned is not a member of the Communist party but charged with "continuing association with it," it may well be claimed to have met Burke's test of statesmanship. That will not indeed avert the need for constant vigilance within and without Parliament. The debate on March 25 should have reassured those who fear that the cloak of security may be used to stifle the integrity of science and the ability of the scientific worker to serve mankind. But it is for scientific workers individually and in their professional associations to take up the challenge to fundamental thinking and constructive action which Mr. Murry throws down to them in *The Free Society*; in that way only can freedom be ultimately safeguarded in science or among the free nations of the world.

—*Editorial. Nature. Ap.* 10, '48. *p.* 537-9.

It is clear both from the bold and forthright report of the President's Committee on Civil Rights and other facts of common knowledge that the liberties which have so long distinguished our nation are in danger from within, as well as from without. Irremediable tragedy only can result if the advice of the President's Committee is ignored. We the undersigned members of the Yale Law faculty take this opportunity to urge immediate and decisive action. This nation needs not alone to be reminded that our government is one fashioned for courageous men, who prefer the conceded hazards of living in liberty to the indignities of the police state; it needs also to reaffirm its faith and to secure its freedoms by vigorous and appropriate measures now.

We are not insensible that in a world becoming increasingly divided, our government must take all rational precautions against acts which threaten, or seem to threaten, our national security and existence. Precautions cease to be rational, however, when they defeat the very ends they are designed to secure. We need not create a police state to escape a police state. It can make little difference to the citizen who loses his liberties and dignities as a human being whether his loss comes from an enemy or from a native oppressor who subverts democratic government in the guise of protecting it.

There is in our history no evidence that our faith in freedom of thought and speech is not well founded. For a hundred and fifty years the most violent dissidence of political expression has been allowed, not only as a monument to "the safety with which error of opinions may be tolerated when reason is left free to combat it," but in the abiding belief that "the ultimate good desired is better reached by free trade in ideas." It is not now apparent why the American people should be so wanting in courage or so skeptical of our foundations as to fall victim to the fears of frightened men either inside or outside the government. It is, however, unhappily true that America appears to be embarking on an era similar to that which followed the first World War. There are alarming signs that persecution for opinion, if not soon curbed, may reach a point never hitherto attained even in the darkest periods of our history. With it, we may expect racial, religious and every other kind of bigotry which, if it is to run its full course, can loose such a flood of intolerance as utterly to destroy the civil liberties without which no democratic society can survive.

A pattern of suppression is today evolving at the highest levels of the Federal Government. The more alarming aspects of the situation include the President's Loyalty Order of last spring, the recent "State of Security Principles" by the Department of State and the current performance of the Un-American Activities Committee of the House of Representatives. The procedure followed by the Committee and that prescribed by the Order and the Statement are such as to subject the citizen to intimidation and abuse without redress and to expose the government worker to loss of reputation and livelihood without the opportunity to defend his honor or his job.

It is the right and the heritage of every American freely to form political opinion and to express it; when accused of offense, to be presented with the charges against him, confronted by his accusers and given a fair opportunity to defend himself before an impartial tribunal. Under the cloak of Congressional immunity or the cloak of anonymity, high officials of the national government are today acting in disregard and in defiance of the American tradition of civil liberties and, in our considered judgment, in violation of the Constitution of the United States. It is, we believe, high time that the executive and legislative branches of the United States Government foreswear belief in witches and, by practicing democracy, set an example to those parts of the world which we hope to have embrace its principles. We, therefore, urge (1) that the House of Representatives immediately abolish its Committee on Un-American Activities, and (2) that the President and Secretary of State revise their present policy with regard to governmental employees suspected as disloyal or as security risks, so as to bring that policy into conformity with both the spirit and the letter of the United States Constitution.—*Manifesto by twenty-two members of the Yale University School of Law, November 22, 1947, American Bar Association Journal. Ja. '48 p. 16.*

There is still another risk involved in a policy based solely or mainly on opposition to communism. Just as such a campaign may put our imprimatur on anti-democratic movements in Europe and Asia, so at home it will serve as a cloak for the worst anti-democratic forces in American society. The term Communist has been so tortured and twisted that it has become necessary to issue special bulletins on how one of the vermillion breed may be identified. Just as the Communists have used liberal organizations of all kinds to advance the political interests of the USSR, so American reactionaries under the cloak of an anti-Communist crusade have waged war on some of the most cherished principles and policies of a democratic society. Collective bargaining, consumers' operatives, the TVA, public health and recreation programs, the social security law, conservation, federal aid to education, civil liberties, the Emancipation Proclamation and Declaration of Independence, have at one time or another been denounced as communistic. Individuals, including some of our most distinguished citizens. . . . have been tarred with the same brush.

Once we embark upon a thoroughgoing anti-Communist crusade how can we make the fine distinctions that may be necessary if we are to avoid such bizarre results and prevent the crusade from becoming a full-fledged assault not only on communism but on democracy in America and throughout the world? We ought not to play into Stalin's hands by giving his Communist stooges credit for so much that is good in our world. Moreover, shouting wolf at every progressive person and policy may make us hard of hearing when our security is really threatened.

I recognize the insidious and baleful influence of Communists in America and elsewhere. I believe the record justifies the popular conviction that Communist parties and party members here—as in Europe—are for all practical purposes agents of the present Russian government. As such I believe we are justified in forbidding their employment in responsible posts in our government.

But the one thing we must not do, as George Soule says, is, "through fear of communism to make ourselves into the likeness of that which the Communists assert we are. They might win if they could conduct the struggle in terms of their own making."

What I have been saying can be summarized as follows: It is not enough for the United States to be against communism and fascism. It is not enough even to be against poverty, insecurity, feudalism, and fear, in whose rotten soil the seeds of communism and fascism thrive. The United States of America, if it is to be true to its traditions, if it is to justify the leadership and power with which it has been invested, must not only be *against* these evil things; it must be aggressively *for* the affirmative values that lie at the heart of our Western civilization. It must be *for* freedom of speech and press and religious worship; for equal justice under law without discrimination of color or race, or class or creed; it must be *for* a more equitable and efficient use of the resources of the world; and for a more equitable distribution of goods and services. And it must be for these things in Spain and China, as well as in France and Italy. We must remember also that the frontiers of freedom are to be found not only in Europe and Asia, but here in America, too. America can once again become the *hope* of the world, a hope founded on a global crusade not against communism and fascism but *for* the Four Freedoms and their fulfillment. Why should we be fearful that Communist propaganda will undermine our influence everywhere? Why not answer the *Comintern* with a *Demintern*? Have we no faith that the people of the world—including the Russian people, too—will in the end choose a system based on freedom and the dignity of man, as against a totalitarian system that promises security at the price of freedom? If it were a simple choice between freedom and security, they would no doubt choose security. We must, therefore, demonstrate that a democratic society can provide not only freedom but security as well. Only thus can we push forward the frontier of freedom and ensure the salvation of Western civilization.

To prove worthy of our heritage and our destiny we must practice what we preach. Only when the principles in which we profess belief are translated into actual behavior can we be sure that our foundations are secure. . . .

If America as the exemplar and defender of freedom is to endure, it must give more than lip service to those basic principles that undergird Western civilization. . . . It must translate these articles of faith into its daily thought and action. If we do this we too shall build our house upon a rock and neither the black tide of fascism nor the red flood of communism can prevail against us.—*Peter H. Odegard, President, Reed College. In "Frontiers of Freedom." The Walter J. Shepard Foundation, Ohio State University. Ap.* 28, '48. *p.*19-22.

THE CASE FOR OUTLAWING THE COMMUNIST PARTY

CAN THE COMMUNIST PARTY BE CONSTITUTIONALLY OUTLAWED? [1]

In spite of a rather widespread view that our Constitution would not permit the *outlawing* of the Communist party, it is submitted that such a view is wholly erroneous, since the Communist party is plainly being used throughout the world as the agency of a great power in its efforts to overthrow other governments. No government can exist which cannot protect itself against revolution or seditious conspiracies. Current history proves beyond reasonable doubt that the Communist party is engaged in seditious conspiracy, international in scope, supported, first, by the Comintern, and now the Cominform, and its overt acts include the overthrow of ten governments within as many years.

The idea that the Communist party cannot be outlawed seems to stem from a supposed right to revolution and to the sacrosanct status accorded this alleged right to revolution by the writers on free speech. There can be no right to revolution, since that is the negation of government, any more than there is a right to kill, though homicide might be *justifiable* under certain circumstances, as in self-defense or during war. But revolution is not even justifiable where there is a reasonably practical method of amendment, as under our Constitution. Free speech fanatics would permit anyone to advocate the overthrow of government by violence. They find it easy to buttress their argument by quotations from the Declaration of Independence and the addresses of our revolutionary patriots. By our Declaration of Independence the overwhelming majority of the people threw off the shackles of a foreign tyrant, after all other means had

[1] By Frank B. Ober, Maryland Bar (Baltimore). *American Bar Association Journal.* 34:742-7. August 1948. Reprinted by permission.

failed. It would be a gross distortion to think that our patriots were singing the praises of a bastard revolution by a *minority* seditious group in our country, aimed at placing our *own* people under the yoke of a *foreign* despot. That is not revolution, but treasonable conspiracy.

There is, of course, a vast difference between advocating free speech in relation to domestic violence, at times when it constitutes no serious threat, contrasted with that which is part of an international conspiracy under the Soviet-dominated world organization. The argument that it is better to let individual agitators blow off steam, in the traditional Hyde Park manner, has considerable merit where not endangering national survival. It is also true that the dangers from subversive organizations at the time of World War I were much exaggerated and therefore there was some basis for the criticism directed against the administration of restrictive laws of that era. The First Amendment radicals were first formulating their arguments before the critical year 1938, when Hitler, through his series of conquests, demonstrated successfully how an enemy power can use seditious fifth columns, and long before the conquest by Russia of the East European countries through the use of their own minority Communist parties.

If it once be recognized that the Communist party is a conspiratorial organization and the spearhead of a threatened foreign attack upon us, there should be no reasonable doubt as to the *constitutionality* of laws outlawing it entirely as a legal political party, and hence also of properly drawn laws seeking to control this menace.

There is, of course, a sharp difference of opinion as to the political wisdom of outlawing communism. Opponents glibly state that it would be un-American to outlaw a legal domestic political party, and add as a crushing *reductio ad absurdum* that if we outlaw the Communist party, next we will outlaw the Republican and Democratic parties. This is a vast oversimplification—(1) the conquest of East Europe shows the so-called *party* is an agency of Moscow; (2) the outlawing of the "party" would deprive it of one of its greatest weapons of mass appeal —that is to say, propaganda through a legal political party, so eagerly desired by official Comintern policy and so fatuously accorded by the extreme legalism of democratic governments; (3) the idea that outlawing would drive it underground and make it more dangerous has lost all plausibility, since recent events in Czechoslovakia disclosed the secret armed underground coexists with the legal political party. To cut off one prong of this pincers movement cannot strengthen the other. (4) Communist parties, while small in numbers, gain a huge advantage from a legal status of adding to their voting strength many groups of malcontents. Panaceas are freely offered—as in the Italian elections—and influence gullible voters who are not really seditious and do not realize their danger. Legalization of the party has not saved recent Soviet victims from enslavement. (5) The Canadian spy trials clearly show that the Communists keep secret members who can be used for espionage purposes, even where the party is legal. Of course, the party can change name, and has done so already seven times, but there has been no practical difficulty in tracing it through its leaders and otherwise; nor is its recent change in professed objectives convincing. (6) Finally, the Communist party is not a *political* party at all in the American sense of a loose association tolerating limitless divergence of opinion. It has party cards, dues paying memberships, requires implicit obedience to the shifting party line determined by the Comintern under Russian direction, with the penalty of expulsion. It is not indigenous to this country, but a section of the Comintern which has preached violence from its inception. The vast majority of its leaders, as pointed out by the FBI, are aliens or have foreign connections, mostly Russian, and its top leaders—like Foster and Browder— are Moscow-trained members of the Comintern and travel constantly to Moscow for instructions. The current political arguments against "outlawing" this conspiratorial, treasonable organization, on the theory it is a *political* party, blithely ignore these facts. The difficulties of drafting effective legislation are enormous—but Congressional efforts to find a solution deserve support rather than ridicule.

Congress may pass laws, but they are only scraps of paper without vigorous enforcement by the Executive.

The Executive department has been subjected to criticism on this score. As the Nixon Subcommittee said:

> Had the law enforcement authorities vigorously enforced existing laws against Communists in the United States, the growth of the movement would undoubtedly have been stultified, so that it would not constitute the serious threat to our national security that it now does.

Prior to 1940 the Civil Service Commission required Communists, otherwise qualified, to be appointed to all federal jobs —even in national defense agencies. Efforts by the Executive to purge the government services of Communists were not very vigorous, to say the least, until the Executive Order of March 1947 set up a new loyalty program, requiring investigations of present and future employees, naming by the Attorney General of subversive organizations, and removal of disloyal employees. The Attorney General has listed 103 subversive organizations under this order. The portion of this order proscribing mere membership in subversive organizations, while upheld by a district judge, may be contrary to the constitutional views of some of the present members of the Court because of the *ex parte* character of the Attorney General's investigation and because of imputation of personal guilt from mere membership.

The question of whether penalties should attach to membership alone should, it is believed, depend upon the character of the proceedings. Chief Justice Stone, in his dissent in the *Schneiderman* case, disposed of the claim that membership in the Communist party is meaningless, in deportation cases where naturalization is not a matter of right, in this language:

> It might as well be said that it is impossible to infer that a man is attached to the principles of a religious movement from the fact that he conducts its prayer meetings, or, to take a more sinister example, that it could not be inferred that a man is a Nazi and consequently not attached to constitutional principles, who, for more than five years, had diligently circulated the doctrine of *Mein Kampf* . . . . A man can be known by the ideas he spreads as well as by the company he keeps, and when one does not challenge the proof that he has given his life to spreading a particular class of well-defined ideas, it is convincing evidence that his attachment is to them rather than to their opposites.

In the executive loyalty order similar considerations would seem to apply, for the reason that there is no vested right to an office. Where criminal guilt is the issue, however, a more troublesome question would arise. But in the Subversive Activities Act, as pointed out, Congress has required personal knowledge by the member of the objectives of his organization.

What have our states to do with this problem? The states, under our federal Constitution, retain their police powers and have the primary obligation of maintaining their own internal security and, as such, the duty to combat seditious organizations. Indeed, the states have war powers themselves, including the right of defense against invasion. Many of the states passed statutes directly prohibiting the advocacy of, or membership in organizations seeking the overthrow of government by violence, about the time of World War I, when criminal syndicalism was widespread.

The former Supreme Court upheld these statutes in the *Gitlow, Whitney* and the *Burns* cases, and while in some cases it construed them narrowly, it never held them invalid. As Mr. Justice Sanford said in the *Gitlow* case, in 1925, in incisive language which today has taken on new meaning:

> That a state, in the exercise of its police power, may punish those who abuse this freedom by utterances inimical to the public welfare, tending to corrupt public morals, incite to crime or disturb the public peace, is not open to question . . . .
>
> And for yet more imperative reasons the state may punish utterances endangering the foundation of organized government and threatening to overthrow by unlawful means. These imperil its own existence as a constitutional state. Freedom of speech and press, said Story, does not protect disturbances to the public peace or the attempt to subvert the government . . . . In short, this freedom does not deprive a state of the primary and *essential right of self-preservation which, so long as human governments endure, they cannot be denied* . . . .
>
> If the state were compelled to wait until the apprehended danger became certain, then its right to protect itself would come into being simultaneously with the overthrow of the government, when there would be neither prosecuting officers nor Courts for the enforcement of the law. [Italics supplied]

Between 1937 and 1940, four new judges were appointed to the Court and a new attitude *toward indirect* state efforts to control sedition appeared. Many, if not most, states had attempted to counteract subversive activities by the patriotic ceremony of saluting the flag and a pledge of allegiance. This custom had prevailed in many public schools for generations. The new Court, at first in the *Gobitis* case, adhered to its previous decisions upholding such statutes.

But three years later, in the *Barnette* case, it reversed itself, overruling its five previous cases. (Justices Reed, Roberts and Frankfurter dissented.) The reversal would not have taken place but for the shift of three new judges from their own position of three years before. Religious sects have claimed exemption from many laws, such as compulsory vaccination, inspection laws, testimonial duties, compulsory medical treatment and the obligation to bear arms. But, prior to the *Barnette* case, they had been compelled to comply with legislation "of general applicability, even though the religious consciences of particular individuals rebelled at the exaction." Yet, one tiny religious sect, which objected to this effort of the state to inculcate Americanism and thus combat sedition, has been permitted to defeat this objective by destroying the sense of unity which makes such ceremony of value and to limit the police power of the state.

The *Barnette* case cited with approval the 1931 *Stromberg* case, where the Court had upheld, against a California statute, the right of a Communist school to require the saluting of the Red Russian flag. The contrast in results is startling, however much the latter case may be justified on technical grounds.

Some states have outlawed the Communist party by refusing to allow it to appear on the ballots, but the constitutionality of these laws has not yet been passed upon by the Supreme Court.

The new Court's lack of sympathy for indirect state efforts to cope with sedition is further evidenced in the *Davidowitz* case, by the striking down of the Pennsylvania law, which, in the exercise of the police power, required registration of aliens.

The foregoing review indicates that the result of the decisions of the new Court has been to block the continuous, if not always well-planned, efforts of Congress and the states to preserve our government from communism and other seditious movements. Everyone is at liberty to advocate change in our government by the orderly methods prescribed by the Constitution. The moment he urges the substitution of the bullet for the ballot he becomes an enemy of society and should be treated as such. Freedom of speech should stop short of seditious activities.

The reversal of constitutional landmarks by the new Court in other fields has become so customary as to cause no surprise. Perhaps much of the explanation lies in the characteristics and background of the new appointees to the Court, but such an inquiry would carry us far afield. However, five general comments on the attitudes of the new Court seem justified.

First: The Court, in its disposition of cases involving communism, seems curiously blind to the lessons of current history which confirm so clearly the documentary evidence as to communism's technique of infiltration and violence, its essentially conspiratorial character, and its plain purpose to establish a beach-head for foreign aggression. As Mr. Justice Holmes has said. "A page of history is worth a volume of logic."

Second: The Court has applied the views of extremists on free speech without giving due consideration, it is submitted, to the necessity of survival. The Court has destroyed any presumption of the validity of legislation in the field by the so-called "preferred status" it gives the Bill of Rights. *Whatever the merits of the "preferred status" accorded the First Amendment in other fields, it is the apotheosis of absurdity to permit a Communist to invoke the very Constitution he is trying forcibly to destroy, to aid him in its destruction.* Traitors and seditious organizers are, like others, entitled to a fair trial under our Bill of Rights, but it is totally and wholly different to give them a "preferred status" when they are hiding behind the First Amendment in advocating the forcible overthrow of our government. Surely, in such a contest the survival of the government is entitled to the preferred status. What does it profit us to have freedoms if they be used to advocate the betrayal of the Constitution which guarantees them?

Third: In sedition cases, which are so closely related to national defense, the presumption in favor of legislative validity is ignored by a Court which has upheld in other fields the greatest extension of legislative power in our constitutional history. The Supreme Court attempts to justify its upsetting of statutes by an unwarranted use of the dictum of Mr. Justice Holmes, that there must be a "clear and present danger of the substantive evil which Congress had the power to prevent." As Mr. Justice Frankfurter, concurring in the *Pennekamp* case, said:

Neither Mr. Justice Holmes nor Mr. Justice Brandeis nor this Court ever suggested in all the cases that arose in connection with the first World War, that only imminent threats to the immediate security of the country would authorize courts to sustain legislation curtailing utterance. Such forces of destruction are of an order of magnitude which courts are hardly designed to counter.

For the Court to apply a veto power to sedition laws and deny the power of the coordinate branches of government in this field is an arrogation by the judiciary of a power far beyond that ever previously used. May we not hope it will yet renounce the views of the "self-canonized liberals," who are unwilling to sacrifice an ounce of free speech dogmatism for a pound of democratic survival, and return to the more fundamental doctrine that this freedom, like others, must be subordinated to self-preservation? Just as the war power is based thereon in a shooting war, so also, it is submitted, this basic right must have priority, especially in a cold war.

Fourth: The new Court, in invalidating state legislation in this particular field, has almost completely abandoned the principle which gives wide latitude to state legislation under its police power and is the chief strength of a federal system of government. By assuming a judicial supervisory power in the name of *preserving* one freedom, it defeats the efforts of the states to defend themselves.

Finally: The Court has been astute in inventing new doctrines to reach the almost predetermined result in this particular field. For example, it refused to follow principles applicable in other fields: In the *Schneiderman* case, by upsetting concurrent findings of fact by both lower Courts; in the *Bridges* case, by upsetting the facts as found by a well-qualified administrative officer on substantial evidence; in all cases in this field, by paying little or no regard to the Court's previous decisions; by the invention or extension of the preferred status and clear and present danger doctrines to this field—thus reversing the presumption in favor of validity of state and federal legislation; and by setting up such severe requirements as to burden of proof in sedition cases as to defeat government efforts to curb communism.

America is faced today with a struggle for existence against an enemy which has developed the new technique of seditious fifth columns in our midst. Congress, the states and, somewhat belatedly, the executive, are alive to the dangers, as are the people at large and the lower federal courts. Our diplomatic efforts, the billions being expended in the Marshall and Truman plans, the peacetime draft law—all attest the grave danger of Russian communism to our industrialized nation, which is so vulnerable in this atomic age. Surely, the time has come when legislative efforts to control sedition should be accorded the presumption of constitutionality to which they rightfully are entitled, instead of being frustrated by legal sophistries.

We lawyers, who tend to be traditionalists and conservatives, have been slow to recognize the menace of this Trojan horse. We have dogmatically adhered to constitutional absolutes and individual rights, which were adopted primarily for protection against domestic tyranny, and thus have blurred over important distinctions. It is one thing to afford to seditious aliens the guarantee of a fair trial; it is quite a different thing to permit them to hide behind one constitutional guarantee in order to carry on their seditious activity in advocating the violent destruction of the government and the assassination of our Constitution.

To conclude, it is time for us to reorient our thinking and for a militant Bar to recognize that our most important obligation is to preserve the *whole* Constitution. We should direct our efforts toward that end instead of encouraging the exaggerated application of civil rights to a field which threatens our national survival. Indeed, in view of the attitude taken by the majority of the new Court, it may yet be necessary to consider the adoption of a constitutional amendment which will restore the preferred status of the Union itself and more nearly attain some of the purposes set forth in the very preamble of our Constitution, "to insure domestic tranquillity" and "to provide for the common defense" and "to secure the blessings of liberty to ourselves and to our posterity."

SHOULD THE COMMUNIST PARTY IN THE UNITED STATES BE OUTLAWED? [2]

When World War II ended I felt that the key question as to future peace would arise if bad policies were followed by the Soviet Union of Russia and by the world Communist party directed from Moscow, I therefore gave special study to their actions, to their methods, to their party intentions. I journeyed to many of the European countries and to Russia and questioned leaders of many nations for a first-hand look-and-listen trip. I followed closely the results of the peace conferences of Potsdam and Yalta and the developments in country after country.

I have reached the conclusion that the Communist organizations in the world are absolutely directed by the rulers of Russia in the Kremlin. I have reached the conclusion that the objectives of these Communist organizations in the world are to overthrow free governments, to destroy the liberties of men, and to bring other countries under the domination of the dictators of Russia. I have watched country after country in which these Communist organizations have taken every legal advantage but have recognized none of the corresponding obligations and moralities.

The most recent and extreme instance is Czechoslovakia. The Communists never had the support of a majority of the people of Czechoslovakia, but they were given full legal standing and Communists were appointed to some of the ministries of government. The people of the country were free, they were rebuilding from the war, there was no tyranny, there was no threat to Russia, there was a politeness and a friendliness toward the Communists, but the Communist organizations, directed from Moscow, took all of these legal blessings and at the same time moved underneath the surface, established Communistic committees in all the departments of government, in the big labor unions, in key industries,

[2] By Harold E. Stassen, former Governor of Minnesota, in debate with Thomas E. Dewey, May 17, 1948. *Vital Speeches of the Day.* 14:482-4+, June 1, 1948. Reprinted by permission. For Governor Dewey's speech, see p. 237-48.

and in the universities and colleges. Then a few weeks ago, the overground and underground moving together, Czechoslovakia was betrayed, the liberties of the people were wiped out, and another country was brought under the domination of the Kremlin. These developments do give rise to a danger of war.

Analyzing what they mean, it seems clear to me that the free countries, including America, do not now have adequate laws to safeguard themselves in the face of this menace. I consider it to be clear that these Communist organizations are not really political parties, they are actually fifth columns, they are Quisling cliques. If we are to have the best chance of winning through for freedom without the horror of a third world war, the free countries must take action to protect themselves against this fifth column in this unsettled period which has been called a cold war.

I do not think it is generally realized in America that we do not now have any law to effectively oppose the actions of these Communist organizations, either overground or underground. There is now no law in America to prevent the Communist organizations from secretly developing organizations of hidden members, from carrying on secret conspiracies, to promote strikes, to establish hatred of religions and races in America.

Neither is there any present law to prevent the Communist organization from maintaining large offices of telephone switchboards and a network of communication to be used in reaching and coordinating these underground activities and in recruiting new members.

In facing up to the problem, we must maintain complete constitutional rights and liberties in America. The right of free speech, of free press, of freedom of conscience and freedom of religion must be kept inviolate. It must always be open to any individual in this country to protest, to object, to dissent. But there is no constitutional right to carry on organizations above ground or below ground directed by the rulers of the foreign power with the purpose of overthrowing the government of the United States and taking away the liberties of its people.

I, therefore, have urged for some months that we need a new law to directly outlaw these Communist organizations. Governor Dewey has insisted that our present laws are adequate. I submit that a new law is needed. It should directly make it illegal after its passage to carry on any organization, either above ground or below ground, which is directed by the rulers of a foreign power for the purpose of overthrowing the government of the United States, destroying the liberties of its people and bringing this country under the domination of the rulers of a foreign power. Such a law would not outlaw ideas, it would not outlaw thoughts, it would make illegal organized conspiracy of fifth columns. Such a law is constitutional under Article 4 Section 4 of the United States Constitution. A very eminent lawyer, the honorable William L. Ransom, past president of the American Bar Association, agrees on its constitutionality in an able article in the *American Law Journal* this month. The language of the Supreme Court in *Ohio v. Akron* indicates that the Supreme Court would uphold its constitutionality. In fact, the national Congress is right now moving to do this very thing.

A law has been introduced known as the Mundt-Nixon bill, which provides that it shall be unlawful to attempt in any manner to establish in the United States a totalitarian dictatorship, the direction and control of which is to be vested in or exercised by or under the domination or control of any foreign government, foreign organization or foreign individual or to attempt to perform any act toward those ends.

The report of the committee that investigated the Communist activities specifically found that the Communist organization was an organization whose basic aim, whether open or concealed, is the abolition of our present economic system and democratic form of government and the establishment of a Soviet dictatorship in its place.

Now, the chairman and secretary of the Communist party of America have protested that this bill would outlaw their organization. I agree that it would and I say that it should. The United States Congress indicated in a preliminary way their approval of the bill when they voted last Friday, by a vote of 296 to 40, to bring it up for action on Tuesday. It might well be amended to some extent before it is finally passed by both Houses, because in some cases directed against individuals it goes even beyond what I have urged. But I do believe that it will pass in the near future in a form that will definitely outlaw these Communist organizations in both their underground and overground activities.

I further believe that this will be a precedent for similar action by the other free countries of the world and that effective means will be developed to safeguard against the fifth-column infiltration of the Communists.

Now, I recognize full well that there are some who have sincerely opposed my position in this matter. I am not certain of the reasons for Mr. Henry Wallace's opposition to my position, but I am confident that Governor Dewey's opposition is completely sincere. But I respectfully ask him to reconsider his opposition as I believe he is mistaken. His position in effect means a soft policy towards communism and all the evidence around the world shows that a soft policy wins neither peace nor respect nor improvement from the Communists. We must not muddle communism with legality. They grasp every concession made and continue their undermining action.

Consider these facts: There are now eleven countries of the world under the domination of the Communist leaders in Moscow. They are Russia, Poland, Czechoslovakia, Hungary, Yugoslavia, Romania, Bulgaria, Albania, Estonia, Latvia and Lithuania. In none of these eleven did the Communists ever receive majority support of the people in a free election. The last three were taken over by force during the war and held ever since. In every one of the remaining eight, the Communists used the legal recognition of Communist organizations as an underground nerve center and recruiting station for their underground movements, until they had seized power and brought the nation under the dictation of the Communist Politburo.

Russia was the first Communist-dominated nation. It came under this dictatorship through a combination of two main reasons: First, the bad government of the czar. Second, the organization developed by the legalized Bolshevik party, which formed throughout Russia and elected six members to the Russian Parliament in the last election held in that country before the Communists came to power.

There seems to have been some mistaken idea that the Communists were outlawed in Russia. This is not correct. The Bolshevik party was active in Russia right up to the first war with Germany. The Communists carried on a nationwide election campaign in Russia in 1912 and elected six members to the Parliament or Duma.

They used this means of developing their revolutionary organization, and when they were caught in the attempted revolution and in various sabotage, in train wrecking and bombings, they were severely punished, but they were not outlawed as an organization. When this present Communist party did come into power in Russia, they promptly wiped out all other political parties and took the whole peoples under a firm and dictatorial grip. In each of the other countries—Poland, Hungary, Yugoslavia, Romania, Bulgaria, Albania and finally Czechoslovakia—the Communists used the blessing of legality as an aid to organizing an underground movement, and finally betrayed the liberties of the people and brought them under the domination of the Kremlin in Moscow.

These are the facts which today cause a menace to Scandinavia and western Europe. These are the facts which today present a danger of future world war.

Another mistaken impression is the claim that if we outlaw the Communist organization, we thereby endanger the liberties and civil rights of other people. This is not true. In Canada the party was outlawed for years and the people lost none of their liberties. In fact, the Communists were permitted to operate legally again under the name of the labor progressive party in 1943, and soon afterwards, in less than three years, it was found that the Communists were working directly with the Russian embassy at Ottawa in a spy ring.

In order that we might narrow down our discussion and find out just exactly what the differences are in our positions, I should like to ask Governor Dewey specifically these questions:

1. Do you agree that the Communist organizations throughout the world are directed from Moscow?

2. Do you agree that the objective of the Communist organizations throughout the world is to overthrow free govern-

ments, destroy liberties, and bring the countries under the domination of the Kremlin?

3. Do you agree that Communist organizations throughout the world are a menace to future peace?

4. Do you agree that because of this menace to world peace, it is necessary that we acquire American young men to serve in our armed forces and to take military training?

To make my position, then, clear, I say very definitely that it does not add up to me to say that loyal, patriotic young Americans must, of necessity, be drafted; that their liberties must be taken away in order to make America strong in the face of the menace to peace caused by Communist organizations, but that none of the privileges and blessings of legality should be taken away from the Communist organizations themselves, which in fact are causing the menace that makes the drafting necessary.

The fundamental principles of human liberty upon which this nation is founded are drawn from our basic religious concepts. Our founding fathers did believe that man has a spiritual value; that he is endowed by his creator with certain inalienable rights; that he should have a human dignity, a respect for the welfare of others; that there is a brotherhood of man.

The constitutional rights in America are based on that concept. When one speaks of the constitutional right of organizations that are seeking to destroy freedom there is a misconception of the deep basis of constitutional rights. There is no such thing as a constitutional right to destroy all constitutional rights. There is no such thing as a freedom to destroy freedom.

The right of man to liberty is inherent in the nature of man. To win it and to maintain it requires courage and sacrifice, and it also requires intelligence and realism and determination in the establishment of the laws and the systems of justice to serve mankind.

I submit that the Communist organization in America and in the freedom-loving countries of the world should be outlawed.

REBUTTAL

Apparently we have narrowed this question down very much. It hinges now primarily on the Mundt-Nixon bill. The Mundt-

Nixon bill says, "It shall be unlawful for any person to attempt in any manner to establish in the United States a totalitarian dictatorship, the direction and control of which is to be vested in or exercised by or under the domination or control of any foreign government, foreign organization or foreign individual, or to perform or attempt to perform any act with the intent to facilitate such end."

Now I hold that that directly fits and applies to the Communist party organization in the United States and in the world today.

The question then is: Does it so apply? Obviously you cannot and should not draft your law in such form that a mere name results in an outlawing. It is being directed by a foreign power, with the purpose of undermining the liberty of the American people and overthrowing our government which is the key point. They are so doing. There should be no doubt of that.

Here is a quote from Louis Budenz who left the Communist party. He said: "We must understand then before we get to the meat of the matter that we are dealing with a conspiracy to establish Soviet dictatorship throughout the world."

Many such instances—Generalissimo Stalin himself said in the speech to the American delegation in 1928, and they are now reverting to that policy, the Communist party of America as a section of the Third Internationale must pay dues to the Comintern. All the decisions of the Congress of the Third Internationale are obligatorily carried out by all the parties affiliated.

In other words the decisions in Moscow by the Kremlin must be carried out in America, so that definitely and directly the Mundt-Nixon bill will outlaw the Communist party as it is now functioning in America and in the world.

In fact, perhaps we are coming down to a point where we can reach agreement. Although I heard the Governor say that he did not think the Mundt-Nixon bill would outlaw the Communist party. I did not hear him say whether he would support that bill. Now, if he will say that he approves of and will support the Mundt-Nixon bill, I will be satisfied that we have reached an agreement that we have thereby outlawed the Com-

munist party as it actually operates and, therefore, we can go on
to these other very important issues in this campaign.

I reiterate, if the Governor feels that he can support the
Mundt-Nixon bill, I will agree that that is sufficient to outlaw
the party as it is now constituted, and he can go on to other important issues in the development of Oregon and in America.

On the matter of the Communist party in Russia, the actual
report, "The History of the Communist Party," which is an established work on what happened in Russia, states very positively
that the Communists were not outlawed; the Bolshevik party, so
to speak, were not outlawed in Russia, and elected six members
to the last Duma in the last elections which were held. So, I of
course realize that we cannot in these few minutes left in the debate check references, but I submit to the Governor that he should
look up his references in the history of what happened to Russia.

Now then, the Governor says that we have effective laws now
—seventeen of them—that all they need to do is use them. May
I ask then why is it that the Communist party organization has
been growing so strong in New York?

New York is the national headquarters of the Communist
party of America. New York, with 9 per cent of America's population, has 40 per cent of the Communists in America. New
York is the capital Communist center in America, and from that
center, from the national headquarters in New York, they have
been reaching out and infiltrating in the labor organizations of
America, they have been prejudicing the sovereignty of this country and the harmonious relationships in labor.

Clearly, does the Governor not agree that they have been
operating underground now?

It is not a matter of driving them underground by the passage
of a law. They are underground and overground and they themselves pick out which one best serves their purposes in each
instance.

Now, I submit so far as I have observed, there has only been
one conviction of a Communist in New York in the last eight
years and that was the publisher or editor of the *Daily Worker,*
and he was convicted for a libel against another editor that really
had no connection with Communist activities.

If there are these laws now that are adequate, why have they not been used in New York?

Why have they not been used in the Federal Government, and has the Governor of New York called upon the Federal Government to use Federal law in cooperation with the state?

We found in a limited way in Minnesota, where we did have some Communist infiltration in 1938, which was causing strikes and violence and killings on the streets of Minneapolis, we found that we could make progress if we cooperated with the Federal Government, the state government and the local government, moving together with the assistance of the loyal, patriotic American workmen; that we gradually weeded them out. We found we were greatly handicapped in completing the job because there was no law that directly related to the manner in which the Communists took their orders from a foreign power.

Let's be specific. If an underground order came from the Kremlin to the Communists in America, and they held a secret meeting at which it was agreed that they were going to seek strikes in certain essential industries and stir them up, we will say, industries that were going to develop some great dynamos or hydroelectric power, some great generators, or in another way interfere with the potential of this country, even though every fact of that secret move was discovered, there is no law under which we could act.

Or, suppose the underground word came and said that the Communists should move in around the Panama Canal and Alaska, and establish themselves in various jobs, and secret meetings were held where that was arranged. There is no law on the books of this country that would permit us to move directly against that conspiracy.

Under the present laws, you would have to wait until a move of force was made, or until they uncovered their hand in a very flagrant way.

What we need is a law that goes directly to the problem of the way in which the Communist organizations have been operating since the end of the war. They are the threat of war. We should not stumble along with laws that are out of date. We should bring our thinking up to date.

This is not a matter of outlawing any ideas. It is not a matter of any thought control.

What constitutional provision would prevent the kind of a law like the Mundt-Nixon bill? Which article of the Constitution would it violate? I know of none that says that an organization may carry on in the manner in which the Communist organization is carrying on now.

Therefore, it is open for legislative action. And I submit to the Governor that he earnestly reconsider his position and specifically, if he will say that he will now agree to support the Mundt-Nixon bill unequivocably.

Then I will agree that we have reached a point of union on this important issue, and we will go forward with a constructive campaign in Oregon on those other very important questions that are before the people of this great state and before our America in the wake of war.

ARE COMMUNISTS TRAITORS TO AMERICA [3]

The trial of the twelve leaders of the Communist party in the United States will very likely cause a good deal of confusion regarding civil rights among many Americans unless we fix clearly in mind what communism stands for, what it actually seeks and how it goes about getting it.

The central question which needs to be asked—and answered by conclusive evidence, not by epithet or prejudice—is this: Is the Communist party simply another political group within the framework of American democracy?

If it is, if its first loyalty is to the Government of the United States and if it only seeks political change, however radical, through constitutional means, then its adherents should be left totally free to exercise their rights as American citizens. If this is the truth, then the arrest of the American Communists is unjust and they are right in calling the Grand Jury indictment a "political frame-up" and a "witch-hunt."

    [3] By Roscoe Drummond, Chief, Washington Bureau of the Christian Science Monitor. *American Mercury.* 67:389-96. October 1948.

But if the Communist party is not just another political party, if its first loyalty is not to the Government of the United States, if it is, in fact, an international conspiracy provably subversive in method and in purpose, then its American adherents have themselves given over their civil rights to a foreign power. If this is the truth, then in arresting the Communist leaders, the American government is alertly and rightly acting in self-defense, in self-preservation, in order to avert subversion before it is too late.

Most American are familiar with some of the evidence indicating that the Communist parties are not political parties at all in the democratic sense and, wherever they operate, serve as instruments of Soviet foreign policy.

We are aware that after Earl Browder had served his purpose of enabling the Communist party to reverse its previous position so as to cooperate in a common front after Hitler attacked Russia, he was, as soon as the war was over, tossed out of his post at the direction of Moscow. William Z. Foster, now under arrest, was put back in.

We are aware that when Moscow was cooperating with Hitler in 1939 and 1940, the Communist party in the United States tried to block the American Government's opposition to Hitler, and that when Moscow stopped cooperating with Hitler, the Communist party in the United States instantly stopped trying to block American opposition to Hitler.

We are aware that what is happening to Marshal Tito in Belgrade is proof that a Communist leader is never permitted to put the interests of his own country ahead of international communism, which means communism run by and for the Soviet Government. Marshall Tito found this out when he tried to be a *Yugoslavian* Communist in Yugoslavia: he learned to his sorrow that he could remain in good standing with Moscow only by being a *Soviet* Communist in Yugoslavia.

These are some of the acts which reveal that the Communist party, whether in America or Italy or Czechoslovakia or Finland is the tool and agent of the Soviet Government, without independence and obedient to every turn and shift of Kremlin policy.

But the proof goes deeper than this. The most conclusive and incontrovertible evidence is not what others say the Communists are up to but what the Communists themselves, in their less guarded moments, say they are up to.

When the Communist party in the United States somersaults overnight from bitter, strike-laden opposition to support of the American armament program, as it did in 1941, for the sole reason that Hitler reneged on his compact with Stalin; when Browder is removed from the chairmanship of the party at a nod from Moscow; when Tito is given a 3000-word denunciation by the Cominform as a "Trotskyist," a "nationalist" and a pursuer of a "hateful policy toward Russia" because he wanted to put Yugoslavia first—these actions are not casual or personal, and they are not surprising or unexpected. They are not accidental violations of Communist policy; they carefully conform to Communist policy—to the policies and purposes of the Communist International which can be cited chapter, verse—and sub-verse.

I should like to report:

That there is no such thing as an *American* Communist party.

That the Communist party which has been set up in the United States is avowedly a "section" of the Communist International.

That its decision can be instantly and legally reversed by the Politburo in Moscow.

That its officials hold office at the behest of Moscow.

That its members have actually signed over to the Soviet-controlled Executive Committee of the Communist International (ECCI) their American civil and constitutional rights to think and act as free men.

These are the basic truths about the Communists and the Communist party in every country, including the United States, and I draw them not from the "imperialistic press" of the West, not from writings of the critics of communism, but from official, incontrovertible, Communist documents—*The Constitution and Rules of the International Communist Party.*

As a means of determining whether Communist parties are like other political groups within a democracy or whether they are obedient instruments of an international conspiracy, I ask

Americans to consider the following questions and to examine the answers which come from the *Constitution and Rules of the International Communist Party.*

Q: Is the Communist party in the United States indigenous to America?

A: The *Constitution and Rules of the International Communist Party* states that every Communist party in every country is only a "section" of the International.

Q: Is the Communist party in the United States free to govern its own affairs, make its own policies?

A: Section III of the International Constitution provides that the Executive Committee of the Communist International shall "give instruction to all sections and control their activities."

Q: Must the Communist party in the United States follow the policies of the International?

A: The *Constitution and Rules* stipulate that "the decisions of the Executive Committee of the Communist International are obligatory for all sections."

Q: Can the International overrule the wishes and actions of the Communist party in the United States?

A: From the *Constitution and Rules*: "The Executive Committee of the Communist International has the right to annul or amend decisions of party congresses and central committees of individual parties and make decisions which are obligatory for them."

Q: What happens if American or Czech or Finnish Communists rebel?

A: "The Executive Committee of the Communist International," states the Constitution to which all have subscribed, "has the right to expel sections [parties], groups and individual members of sections."

Q: How does the Communist International check up on the work and loyalty of its various national subdivisions?

A: By its Constitution the Executive Committee of the Communist International "has the right to send their representatives to the various sections, to participate in their meetings, to speak in opposition to the central committee of a given section, to send instructors to the various sections."

Q: Are there further methods of Kremlin control over the American and other Communist parties?

A: The Constitution of the International creates a "Control Division" with powers "to investigate matters concerning the unity of the sections, the conduct of individual members, complaints against the actions of the central committees and concerning members, and to audit the accounts of the Third International." The Rules provide further that "the central Committee [of the various parties] must send the Executive Committee of the Communist International minutes of their meetings and reports."

Q: Can officials of the Communist party in the United States resign from party office if they don't like what the party calls upon them to do?

A: No. The Rules provide against any such independence. The International Constitution stipulates that "resignation from office is disruptive. Leading posts in the party do not belong to the occupant but to the Communist International. Elected members may resign only with the consent of the Executive Committee of the Communist International. Resignations accepted by the central committees of sections [parties] without the consent of the ECCI are invalid."

Q: Can members leave the Communist party freely?

A: Paragraph 37 of the Rules provides that no member of any Communist party is allowed to leave his country without the consent of the central committee and that if he changes domicile he is compelled to join the party in the country where he goes.

Is the Communist party a genuine and indigenous political party within the framework of American democracy? The foregoing are the facts, indisputable facts. I believe they do not need to be argued. They show that the American Communists are totally under the orders of the Soviet-controlled Executive Committee of the Communist International, and their party is subject to foreign inspection and domination, that the Communist party operating in the United States is not an autonomous body, and that American Communists have already given over to a foreign agency the civil rights of free thought and action which they now want to claim for themselves under the American Constitution.

These are the facts in evidence. I believe that when they are brought fully into the open, as the *American Mercury* is constantly helping to do, the American people will have no trouble deciding that the Communist party in every country is the subversive tool of a foreign government and can treat it accordingly without any impairment of civil rights and constitutional liberties.

And there are other facts which add proof upon proof that the Communist party in the United States is disloyal to America and seeks to destroy the very liberties which it wants to use for itself until it can abolish them for others entirely.

This fact—that American Communists have renounced their patriotism to the United States and have pledged themselves to practice national treason.

Proof: "Every party must renounce social [national] patriotism . . . and pacifism," declares the Constitution of the Third International. "Every branch and member of the universal Communist party is pledged to indulge in national treason in case of war with the Soviets—no matter who, in such a war, should be the aggressor.

"Each affiliated party is obliged to render every possible assistance to the Soviet Republics . . . carry on propaganda to induce the workers to refuse to transport military equipment, and by legal or illegal means propagandize the troops.

"The object of the struggle, which must inevitably turn into civil war, is to obtain the political power. Eventually the proletariat must resort to armed uprising. . . . The party must always adapt itself to the idea of the Soviets. . . ."

And this fact—that the visible, legal part of the Communist party which protrudes above ground is only a façade and is subordinate to and controlled by the illegal Communist underground.

Proof: "The general state of things in Europe and America," according to the official theses of the Communist International, "makes necessary for the Communists of the whole world an obligatory formation of the illegal Communist organizations, along with those existing legally.

"The Communist parties must learn systematically to unite legal with illegal work, but all legal work must be carried on under the control of the illegal party. Parliamentary groups must be fully and absolutely subject to the party, regardless of whether the party as a whole is legal or illegal."

And this further fact—that the Communist party is openly dedicated to the use of force to achieve its end, which is Communist control of every government it can lay its hands on.

Proof: "Unless the bourgeois system [which means any non-Communist system] is overthrown," says the platform of the Communist International, "the repetition of war is inevitable. To overthrow the international bourgeoisie and create an international Soviet Republic, all means will be used, including force of arms.

"To admit the idea of a peaceful reformist passage to socialism is to give proof of extreme petty bourgeois obtuseness.

"Only a violent defeat of the bourgeoisie will guarantee complete submission."

These are the explicit and committed purposes of the Communist International of which the Communist party in the United States is one "section." Every Communist party member in every country has accepted these purposes as his own and he has pledged that he will subordinate his will to the discipline and direction of the Soviet-controlled Executive Committee of the Communist International as its *Constitution and Rules* disclose.

The venomous Cominform blast at Marshal Tito becomes entirely clear in the light of this evidence of what communism stands for, how it works and whom it is intended to serve. Obviously the Yugoslavian Communists were becoming too Yugoslavian, and the fact that Moscow acted to try to unseat Tito is open evidence that the Communist parties are the tool and agent of the Soviet government. This is not a new fact; it is an old fact newly proven.

Apparently Marshal Tito had assumed that it was possible for him to be a patriotic Yugoslav and a loyal Communist party leader at the same time. He had evidently forgotten the rules, for the Constitution of the Third International declares: "Every party must renounce social [national] patriotism."

A few months ago William Z. Foster, the indicted chairman of the Communist party in the United States, testified before a

Senate committee hearing on the Mundt-Nixon Communist-control bill. Judged by the principles of democracy, Mr. Foster made the most startling and incomprehensible statements. But in the light of the Constitution and rules and platform of the Communist International, here quoted, his testimony stands as the logical outgrowth of the commitments which he has accepted.

If there remains any non-Communist American who fails to see that communism is an aggressive, subversive conspiracy run from Moscow, it is well that Mr. Foster has now publicly, if not too willingly, testified:

That American Communists would not support the United States if it were attacked by the Soviet Union.

That American Communists would not in any circumstance obey any of the proposed legislation restricting Communist activities, even though it became the law of the land.

That American Communists would seek to end any war in which the United States and the Soviet Union might become engaged—on Soviet terms.

This testimony is carefully and faithfully extracted from the record. The single, central, all-vital fact which it underlines is that the Communist party is a Soviet agency within the United States, loyal only to the Soviet Union, and its obedient instrument. By the very rules and constitution of the Communist International, Mr. Foster cannot, any more than Marshal Tito, let loyalty to his own country conflict with orders from the Soviet-controlled Executive Committee of the Communist International.

There was one little point in his testimony at which Mr. Foster wavered just a bit from pure Communist doctrine—no doubt for a reason. Though inconsistent with some of his earlier testimony, he allowed himself to say that he wasn't sure whether American Communists would or would not actually disobey military orders if the United States and Russia got into war.

Either Mr. Foster hasn't read all the rules—hardly probable —or, as a tactic—very probable—he was momentarily blurring the role the American Communists would play. But the Constitution of the Communist International allows for no doubt and no deviation on this point if it should be reached. It is explicit and binding. It says:

"Every branch and member of the universal Communist party is pledged to indulge in national treason in case of war with the Soviets—no matter who, in such a war, should be aggressor." And it declares further: "Each affiliated party is obliged to render every possible assistance to the Soviet Republic."

The Grand Jury indictments of Foster and his associates charge them with conspiring "to organize the Communist party of the United States as a society, group, assembly of persons who teach and advocate the overthrow and destruction of the Government of the United States by force and violence."

The courts, ultimately the Supreme Court, will decide whether the American Communists are being "framed," as they contend, or whether they are guilty, as charged. They will have an American trial and they will be judged on the evidence by a jury of their peers.

The question which was posed at the beginning of this article and which, I hope, every American will ponder and answer for himself is whether the Communist party is an honest, genuine political group acting within the framework of American democracy, or whether it is a conspiring agent of a foreign government and a total enemy of those precious American freedoms which its members want, for a time, to use until they can destroy them?

Many times the Communist party has sought to elect a Communist as President of the United States and would be overjoyed to get its members into Congress. Why? To preserve the Constitution of the United States, as every President is sworn to do? To protect and strengthen democratic government?

Let the Communists answer those questions. The true answer is contained in the statutes and rules and constitution of the Third International. The answer, and I quote, is:

"Only the violent defeat of the bourgeoisie [which in Communist parlance is any non-Communist government]—the annihilation of their entire government apparatus from top to bottom, parliamentary, juridical, military, municipal . . . only such measures guarantee complete subjugation."

"Parliamentary [democratic] government can in no way be a form of Communist society. . . . The task of the proletariat consists in blowing up the whole machinery and all parliamentary institutions."

"Communism repudiates the possibility of winning over parliaments. Its aim is to destroy parliaments."

"The Central Committee must have its permanent representative in the [party's] parliamentary faction, with the right of veto. . . . Each candidate must sign a paper that at the first request of the Central Committee . . . he will give up his mandate. Each Communist representative must remember that he is not a 'legislator,' bound to seek agreements, but an agitator, detailed into the enemy's camp to carry out party orders."

"The Communist party enters such [parliamentary] institutions not for the purpose of organization work . . . but to blow the Parliaments up from within."

In view of these facts can it be contended that the Communist party is a genuine, honest political group working within the framework of American democracy?

In view of these facts can it be contended that American Communists deserve the protection of the American Constitution?

The courts will soon decide whether William Z. Foster is guilty of teaching and advocating the overthrow of the American Government by force and violence. But if the American Communist leader, Foster, is innocent of conspiring to destroy American democracy, he is guilty of being disloyal to the Communist tenets he has accepted. The Yugoslavian Communist leader, Tito, tried to have it both ways and found he couldn't.

WHO'S UNDERMINING CIVIL LIBERTIES? [4]

The danger to civil liberties does not come entirely from the frontal attacks on the Bill of Rights. There is a grave danger which, curiously enough, comes from the actions of its friends—from the host of well-meaning people who are de-

[4] By Lawrence Fertig, Columnist on *New York World-Telegram. Plain Talk.* 2:6-9. August 1948. Reprinted by permission.

fenders of the democratic process but are, however unconsciously, chipping away at its foundation.

The present situation arises out of a problem of how to fight Communists. One of the basic principles of civil rights is that, except for criminals, there must be only one class of citizenship. Every citizen of the United States is a first-class citizen and as good as any other, just so long as he obeys the law. It logically follows that no public official has the right to discriminate against any citizen because he belongs to some organization which that official does not like. If some Secretary of State, for instance, were to rule officially that under no condition would he hire a Republican or a Catholic, he would be forced to resign in short order because of the protests of an irate nation. It is true that no one has the *right* to a job in a government office and that administrative officials are privileged to select for their departments only those applicants who, in their opinion, are especially fitted for the work. But it is also true that public officials are, in effect, custodians of the public welfare and as custodians they must not discriminate against any groups which are legally constituted in our society.

But there is discrimination going on—and it is practiced with the consent and approval of the civil liberties defenders. There is an official ruling to the effect that no Communist may be hired in a position of trust in the Atomic Bomb Development. There is an official ruling that no Communist may be hired in a position of trust in the State Department. It is a fact that the Civil Liberties Union has not officially protested against this policy and it is also a fact that the staunchest de-- fenders of the Bill of Rights privately admit that the Secretary of State and the head of the Atomic Bomb Commission are absolutely right in refusing to give jobs to Communists. On the record the civil liberties defenders acquiesce in treating a legally constituted minority on a different basis from all other groups.

This acquiescence comes about because they know very well that Communists owe their allegiance to a foreign power and cannot be trusted. It would be the sheerest folly to place a Communist close to atomic bomb secrets or close to confidential information in the State Department. But while this is undoubtedly a sensible, practical policy, it leaves the civil liberties defenders out on a limb. It makes them guilty of approving the principle of "guilt by association" which they continually fight against. Of course they can take refuge in the fact that high public officials are not supposed to give important jobs to people they do not trust. But it is a matter of official ruling that these public officials must not trust any individual because he is a Communist. Here is a clear case of discrimination against a legally constituted group.

It must send shivers down the spine of many good people to think that some administrator in the future could just as readily outlaw other minority groups. The civil liberties defenders would be in no position to raise objections because they have already surrendered their principle. They have already admitted that a high public official has the right to discriminate against a group of citizens of whose policies he does not approve.

This confusion in the civil liberties position comes about because these people simply will not face the facts. They will not acknowledge the fact that they are facing a deadly conspiracy to act, and not a body of ideas to be debated in the public forum. They still insist that those who propose measures to curb the Communists are advocating "thought control." The fact is that no one with the faintest understanding of civil liberties proposes to control thought or free speech. Communists or Socialists or Fascists, for that matter, should be privileged to think what they want and talk as much as they please. There should be no attempt to curtail speech or thought. But it is obvious that the Communist conspiracy, while it is based upon thoughts, is primarily concerned with actions. It is concerned with working in behalf of a foreign power; it is concerned with laying plans to overthrow this government by force; it is concerned with planned infiltration into organizations like labor unions, communal groups, etc., with a view to taking them over or destroying them completely. The defenders of civil liberties refuse to acknowledge that this new type of conspiracy requires a new approach in the defense of our rights. The Communist conspiracy is pledged to the overthrow of the Bill of Rights by actions, by deeds, by conspiratorial maneuvers. To meet this danger, the defenders of civil liberties merely repeat such soporifics as "ideas must meet their test in the market place."

The only way the civil liberties defenders can extricate themselves from the present dilemma is to face the fact that they are dealing with a conspiracy and not with pure ideas; and to urge actively that the leaders be publicly tried in a court of law for conspiracy. There is no intention to restrain Marxists from talking *ad nauseam* about the exploitation of labor, cruelty of employers or the necessity for a totally new system. That is their privilege under the law.

It must be clearly understood that what we are talking about here is a public trial of the leaders of the Communist party and nothing else. The huge mass of evidence now in the hands of the FBI, the Attorney-General and many other organizations and individuals who are acquainted with this conspiracy must be placed on the record. On the basis of circumstantial evidence a conviction in this case would be practically certain. The result would be that a Communist would never again be able to say that he is as good as any other American citizen. It would be made clear as day that his activity as a Communist does not entitle him to the protection of the law or the respect of other American citizens. He would be legally stamped as the jackal in our democratic society.

Strangely enough the Civil Liberties Union itself has leaned over backward in its defense of the Communists and has even taken the official position that the Communists do not advocate violence or act as foreign agents. One would expect this organization to defend Communist rights but *not* to defend their lily-white innocence. Yet we find the Civil Liberties Union making the flat statement that the Communists are not violating any laws. In a pamphlet entitled "It's Not Only Communists' Rights," they say, "If the Communist party, as alleged, advocates violence or acts as a foreign agent, criminal statutes can be invoked. *That they have not been indicates that there is no such case to be made.*" In view of this bald statement one can hardly blame many people for thinking that the American Civil Liberties Union not only defends the right of individual Communists but at times actually assists the Communist party in its propaganda campaign.

Not being a lawyer, the writer does not claim to know whether there are adequate laws under which the Communist party can be tried and stigmatized. Governor Dewey in his radio debate with Mr. Stassen said there were twenty-eight such laws. When Mr. Stassen asked whether Mr. Dewey did not agree that the Communist party was under direction of a foreign power, Mr. Dewey replied, "Certainly." When Mr. Stassen asked whether it aimed to overthrow this government by force, Mr. Dewey replied, "Certainly." Yet it is interesting that there have been no attempts at conviction in the State of New York and it is high time that this deficiency be corrected.

It will be objected that the trial of the Communist party will drive Communists underground. But it may be asked by whose authority such a trial is sidetracked if, as is perfectly evident, the Communist party is today violating the law. Should we permit its members to violate the law in order not to drive them underground? Do we refuse to prosecute robbers, murderers, or other law violators because we are afraid to drive them underground? Besides it has long been obvious that the Communist party is already seven eighths underground and it would make very little difference if the other one eighth were also submerged.

If there is no adequate law upon the statute books now under which the Communists can be tried for their nefarious activities, then it might be well to pass as a statute, Section 4 (a) of the Mundt-Nixon bill which states "It shall be unlawful for any person to attempt in any manner to establish in the United States a totalitarian dictatorship, direction and control of which is to be vested in, or exercised by, or under the domination or control of any foreign government, foreign organization or foreign individual."

The civil liberties defenders in this country can no longer maintain a passive attitude toward the Communist party. They can no longer refuse to recognize the nature of its conspiracy. They are duty bound to take the lead in advocating a fair and honest trial for this conspiracy on the ground that it violates the law. By doing so they will extricate themselves from their present dilemma and give a solid unassailable base to their defense of all minority groups in peacetime. By their official position they must recognize what they secretly and privately admit—that members of the Communist party cannot be trusted in their allegiance to this country. That the Communist party works day and night as a conspiracy to achieve the objectives of a foreign power. Once the Communist party has been tried and found guilty, its members may assume some other name and form a new party with the same objectives as the old one. That remains to be seen. If it happens, then the party should be tried. But it is high time that we stopped closing our eyes to the conspiracy which is evident to everyone.

THE TRUTH ABOUT COMMUNISM [5]

I doubt whether most Americans clearly know what communism is. If they did they would have fewer heart-searchings over what to do about it.

I intend to tell what it is, not out of hearsay, but out of its own documents.

The *Constitution and Rules of the International Communist Party* proves that there is no American party or movement; what calls itself so is merely a "section" of the International, directly governed by the Executive Committee of the International Communist Party (ECCI) which exercises complete control over it, and over all parties of the world.

According to Section III of the Constitution, the ECCI "gives instruction to all sections (parties) and controls their activities."

"The decisions of the ECCI are obligatory for all sections."

"The ECCI has the right to annul or amend decisions of party congresses and central committees of individual parties and make decisions which are obligatory for them."

"The ECCI has the right to expel entire sections, groups, and individual members of sections."

"The ECCI . . . has the right to send their representatives to the various sections . . . to participate in their meetings . . . to speak in opposition to the Central Committee of a given section . . . to send instructors to the various sections."

[5] By Dorothy Thompson, Author, Newspaper Columnist and Lecturer. 17p. Public Affairs Press. Washington, D.C. 1948. Reprinted by permission of the Bell Syndicate.

Thus, the American Communists are entirely under the order of the ECCI, consisting of Russians, Poles, Yugoslavs and what not, but actually ruled by the Politburo of Russia.

Foreign control is further exercised through the "International Control Division." Its powers are: "To investigate matters concerning the unity of the sections . . . the conduct of individual members . . . to examine complaints against the actions of the Central Committees . . . and concerning members . . . and audit the accounts of the Third International."

Thus, every American Communist, and every Communist anywhere, is subject to foreign inspection and discipline.

The relationship between the national parties and the ECCI is fixed in the Constitution and Rules.

"The Central Committees [of the various parties] must send the ECCI minutes of their meetings and reports."

An American Communist may not resign from office without the consent of the ECCI. "Resignation from offices is . . . disruption . . . Leading posts in the party do not belong to the occupant but to the Communist International . . . Elected members may resign only with the consent of the ECCI. Resignations accepted by the Central Committees of sections without the consent of the ECCI are invalid."

Thus the International even controls who may or may not be or remain an official of the "American" party.

According to Paragraph 33 of the Constitution and Rules every Communist party must contribute to the support of the International which fixes the amount of the contribution. The International taxes American Communists.

According to paragraph 37, no member of a Communist party may leave his country without the consent of the Central Committee and if he changes domicile is compelled to join the party in the country where he goes. This is evidence enough that each "party" is merely a section of one party.

The American Communist party is not an autonomous body. Its members, who claim their rights under the American Constitution have already relinquished every personal right to an international, actually Russian body. Their claim to participate in the political life of America is as preposterous as would be the claim of the Yugoslav Communist party to participate, because the American, Russian, Yugoslav, Bulgarian, etc., parties are all the same organization.

Mr. Wallace has welcomed Communist support. Asked in Milwaukee whether American Communists were foreign agents, he replied, "I don't know." We recommend to him a little research.

What calls itself the American Communist party and is more accurately described in the Constitution of the Third International as a "section" of the International is an illegal organization, pledged to illegal methods, to secrecy, and, at the right moment, to armed rebellion. This is proved by the program, statutes, and theses of the International Congresses. Much could be quoted if space permitted, but the following "theses" should suffice:

"The general state of things in Europe and America makes necessary for the Communists of the whole world an obligatory formation of illegal Communist organizations, along with those existing legally."

"Only a violent defeat of the bourgeoisie—the annihilation of their entire government apparatus from top to bottom, parliamentary, juridical, military, bureaucratic, administrative, municipal . . . only such measures guarantee complete subjugation" (to communism). It must be understood that in Communist parlance the word "bourgeoisie" has come to mean every person, form of state, or social order that is not Communist, including such Socialist systems as that of the British Labor Party, New Dealers, or European Social Democrats.

"In every organization, union, association—political, professional, military, educational nuclei must be formed, mostly open, but some secret."

"The absolute principle of combining legal with illegal work is determined."

"Communist parties must create legal publications, in which Communists, without calling themselves such, and without mentioning their connection with the party, would be taught to utilize the slightest possibility allowed by the laws . . . and . . . also . . . illegal sheets . . . giving undiluted revolutionary information and slogans."

"Communists can have no confidence in bourgeoise (non-Communist) laws . . . Wherever there is martial law, illegal work is necessary. Communist groups should be formed within every military organization. Refusal to carry on or participate in illegal work must be considered treason to the cause."

"Every party must renounce social patriotism . . . and pacifism."

Every branch and member of the universal Communist party is pledged to indulge in national treason in case of war with the Soviets—no matter who, in such a war, should be aggressor:

"Each affiliated party is obliged to render every possible assistance to the Soviet Republics . . . carry on propaganda to induce workers to refuse to transport military equipment, and by legal or illegal means propagandize troops."

"The object of the struggle, which must inevitably turn into civil war, is to obtain the political power. Eventually the proletariat must resort to armed uprising. . . . The party must always adapt itself to the idea of the Soviets. . . ."

Where "legal" parties exist, the legal structure is subject to the illegal. Thus:

"The Communist parties must learn systematically to unite legal with illegal work, but all legal work must be carried on under the control of the illegal party. Parliamentary groups must be fully and absolutely subject to the party, regardless of whether the party as a whole is legal or illegal."

It is such a party, consistently pledged to law-breaking, whose support has been welcomed and counsels heeded by . . . [a] candidate for the highest American office. The party is a self-described criminal conspiracy whose members, in joining it, resign from all loyalty to the American or any other "bourgeoise" constitution. Constitutional rights, however, can be granted only in return for constitutional loyalties. The party should be outlawed, and all connections with it penalized.

In a statement made in Milwaukee, Henry Wallace said: "Like the Quakers and Methodists, Communists want peace."

Seldom has a remark of more ineffable idiocy been uttered. A basic thesis of communism is that war, international and civil, is inevitable, until the whole world is organized in a union of Socialist and Soviet Republics. Pacifism, reformism, "peaceful change" and Leagues of Nations are considered to be useless; the world can have peace only after the "violent" over-throw, by "pitiless" means, of all non-Communist social orders. . . . Communists do not widely publicize the memoranda of their congresses, but they are available, and they deny that communism means peace. Communism means unremitting struggle, by all available means including armed force, until it triumphs throughout the globe.

In reading Communist documents, always keep in mind that the world "bourgeoisie"—as made clear by the documents themselves—includes all anti-Communists, Socialists, Democrats, Reformists, labor unions, and all state institutions, constitutions, parliaments, judiciaries of non-Communist social orders. These are to be overthrown "from top to bottom" and "necessarily" by extreme violence. This is reiterated over and over in the platforms of the Communist International. To quote:

"Unless the bourgeoise system is overthrown, the repetition of war is inevitable. To overthrow the international bourgeoisie and create an international Soviet Republic, all means will be used including force of arms."

"Without revolutionary overthrow . . . no talk of disarm-ament or democratic reorganization of the League of Nations will be capable of preventing war."

"To admit the idea of a peaceful reformist passage to social-ism is to give proof of extreme petty bourgeoise obtuseness."

"Only a violent defeat of the bourgeoisie . . . will guarantee . . . complete submission."

"Only such a party is able to lead . . . in the most pitiless, decisive last struggle."

"The conquest of political power by the proletariat does not put an end to the struggle . . . It makes the struggle broad, pitiless, acute . . . All the groups, parties, leaders of the labor movement . . . on the side of reformism . . . are unreliable. The struggle is such that at any moment it may replace the weapon of criticism by the criticism of the weapon."

"That, which before the victory of the proletariat, seems but a theoretical difference on the question of "democracy" becomes, after victory, a question which will be decided by force of arms."

"Parties joining the Third International must recognize the necessity of a complete and absolute rupture with reformism."

"The Communist International has declared a decisive war on the whole bourgeoise world."

"The proletariat must resort to armed uprising . . . Labor organizations will not suffice."

"Intensified class struggle . . . turns into civil war . . . . The proletariat must form its state organization as a fighting organization."

"The Communist International . . . mercilessly exposes all forms of the doctrine of class peace."

"Gandhism . . . pacifism . . . must be strongly combatted by communism."

"The Soviet state is the armed proletarian state." . . .

The *New York Herald Tribune* recently solicited from William Foster, head of the Communist party in the U. S., answers to key questions concerning the aims of the party in this country. Mr. Foster's answers are calculated to demonstrate that the Communists are a constitutional party and do not receive orders from Moscow. The answers are both correct and false; but utterly misleading to anyone unfamiliar with the dialectics, theses, and tactics of communism.

Communist parties do not receive orders in the sense that everything is referred to the Kremlin. That is unnecessary. Policies, strategies, and tactics are agreed upon in meticulous detail; a continuous liaison between the parties is carried on through secret personal connections, correspondence, and even gleaned from public statements of Soviet leaders and press. It hardly could be a coincidence that the *New York Daily Worker*, the *London Daily Worker*, and Communist newspapers of the continent treat world affairs almost identically.

The "correct" attitude of Communist parties toward "bourgeois democracies," such as ours, was laid down—with some revisions of past tactics—in the Seventh International Communist World Congress held in Moscow in August 1935. Hitler had come to power, banning the most powerful European Communist party and jailing its leaders and members. The Communists were seeking allies, which was the easier since

Hitler was not only anti-Communist, but also persecuted Jews and all anti-Nazis.

Therefore, this "popular front" Congress changed its tactics, without moving an inch from its fundamental revolutionary aims, which were repeatedly reaffirmed by all speakers. In the customary memorialization of the Communist parties to Stalin, "leader of exploited and oppressed throughout the world," he was thanked because "You have taught us to combine Bolshevist efficiency and irreconcilable revolutionary spirit with the necessary flexibility."

It was recognized and stated that "bourgeois democracy" offers opportunities for successful organization and agitation that fascism does not. It is, therefore, temporarily preferable.

This was brought out by the most extended speech of the Congress, made by Dr. D. Z. Manuilsky, now Ukrainian delegate to the United Nations. He called for a "policy of revolutionary activity backed by the Soviet Union." A step in this activity was to seek collaboration "with such social groups as are neither supporters of the proletarian dictatorship or social revolution," in the struggle "against war and fascism."

He expressed the conviction that "as a result of years of successful struggle [within the Communist movement] for the complete Bolshevization of all the parties, we have achieved an iron unity which enables us in the given, concrete situation, to formulate a united, revolutionary party." This united party, he went on to explain, was to be formed by including Social Democrats who, in the face of fascism, were ready to break with their former compromises with the bourgeoisie. But this collaboration was not to represent any basic Communist compromise whatsoever.

"We are in favor of a united party that serves the interests of the proletarian revolution."

Five conditions were laid down for such unity:

1. "The party must be absolutely independent of bourgeoisie parties.

2. "All connections with the bourgeoisie must be destroyed.

3. "The necessity of the revolutionary overthrow of the rule of the bourgeoisie and the establishment of the Dictatorship of the Proletariat in the form of Soviets must be accepted.

4. "There shall be no support of the bourgeoisie in the event of 'Imperialist' war, and

5. "The party shall be built on 'democratic centralism.'" In plain English, that means blind obedience.

Mr. Foster was a delegate to that conference and voted for all its resolutions. And these are exactly the conditions imposed on the postwar "unity" parties in Europe. These are coalitions, only in the sense that the left-wing Social Democrats have accepted Communist theses, leadership, and authority. Mr. Foster also accepts them. . . .

Mr. Foster's "loyalty" to the United States consists in believing that it is to the best interests of the United States eventually to join a World Union of Socialist and Soviet Republics under Russia's leadership. That does not preclude treason, if treason has any meaning whatsoever.

All Communists speak of the Soviet Union as their "Fatherland." At this seventh Congress, Marcel Cachin, one of the French delegates, said, "Comrades, all the parties of the Communist International have never been more attached than at the present time to their Fatherland, the Soviet Union."

When Dimitrov, long head of the Comintern and now head of the Bulgarian Government, faced the German Supreme Court in the Reichstag Fire Trial, being unjustly accused, he said:

"I am defending my political and revolutionary honor . . . my Communist ideology, and the significance of my whole life. . . . Therefore every word I say is the absolute truth. For me, as a Communist, the highest law is the program of the Communist International, and its Supreme Court is the Control Commission of the Communist International."

Dimitrov did speak the absolute truth. The question which should have been put to Mr. Foster was whether his own position is that of Dimitrov. If it were not, he would not be for five minutes longer head of the American Communist party.

The object of parliamentary or congressional government is to establish a consensus by deliberation between the various interests and opinions of the population as expressed through elected representatives, dependent for reelection on the satisfaction of a majority of their constituents. Legislation in the United States is subject, in addition, to the ruling of the Supreme

Court that it is within the Constitution. These are the assumptions of our government.

When, however, Communist parties, exercising their legal rights, elect representatives to parliamentary bodies—either by promoting open Communist candidates, or others over whom they can exercise control—they do not do so on such assumptions. Their object is not to secure "agreements" or "compromises," but to use the tribunes of governments for disruptive agitation, and destroy the representative system from within.

They do not hold themselves responsible to the voters, or to their own consciences, but to the Central Committee of the Communist Party, to which they must agree formally, in advance, to surrender their offices on demand. That branch of the party which thus controls government representatives like puppets on strings, is the illegal party which, as we have demonstrated in previous articles, is subject to the Executive of the Communist International. Any Communist, sitting in any "bourgeoise" government, represents only the Communist International.

In the Statutes and Theses of the Second International Communist Congress, which have never been changed, we read this:

"In particular, one of the nuclei of Communists deserves especial care; namely those members of the party who are members of bourgeoise government institutions. . . . Such a tribune has special importance in the eyes of the backward masses. Therefore, from this tribune Communists must carry on their work of propaganda, agitation, and organization."

"Deep hatred against all parliaments is perfectly justified. . . . Therefore all Communist parties must be very strict in their attitude toward their parliamentary factions, demanding their complete subordination to the control and directions of the Central Committee of the party. They shall . . . subject their speeches to careful analysis in Party meetings . . . to exclude all who show a tendency toward the Second International [democratic socialism]."

"Parliamentary [representative] government can in no way be a form of Communist society. . . . The task of the proletariat consists in blowing up the whole machinery and all parliamentary institutions. Communism repudiates the possibility of winning over parliaments. Its aim is to destroy parliaments. . . . The Communist party enters such institutions not for the purpose of organization work . . . or agreement . . . but to blow the parliaments up from within."

Wherever Communists sit in governments of non-Communist countries, they have among them a censor whose word is law.

"The Central Committee must have its permanent representative in the parliamentary faction, with the right of veto. . . . Each candidate must sign a paper that at the first request of the Central Committee . . . he will give up his mandate. Each Communist representative must remember that he is not a 'legislator,' bound to seek agreements, but an agitator, detailed into the enemy's camp to carry out party orders."

Under these conditions, how can it be argued that communists have the "right" to participate in government institutions which they have pledged themselves to destroy, into whose legislative halls they go only to agitate and wreck, which they describe as "enemy camps" and where they are not free agents but subject to international control?

To say that it is "unconstitutional" to outlaw and prosecute such a movement is merely to admit that democracies can devise no legal means to protect themselves. All the hearings called by the Thomas Committee are far less useful than a thorough-going study would be of what communism, according to its own published theses, really is.

The publicly propagandized aims of communism are vaguely liberal. One can read the *Daily Worker* every day for a year without finding any clear exegesis of Communist principle. Like Hitler, Communists, outside their own ranks, promise all things to most men, denouncing only "monopolists," "imperialists" (and failing to provide a glossary for their meaning of these terms), opposing race discrimination, child labor, etc. And everywhere they pose as the friends of all farmers except owners of "vast estates." . . .

Communism aims at the eventual expropriation without compensation of all land, and the reduction of all farmers to the status of propertyless agricultural sharecroppers for the Dictatorship of the Proletariat. The program is set forth in detail in the International Congresses, especially the second and the sixth.

The program recognizes four classes of proprietors: Owners of large landed estates (acreage not fixed; in Poland all over 250 acres); successful farmers of smaller holdings; marginal farmers only one point above subsistence; and those who barely scratch a living.

These are to be absorbed step by step as follows:

"Confiscation of all large landed estates and transference of state and municipal properties, forests, minerals, rivers, etc.," together with "all property used in production connected with such properties, buildings, machinery, cattle, flour mills, dairies, etc., to the proletarian dictatorship."

Compensation of any kind, or retention, even, of household goods, is strictly prohibited.

Parts of such properties are to be initially bestowed upon marginal and subsistence farmers "to the degree necessary to neutralize them and win them over to the side of proletarian revolution."

The poorest, "little farmers who possess by right of ownership or rental small portions of land which barely meet the needs of their families without requiring hired labor," it is calculated, "will side with the proletariat"—especially since they are to be bribed.

The marginal farmers, "small landowners who possess portions of land which, though small, may yield only scanty provision for the family . . . but the possibility of accumulating a certain surplus which, in the best years, could be transformed into capital and which sometimes needs to employ labor . . . must, in the beginning of the proletarian dictatorship, be neutralized. The vacillation of this group is unavoidable."

Eventually all these must become wage workers on state farms, but "transition to collective agriculture must be managed with circumspection, step by step."

But members of the farming class which represents the backbone of all agriculture, the working farmers with sufficient land to yield a considerable surplus over the family's needs, with sufficient capital investment to mean high and efficient production—the class to which a majority of American farmers belong—are "the worst class enemies."

"The land-owning farmers are capitalists, managing their land with several hired laborers, even though they themselves do personal manual labor. This is the most numerous element of the bourgeoisie and the decided enemy of the revolutionary proletariat. . . . Chief attention must be given to the struggle against this element. The revolutionary proletariat must prepare the necessary force for the disarmament of every single man of this class . . . and must deal a relentless crushing blow to his class. In the Russian proletariat revolution this class has been taught what it costs to make the slightest attempt at resistance."

It has indeed. The crushing of resistance in Russia cost millions of dead from starvation, in the only wholesale famine to strike a country inhabited by white men in a hundred years. But no matter: "The Communist International denounces those . . . who . . . oppose . . . on the ground that it might cause a falling off in the production of food stuffs. No program . . . or declarations . . . have any value if the fact is not testified in deeds that Communists put, above all, the development of revolution."

Thus, the Communist program for agriculture, universal for all countries, would expropriate entirely all farmers living above subsistence or its margin, who are eventually to be collectivized. Further proof that this is still the program can be seen in eastern Europe where the step-by-step program is under way with the same results as in Russia—starvation. The relentless breaking of the peasant parties and the execution of their leaders is part of this program.

To summarize the problem: A fundamental error made by Western statesmen, during and since the war, and entertained by many publicists—notably Walter Lippmann—is that the Russians would be, or are, willing to agree to a partition of the world into "orbits" or "spheres of influence," along familiar lines of power politics.

Those who hold this hope have been confusing Stalin with Hitler. Hitler was for the partition of the world, and tried to sell that idea to the British. But Stalin is a Bolshevist—that is, a totalist.

The Russians—to be sure—might, and did, encourage the orbit idea as a means of extending their power by agreement. They play the game of power politics when it is to their interest, using the familiar terms and arguments, stressing the need for strategic frontiers, warm water ports, etc. But they are not thinking basically in such terms at all. Anything that increases Soviet power and maneuverability serves the world revolution, and anything that serves the world revolution serves Soviet power. There is no contradiction here. As Bela Kun, Hungarian Communist revolutionist, said to a correspondent of *Petit Parisien* in 1936:

It is the sacred duty of the national sections of the Comintern to protect the first proletarian state in the world. On this point there can be no hesitation. And speaking generally, it is impossible that the interests of the world proletariat—and the Comintern—should not invariably coincide exactly with those of the Soviet Union.

The Soviet Union and Comintern are genuine believers in "One World." They do not, however, believe that one world can be constructed via the United Nations or such schemes as world federalism. This has not prevented the Soviets from participating in the League of Nations or the United Nations, or shifting their policies in these bodies to suit concrete situations.

When, for instance, in 1935 and 1936 the Soviets had every reason to fear an imminent German attack they fought for the very measures which they now oppose in the United Nations: The definition of aggression; and the duty of the League to preserve the territorial integrity of member states and to apply sanctions against aggressors. But temporary tactics in no way modify the objective all tactics are designed to serve: World domination through war and revolution.

If, from time to time, Stalin or others deny that peace is compatible with a world divided into Communist and non-Communist states—that, again, is tactical. The basic tenet was expressed by Manuilsky in the last World Congress:

It is undeniable that wars will remain inevitable as long as capitalism exists, but it is equally undeniable that we cannot sit with folded hands and fatalistically await the coming imperialist war.

The Soviets and Comintern seek to postpone the "inevitable" war to the most suitable moment for themselves, or to avoid "the last struggle," by using a long armistice successfully to intrench themselves in an invulnerable position from which to squeeze the last recalcitrants into line. But that only a World Union of Socialist and Soviet Republics will end war, is a cardinal principle of the Soviet state and the Communist revolution.

It is, therefore, futile to hope that the Soviets will enter into any international agreement which would bind them to defend a non-Communist state against any aggressor, or subject their own armaments to international control, or submit to the judgments of non-Communist courts, or restrict—under sanctions—their freedom of action. Communists were, entirely logically, unwilling to defend bourgeoise democracies against Fascist attacks until the Soviet "Fatherland" was involved.

The Soviet Union, as we have shown in previous quotations, does not enter a parliamentary body or the United Nations to cooperate, but to agitate and wreck. All non-Communist countries are, by definition, "enemy" states; Fascist states are no different from others, except as they may be immediately more dangerous.

But the power of the Communist movement lies in the fact that it does recognize a requirement of history: One World— and that in this, it has no effective rivals. It is the only supranational, absolutely centralized and disciplined world party and world creed. No powerful democratic state ever has yet clearly formulated and vigorously promoted an alternative plan for collective security involving limitations on sovereignty.

Objections to delegalizing communism are chiefly two. The first is that Communists are guaranteed freedom of activity of the Constitution; the second, that if outlawed the legal organization would go underground.

The first argument assumes that any kind of political activity has, under the Constitution, a natural right. That was not Lincoln's interpretation. Nothing in the Constitution prohibited secession; Lincoln thought, however, that preservation of the Union was the essence of the Constitution.

A continually reaffirmed thesis of communism is that its objectives cannot be realized without ruthless violence nor within the framework of a constitutional order. Is it our counter-thesis that law cannot be invoked against promoters of such catastrophe? Law, it has been said, is made by criminals; first an act damaging to the community is committed and then a law is passed to prohibit its occurring again.

But what if overt acts by an organization with which an American group is subordinately affiliated long have been projected and actually carried out in many other countries? Is it a principle of law that it may not anticipate events? Actually, conspiracy to commit certain acts is itself an overt act. That a definite conspiracy exists and has existed for years to subvert all constitutional orders in the world, and that the American Communist party and its leading members have been consciously allied with it, can be proved.

Popular confusions arise concerning constitutional rights. Rights guaranteed by a state can be guaranteed only within the framework of that state. They cannot be detached from it, as though they were a constitution in themselves, which is what some people would like to do with the Bill of Rights. They are not dissoluble from the intent of the state that guarantees them. The intent and purpose of the American Constitution is formulated in the preamble: "to form a more perfect union, establish justice, insure domestic tranquillity, provide for the common defense, promote the general welfare, and secure the blessings of liberty to ourselves and our posterity."

Now comes an American movement, a subordinate branch of an international movement, which regards the national welfare as indissoluble from and subservient to the welfare of the Soviet state; which conspires to disturb the domestic tranquillity by civil strife; to substitute for the constitutional system a Communist dictatorship of the proletariat; to sabotage the common defense under all circumstances unless the Soviet Union is thereby served; and to withdraw from the people all liberties, to be afterward granted or withdrawn from ourselves and our posterity according to the whim of a dictatorship. And the Constitution demands that this conspiracy be legalized? That is reducing the Constitution to absurdity.

The second argument is dangerous. Communist parties are both legal and illegal, and the illegal structure governs the legal. But legality is an enormous aid to the illegal conspiracy. It prevents forthright action against the chief criminals; it leads to roundabout persecutions; it enables the Communists to deceive simple, generous-hearted, and gullible citizens, and it leads to dubiously legal actions from the government itself.

The present half-legal, half-persecuted position of the party and its members is not justice. It operates to eliminate one evil with another, both evils containing dangers to the constitutional order.

Merely to ban the Communist party as such would be useless. It would revive, as it did in Canada, under another name. A proper law would not even need to name the Communist party. It would very carefully define specific practices and organization for specific objectives as being incompatible with the constitutional order.

Certain activities clearly defined as treasonable should be forbidden American citizens. No citizen of the United States should be allowed to hold membership in or contribute to any organization which receives orders from a foreign state, or the officials of a foreign state, or to associate himself with any organization or movement which is pledged to acts in contravention of American law, or which has ever consciously and deliberately infringed the laws of the United States.

No citizen should be permitted to become a member of or contribute to any organization whose members are pledged, or have ever been pledged, to tender prior loyalty to any state other than the United States, or to defend any state other than the United States in case of war, except as in such a war the United States might formally be allied with another power.

No citizen of the United States should be allowed to hold membership in or contribute to any organization which has as its immediate or remote objectives the overthrow of the Constitution of the United States or its abolition by violence, or by any means not provided in the Constitution itself, or the deprivation of any class, race, group, or region of American citizens of the rights guaranteed them in the Constitution, or of lawfully acquired property except by due process of law.

No citizen of the United States should be permitted to hold membership in or contribute to any organization which advocates openly or secretly civil war, or violence as a means of obtaining political, economic or social objectives, whether such violence be directed against the state, or by the instruments of the state against the people. Nor should any American citizen be permitted to hold membership in, or contribute to any organization which is associated in any way with foreign states, parties, or organization whose tenets include, or have at any time included, advocacy of civil war as a means of obtaining political, social, or economic objectives.

The prosecution of movements or parties is difficult and unsatisfactory. The essence of American law is that the citizen is responsible for his own acts, as an individual. A proper law would establish that responsibility.

GRESHAM'S LAW IN POLITICS [6]

According to a well-known principle of economics known as Gresham's law, bad money will always drive good money out of circulation when the two are in competition. The reason is obvious. The instinctive temptation, in such a situation, is to hoard the good money and work off the bad on someone else. . . .

Since the rise of totalitarianism in its two forms, communism and fascism, there is a serious possibility that Gresham's Law may hold good in politics, as well as in economics. There is genuine danger that some thing which would have seemed impossible in the optimistic, liberal nineteenth century may come to pass; that bad, or tyrannical government will systematically replace good, or free government.

It is the great safety valve of democracy that the voters can turn out, with no resort to conspiracy and violence, an administration which the majority no longer desires. If they change their minds a few years later another change can be made with-

[6] By William Henry Chamberlin, author of books on Soviet Russia; columnist for *Wall Street Journal*. *Wall Street Journal*. p. 6. April 7, 1948. Reprinted by permission.

out benefit of plots or purges, by the simple prosaic verdict of the ballot box.

But this normal swing of the political pendulum is upset when a totalitarian party attracts enough mass support to become a serious contender in an election. Here is where the political variant of Gresham's law begins to apply. A Communist or a Fascist party, under democratic systems, can lose a score of elections and continue to function freely. But let such a party win just one election, or somehow get its hands on the state authority without an election, and the pendulum stops right there, just as if the clock had been smashed. For there are no more free elections. The people have no chance peacefully and legally to reconsider their verdict.

This is something that should be remembered by well-meaning liberals who feel that if a people "wants" communism it should try out this new idea and then reject or modify it if it proves a disappointment. This would be an excellent proposition if there were any means of linking the practice of communism with ironclad observance of political and civil liberties. But experience has shown, without a single exception now that Czechoslovakia has been transformed into the standard east European Communist police state, that political and civil liberties go out the window just as soon as communism comes into power. A people that votes communism in haste has no opportunity to correct its mistake later on. Purges and synthetic plots and a government controlled press, slave labor concentration camps for dissenters and a universal espionage system make it impossible for an opposition to function peacefully and legally.

On European roads in American sectors of occupation one often sees the sign: "Drive carefully. Death is so permanent." A similar warning would hold good for communism. Once it is clamped down it can only be overthrown by war, civil or foreign.

There has been no case as yet when Communists in any country have won more than 50 per cent of the votes in a free election. But should there be such a case, should a Communist-dominated bloc win over the votes, . . . a problem would arise which would be a poser for the most sincere believer in democratic liberties. . . .

This dilemma might have perplexed even the lucid intelligence of Voltaire. It was easy for the French publicist to make a grand gesture of verbal generosity with his: "I disagree utterly with what you say and will defend to the death your right to say it." But would he have said this quite so unreservedly about a party and movement which was determined, on coming into power, not only to liquidate Voltaire but to suppress finally and irrevocably all dissenting opinion? Gresham's law in politics may call for new rules, new standards of judgment.

WHAT ARE WE WAITING FOR? OUTLAW COMMUNISM NOW! [7]

We have studied communism for more than twenty-six years. We cannot understand the propaganda against outlawing the Communist party. It is said it would drive them underground. They are underground now and above board both at the same time, but always ready to assume the one state or the other as suits their objectives. As a matter of fact they are always practicing both to undermine our republic.

The main movement in the United States today and for the past twenty-eight or twenty-nine years is to bore within secretly, i.e., *underground*. That is going on in our schools, our colleges, our labor unions—in fact in every activity of American life. At the same time they are working above board where they can. They are working in the open only as they think that will give them a political standing. And why do they want political standing?

At the seventh World Congress in 1935, Dimitroff, one of the leaders then and now of Soviet communism in Russia, made the following statement in one of the principal addresses to that Congress. He spoke in regard to Germany, and particularly the state of Saxony in which there were important Communist uprisings in 1923 and where the Communists were badly beaten. He said,

But when participating in the government, the Communists should have used their positions primarily for the purpose of arming the pro-

[7] Friends of the Public Schools. Bulletin. 11:7-8. August 1948. Reprinted by permission.

letariat, and Comrades, we demand of every United Front government
. . . that such a government carry out definite and fundamental revolutionary demands required by the situation. For instance, control of the
banks, disbanding of the police, its replacement by an armed workers'
militia, etc.

Are we going to continue being such unutterable fools as to permit them to do that to us?

The following are their official pronouncements of what they
will do when they get a strong enough position inside the government to take a determined open stand. It is said Germany
had a hundred Communists in the German Reichstag when Hitler
rose to power. The same thing was true in the Italian Parliament
when Mussolini rose to power.

In regard to their object for running for political office we
have this from the program of the *Communist International* of
1936:

In universally championing the current everyday needs of the
masses of the workers and of the toilers generally, in utilizing the
bourgeois parliament as a platform for revolutionary agitation and propaganda, and subordinating the partial tasks to the struggle for the dictatorship of the proletariat, the parties of the Communist International
advance partial demands and slogans . . . but must not adopt the view
of sharing power in any form.

Note that official statement, "utilizing the bourgeois parliament
[U. S. Congress, ed.] as a platform for revolutionary agitation
and propaganda." . . . That is why we have Communists in
Congress! They are there for "revolutionary agitation and propaganda." Are we going to permit them to operate above board
in our halls of Congress, to occupy platforms as presidential candidates and congressional candidates to put before children and
uninformed voting citizens, the . . . schemes of communism?
That thing is more deadly dangerous than if we stopped all vac-
cinations and allowed small pox patients to run at will throughout the United States.

In the International Communist Congress for 1936, page 80,
the following statement is made,

If the ruling classes are disorganized, the party of the proletariat is
confronted with the task of disarming the bourgeoisie [everyone except
Communists, ed.] and arming the proletariat [and by organizing] mass
action, including parliamentary activity.

This mass action includes: (a) A combination of strikes and demonstrations, (b) a combination of strikes and armed demonstrations
[and finally] (c) the general strike cojointly with armed insurrection
against the state power.

Again we say, what are we waiting for? Are we going to
let the Communists in our Congress combine with the mass action of the Communists outside to bring on strikes, armed demonstrations and finally the general strike cojointly with armed
insurrection against the state power—terrorism in Congress and
outside through general strikes until we have bloody civil war?
Remember this is no statement by any single Communist.
It is a definite conclusion of the World International Communist Congress of 1936, a Congress that laid down definite procedures, which they are following today. Down that road traveled
Italy, France, Germany and other countries that have come either
to complete governmental chaos or to the very verge where no
one knows when final chaos will result. And we hesitate to outlaw the Communist party and all fellow travelers!!

Within the last half century preventive medicine has become
one of the greatest methods of lengthening life and decreasing
deaths that has been invented in the history of mankind. Preventive activity against treason applied to our educational system
and our governmental operations will save our nation in the future from vastly greater evils than preventive medicine is saving
us today. Let us apply some common sense by applying preventive action against treason now and in the future.

Now read what William Z. Foster, present head of the Communist party, had to say in his book, *Toward Soviet America,*
page 275, written when he was running for president the last
time. If we will study that we will see what will happen to all
of us who don't bow to the lust of dictatorship should communism get power in America. W. Z. Foster . . . says,

Under the dictatorship all the capitalistic parties . . . Republican,
Democratic, Progressive, Socialist, etc. . . . will be liquidated, the Communist party functioning alone as the party of the toiling masses. Likewise, will be dissolved all other organizations that are political props of
the bourgeois rule, including chambers of commerce, employers' associations, rotary clubs, American Legion, YMCA, and such fraternal orders
as the Masons, Odd Fellows, Elks, Knights of Columbus, etc.

Also note what it cost in human lives and human misery and terror to establish communism firmly in Russia between 1917 and 1935.

According to the October 1935 issue of the *Army Chaplain* (official publication of the Chaplain's organization which includes Active and Reserve Chaplains of all services whether Protestant, Roman Catholic, or Hebrew) the number of people who have been killed or executed since the Soviet regime came into power in Soviet Russia, taking only the known dead, are as follows:

Twenty-eight bishops and higher clergy, 6,778 priests, 6,585 school teachers, 8,000 doctors, 51,860 army officers, 200,850 policemen and other officials, and 11,488,520 peasants and partisans. These make the staggering total of 11,762,611. Nearly 2,000,000 more dead than the total killed in the World War [World War I].

Furthermore, according to an article printed in the *New York Times* and reprinted by the *Washington Post* about July 25, 1934, "probably more than a score of millions of lives had been lost by starvation in the first fifteen years of Soviet control," or up to about the first of 1933. Ripley, of "Believe It Or Not" fame, said in a broadcast on April 5, 1935, quoting from Professor L. Tarassevich, noted Russian sociologist, that thirty million Russians have starved to death since that country turned Communist.

The hour is late. The time for action is here. Outlaw communism and drive every Communist agitator and fellow traveler out of places of responsibility and power whether in schools, colleges, government, business or elsewhere under the Stars and Stripes.

LIBERALS AND THE COMMUNIST TRIAL [8]

I believe it is legitimate for the government to try the Communist leaders under the sedition clauses of the Smith Act of 1940. I make no comment on the question whether they are guilty or innocent. What I do say is that the Smith Act, under

[8] By Morris Ernst, member of board of American Civil Liberties Union. *New Republic.* 120:7-8. January 31, 1949. Reprinted by permission.

which the Communists are being tried, as applied to secret conspiracy leading toward illegal acts, is in accordance with American principles, and that the evil which it seeks to combat is a
serious one.

Let me say at once that I believe Communists have a right to
advocate publicly the overthrow of the United States. I further
believe they even have the right to say publicly that if all else
failed, they would advocate the ultimate use of violence to change
the form of our government. I would be willing to aid in the
defense of Communists who were being tried for making public
statements of this sort.

But we are confronted today with a situation where arguments
about public statements have no relevance. The question is one,
not of public statements but of secret acts, in the course of a
secret conspiracy, which might never become public until it was
too late, until democracy no longer had time or the chance to
defend itself.

The shibboleth of liberals in cases which involve, or seem
to involve, free speech, is Justice Holmes's famous dictum that
the rights of the individual must not be impaired until there is
"a clear and present danger" to the government. Let me ask you:
At what time was there a "clear and present danger" from Quisling in Norway until he came to power? When was there "a
clear and present danger" before the Communist coup in Czechoslovakia? There was no such time. No case in American history
has ever demonstrated to my satisfaction that there was any
"clear and present danger" to our government.

I prefer to the Holmes doctrine that of Justice Brandeis, who
said the overriding question is whether, in the given situation,
society has a chance to counteract what is being done, has the
opportunity to protect itself. If there is a public debate, society
certainly has that chance. But the essence of plotting for a revolutionary coup is its secrecy. If the end to be obtained is illegal,
and the means are secret, the acts of individuals and groups
should be prevented by law whether the size of their effort is
large or small.

Bank robbers use speech, and other means of communication,
when they are planning to hold up a bank. But the police do

not worry about their rights of free speech, or stand aside and wait for "a clear and present danger" until the robbers have entered the lobby of the bank and begun shooting. The police try to stop the conspiracy at the earliest possible moment.

If we don't act now to prevent secret conspiracy looking toward an illegal coup, which is the complete antithesis of the process of the democratic vote, we are in some danger of having laws enacted which really do interfere with the First Amendment and curtail freedom of speech. Any such law would be contrary to sound public policy and should be held unconstitutional, just as I would consider the Smith Act unconstitutional if it were applied to public debate.

It is part of our national mores that you should not pick on anybody smaller than you are; and social psychologists have noticed how often we apply this principle in places where it has no validity. The doctrine of "clear and present danger" says in effect: those who want to destroy our institutions should be permitted to keep on trying until they are almost strong enough to succeed.

Stated in this way, it of course sounds ridiculous, and it is ridiculous for another reason—because it belongs to the eighteenth century rather than the twentieth. Open, public speech is always the weapon of the little guy; whatever is secret is by that very fact already big enough to be taken seriously.

Justice Holmes's doctrine assumes that a secret coup succeeds or fails by a mere count of noses; that in order to win you must have half, or nearly half, the total population on your side. But today we live in a world of such close and intricate technology that under certain circumstances a very small minority may take over a country, by capturing such things as our storehouse of atomic bombs, the radio stations, the long-distance telephone lines, a few airfields.

Roger Baldwin says that we should not attempt to apply the Smith Act to the Communist leaders lest we drive them underground. Without prejudging the case, let me say that the indictment is based on the assumption that they are underground now, that the visible activities of the party are only that part of the iceberg above surface, intended chiefly for camouflage. If the

Communists were clearly above ground, I would agree with Baldwin—and so would the government, and there would be no case.

EXCERPTS

As a result of evidence adduced before various committees of the Senate and House of Representatives, Congress hereby finds that—

1. The system of government known as totalitarian dictatorship is characterized by the existence of a single political party, organized on a dictatorial basis, and by an identity between such party and its policies and the government and governmental policies of the country in which it exists, such identity being so close that the party and the government itself are for all practical purposes indistinguishable.

2. The establishment of a totalitarian dictatorship in any country results in the ruthless suppression of all opposition to the party in power, the complete subordination of the rights of individuals to the state, the denial of fundamental rights and liberties which are characteristic of a representative form of government, such as freedom of speech, of the press, of assembly, and of religious worship, and results in the maintenance of control over the people through fear, terrorism and brutality.

3. There exists a world Communist movement which, in its origins, its development, and its present practice, is a worldwide revolutionary political movement whose purpose it is, by treachery, deceit, infiltration into other groups (governmental and otherwise), espionage, sabotage, terrorism, and any other means deemed necessary, to establish a Communist totalitarian dictatorship in all the countries of the world through the medium of a single worldwide Communist political organization.

4. The direction and control of the world Communist movement is vested in and exercised by the Communist dictatorship of a foreign country.

5. The Communist dictatorship of such foreign country, in exercising such direction and control and in furthering the purposes of the world Communist movement, establishes or causes

the establishment of, and utilizes, in various countries, political organizations which are acknowledged by such Communist dictatorship as being constituent elements of the world Communist movement; and such political organizations are not free and independent organizations, but are mere sections of a single world-wide Communist organization and are controlled, directed, and subject to the discipline of the Communist dictatorship of such foreign country.

6. The political organizations so established and utilized in various countries, acting under such control, direction, and discipline, endeavor to carry out the objectives of the world Communist movement by bringing about the overthrow of existing governments and setting up Communist totalitarian dictatorships which will be subservient to the most powerful existing Communist totalitarian dictatorship.

7. In carrying on the activities referred to in paragraph 6, such political organizations in various countries are organized on a secret, conspiratorial basis and operate to a substantial extent through organizations, commonly known as "Communist fronts," which in most instances are created and maintained, or used, in such manner as to conceal the facts as to their true character and purposes and their membership. One result of this method of operation is that such political organizations are able to obtain financial and other support from persons who would not extend such support if they knew the true purposes of, and the actual nature of the control and influence exerted upon, such "communist fronts."

8. Due to the nature and scope of the world Communist movement, with the existence of affiliated constituent elements working toward common objectives in various countries of the world, travel of members, representatives, and agents from country to country is essential for purposes of communication and for the carrying on of activities to further the purposes of the movement.

9. In the United States those individuals who knowingly and willfully participate in the world Communist movement, when they so participate, in effect repudiate their allegiance to the United States and in effect transfer their allegiance to the foreign

country in which is vested the direction and control of the world Communist movement; and, in countries other than the United States, those individuals who knowingly and willfully participate in such Communist movement similarly repudiate their allegiance to the countries of which they are nationals in favor of such foreign Communist country.

10. In pursuance of communism's stated objectives, the most powerful existing Communist dictatorship has, by the traditional Communist methods referred to above, and in accordance with carefully conceived plans, already caused the establishment in numerous foreign countries, against the will of the people of those countries, of ruthless Communist totalitarian dictatorships, and threatens to establish similar dictatorships in still other countries.

11. The recent successes of Communist methods in other countries and the nature and control of the world Communist movement itself present a clear and present danger to the security of the United States and to the existence of free American institutions and make it necessary that Congress enact appropriate legislation recognizing the existence of such worldwide conspiracy and designed to prevent it from accomplishing its purpose in the United States—*Preamble to the Mundt-Nixon Bill. Plain Talk.* Jl. '48. *p.* 34-5.

Strange as it may seem, fantastic as it may sound to the ordinary man who is not in a labor union or in government or politics or in certain pressure groups, the truth nevertheless is that the so-called Communist party is not a political party at all, as Americans understand the term; that it is a conspiracy, a fifth column for its masters in Moscow; that there is a similar conspiracy in every other country in the world, from China to Chile and from South Africa to Sweden; and that the fifth column in this country does exercise an enormous power.

This power is grotesquely underrated, because the Communist party has deliberately minimized its own importance in order to prevent its victims from taking alarm in time. By using the cleverest of public relations methods, it has circulated the fiction that the Communists are only a negligible handful of "progressives" and that anybody who says otherwise is a blood brother of Goebbels, Franco, Rankin, and Bilbo. . . .

The thing that makes the Communists so effective is that they are not only a religion but an army. Just as in an army a group of commonplace young draftees may be trained rigorously and pitilessly till they are extraordinarily skilled in a rare technique and can accomplish what seems a miracle, so in the Communist fifth column even commonplace people are taught and drilled and supervised until they can coordinate their activities with amazing effectiveness.

The party has public relations experts of singular ability, and is steadily training more. It has its own advertising agencies. In every sizable city it has its own law firms. These lawyers are not merely hired men, working for a fee. They are themselves passionate Communists. Outwardly they may seem no different from other lawyers; but that is because a man may be fanatically religious without shouting hallelujah.

The fifth column even has an appreciable number of business men among its adherents. It has wealthy "angels," not only among movie stars and inheritors of large fortunes but also among men who made their own money in business. . . .

One reason is that the party has been adroit enough to befog the truth. In this it has enjoyed the unwitting assistance of some publishers and congressmen, who have smeared genuine liberals as Communists and have thus led millions to believe that practically anybody who is called a Communist is really a liberal. At times the Communists themselves, especially in government agencies, have fought against anti-Communist liberals by spreading the story that they are Communists.

Further, it is only since 1935, when Stalin ordered his parties all through the world to adopt the popular front method, that the Communists have become so powerful in the United States; and in this period they have succeeded by a process of elaborate deception. Today most of the party members deny their membership; they are listed in the party under false names. Others, known as fellow travelers, are technically not members at all but cooperate completely with members and obey every order.

THE REFERENCE SHELF

The party cooperates through hundreds of unions and other organizations. . . . In the names of fellow travelers and secret party members, it publishes innocent-seeming magazines and news letters.

How do we know all this? By comprehensive and irrefutable proof. By documentary evidence in many cases. By overnight reversals of policy on the part of individuals and organizations whenever Moscow suddenly changes its line. By confidential statements of party members to sympathizers or close friends. By revelations of former party members and fellow travelers who have become disillusioned and told the truth, either publicly or in private.

It is not generally realized that there are many thousands of former Communists in this country who, having lost their Soviet religion, are now resolutely anti-Communist, and that they range from rank-and-filers to the very highest figures, including two of Earl Browder's predecessors as secretary of the party. These men are in the know. They have reported to Stalin personally in Moscow and have received orders from him. They have run the shows here. They understand the game.

In numberless ways the proof is overwhelming.—*Andrew Avery. "The Communist Fifth Column." Chicago Journal of Commerce. Chicago. Je. 24, '46. p. 3-5.*

THE CASE AGAINST OUTLAWING THE COMMUNIST PARTY

WHO IS LOYAL TO AMERICA? [1]

On May 6 a Russian-born girl, Mrs. Shura Lewis, gave a talk to the students of the Western High School of Washington, D.C. She talked about Russia—its school system, its public health program, the position of women, of the aged, of the workers, the farmers, and the professional classes—and compared, superficially and uncritically, some American and Russian social institutions. The most careful examination of the speech—happily reprinted for us in the *Congressional Record*—does not disclose a single disparagement of anything American unless it is a quasi-humorous reference to the cost of having a baby and of dental treatment in this country. Mrs. Lewis said nothing that had not been said a thousand times, in speeches, in newspapers, magazines, and books. She said nothing that any normal person could find objectionable.

Her speech, however, created a sensation. A few students walked out on it. Others improvised placards proclaiming their devotion to Americanism. Indignant mothers telephoned their protests. Newspapers took a strong stand against the outrage. Congress, rarely concerned for the political or economic welfare of the citizens of the capital city, reacted sharply when its intellectual welfare was at stake. Congressmen Rankin and Dirksen thundered and lightened; the District of Columbia Committee went into a huddle; there were demands for the housecleaning in the whole school system, which was obviously shot through and through with communism.

All this might be ignored, for we have learned not to expect either intelligence or understanding of Americanism from this element in our Congress. More ominous was the reaction of the

[1] By Henry Steele Commager, Professor of History, Columbia University. *Harper's Magazine.* 195:193-9. September 1947.

educators entrusted with the high responsibility of guiding and guarding the intellectual welfare of our boys and girls. Did they stand up for intellectual freedom? Did they insist that high school children had the right and the duty to learn about other countries? Did they protest that students were to be trusted to use intelligence and common sense? Did they affirm that the Americanism of their students was staunch enough to resist propaganda? Did they perform even the elementary task, expected of educators above all, of analyzing the much-criticized speech?

Not at all. The District Superintendent of Schools hastened to agree with the animadversions of Representatives Rankin and Dirksen. The whole thing was, he confessed, "a very unfortunate occurrence," and had "shocked the whole school system." What Mrs. Lewis said, he added gratuitously, was "repugnant to all who are working with youth in the Washington schools," and "the entire affair contrary to the philosophy of education under which we operate." The hapless principal of the Western High School, was "the most shocked and regretful of all." The District of Columbia Committee would be happy to know that though he was innocent in the matter, he had been properly reprimanded!

It is the reaction of the educators that makes this episode more than a tempest in a teapot. We expect hysteria from Mr. Rankin and some newspapers; we are shocked when we see educators, timid before criticism and confused about first principles, betray their trust. And we wonder what can be that "philosophy of education" which believes that young people can be trained to the duties of citizenship by wrapping their minds in cotton-wool.

Merely by talking about Russia Mrs. Lewis was thought to be attacking Americanism. It is indicative of the seriousness of the situation that during this same week the House found it necessary to take time out from the discussion of the labor bill, the tax bill, the International Trade Organization, and the world famine, to meet assaults upon Americanism from a new quarter. This time it was the artists who were undermining the American system, and members of the House spent some hours passing around reproductions of the paintings which the State Department had sent abroad as part of its program for advertising American culture. We need not pause over the exquisite humor which congressmen displayed in their comments on modern art: weary statesmen must have their fun. But we may profitably remark the major criticism which was directed against this unfortunate collection of paintings. What was wrong with these paintings, it shortly appeared, was that they were un-American. "No American drew those crazy pictures," said Mr. Rankin. Perhaps he was right. The copious files of the Committee on Un-American Activities were levied upon to prove that of the forty-five artists represented "no less than twenty were definitely New Deal in various shades of communism." The damning facts are specified for each of the pernicious twenty; we can content ourselves with the first of them, Ben-Zion. What is the evidence here? "Ben-Zion was one of the signers of a letter sent to President Roosevelt by the United American Artists which urged help to the USSR and Britain after Hitler attacked Russia." He was, in short, a fellow traveler of Churchill and Roosevelt.

The same day that Mr. Dirksen was denouncing the Washington school authorities for allowing students to hear about Russia ("In Russia equal right is granted to each nationality. There is no discrimination. Nobody says, you are a Negro, you are a Jew") Representative Williams of Mississippi rose to denounce the *Survey-Graphic* magazine and to add further to our understanding of Americanism. The *Survey-Graphic*, he said, "contained 129 pages of outrageously vile and nauseating anti-Southern, anti-Christian, un-American, and pro-Communist tripe, ostensibly directed toward the elimination of the custom of racial segration in the South." It was written by "meddling un-American purveyors of hate and indecency."

All in all, a busy week for the House. Yet those who make a practice of reading their *Record* will agree that it was a typical week. For increasingly Congress is concerned with the eradication of disloyalty and the defense of Americanism, and scarcely a day passes that some congressman does not treat us to exhortations and admonitions, impassioned appeals and eloquent declamations, similar to those inspired by Mrs. Lewis, Mr. Ben-Zion, and the editors of the *Survey-Graphic*. And scarcely a day passes that the outlines of the new loyalty and the new Americanism are not etched more sharply in public policy.

And this is what is significant—the emergence of new patterns of Americanism and of loyalty, patterns radically different from those which have long been traditional. It is not only the Congress that is busy designing the new patterns. They are outlined in President Truman's recent disloyalty order; in similar orders formulated by the New York City Council and by state and local authorities throughout the country; in the programs of the DAR, the American Legion, and similar patriotic organizations; in the editorials of the Hearst and the McCormick-Patterson papers; and in an elaborate series of advertisements sponsored by large corporations and business organizations. In the making is a revival of the red hysteria of the early 1920's, one of the shabbiest chapters in the history of American democracy; and more than a revival, for the new crusade is designed not merely to frustrate communism but to formulate a positive definition of Americanism, and a positive concept of loyalty.

What is the new loyalty? It is, above all, conformity. It is the uncritical and unquestioning acceptance of America as it is—the political institutions, the social relationships, the economic practices. It rejects inquiry into the race question or socialized medicine, or public housing, or into the wisdom or validity of our foreign policy. It regards as particularly heinous any challenge to what is called "the system of private enterprise," identifying that system with Americanism. It abandons evolution, repudiates the once popular concept of progress, and regards America as a finished product, perfect and complete.

It is, it must be added, easily satisfied. For it wants not intellectual conviction nor spiritual conquest, but mere outward conformity. In matters of loyalty it takes the word for the deed, the gesture for the principle. It is content with the flag salute, and does not pause to consider the warning of our Supreme Court that "a person gets from a symbol the meaning he puts into it, and what is one man's comfort and inspiration is an-

other's jest and scorn." It is satisfied with membership in respectable organizations and, as it assumes that every member of
a liberal organization is a Communist, concludes that every
member of a conservative one is a true American. It has not
yet learned that not everyone who saith Lord, Lord, shall enter
into the kingdom of Heaven. It is designed neither to discover
real disloyalty nor to foster true loyalty.

What is wrong with this new concept of loyalty? What,
fundamentally, is wrong with the pusillanimous retreat of the
Washington educators, the barbarous antics of Washington legislators, the hysterical outbursts of the DAR, the gross and vulgar
appeals of business corporations? It is not merely that these
things are offensive. It is rather that they are wrong—morally,
socially, and politically.

The concept of loyalty as conformity is a false one. It is
narrow and restrictive, denies freedom of thought and of conscience, and is irremediably stained by private and selfish considerations. "Enlightened loyalty," wrote Josiah Royce, who
made loyalty the very core of his philosophy,

means harm to no man's loyalty. It is at war only with disloyalty, and
its warfare, unless necessity constrains, is only a spiritual warfare. It
does not foster class hatreds; it knows of nothing reasonable about
race prejudices; and it regards all races of men as one in their need
of loyalty. It ignores mutual misunderstandings. It loves its own wherever upon earth its own, namely loyalty itself, is to be found.

Justice, charity, wisdom, spirituality, he added, were all defin-
able in terms of loyalty, and we may properly ask which of these
qualities our contemporary champions of loyalty display.

Above all, loyalty must be to something larger than one-
self, untainted by private purposes or selfish ends. But what
are we to say of the attempts by the NAM and by individual
corporations to identify loyalty with the system of private enterprise? Is it not as if officeholders should attempt to identify
loyalty with their own party, their own political careers? Do not
those corporations which pay for full-page advertisements associating Americanism with the competitive system expect, ultimately, to profit from that association? Do not those organizations that deplore, in the name of patriotism, the extension of

government operation of hydro-electric power expect to profit from their campaign?

Certainly it is a gross perversion not only of the concept of loyalty but of the concept of Americanism to identify it with a particular economic system. This precise question, interestingly enough, came before the Supreme Court in the Schneiderman case not so long ago—and it was Wendell Willkie who was counsel for Schneiderman. Said the Court:

> Throughout our history many sincere people whose attachment to the general Constitutional scheme cannot be doubted have, for various and even divergent reasons, urged differing degrees of governmental ownership and control of natural resources, basic means of production, and banks and the media of exchange, either with or without compensation. And something once regarded as species of private property was abolished without compensating the owners when the institution of slavery was forbidden. Can it be said that the author of the Emancipation Proclamation and the supporters of the Thirteenth Amendment were not attached to the Constitution?

There is, it should be added, a further danger in the willful identification of Americanism with a particular body of economic practices. Many learned economists predict for the near future an economic crash similar of that of 1929. If Americanism is equated with competitive capitalism, what happens to it if competitive capitalism comes a cropper? If loyalty and private enterprise are inextricably associated, what is to preserve loyalty if private enterprise fails? Those who associate Americanism with a particular program of economic practices have a grave responsibility, for if their program should fail, they expose Americanism itself to disrepute.

The effort to equate loyalty with conformity is misguided because it assumes that there is a fixed content to loyalty and that this can be determined and defined. But loyalty is a principle, and eludes definition except in its own terms. It is devotion to the best interests of the commonwealth, and may require hostility to the particular policies which the government pursues, the particular practices which the economy undertakes, the particular institutions which society maintains. "If there is any fixed star in our Constitutional constellation," said the Supreme Court in the Barnette case, "it is that no official, high or petty, can prescribe what shall be orthodox in politics, nationalism, religion, or other matters of opinion, or force citizens to confess by word or act their faith therein. If there are any circumstances which permit an exception they do not now occur to us."

True loyalty may require, in fact, what appears to the naive to be disloyalty. It may require hostility to certain provisions of the Constitution itself, and historians have not concluded that those who subscribed to the "Higher Law" were lacking in patriotism. We should not forget that our tradition is one of protest and revolt, and it is stultifying to celebrate the rebels of the past—Jefferson and Paine, Emerson and Thoreau—while we silence the rebels of the present. "We are a rebellious nation," said Theodore Parker, known in his day as the Great American Preacher, and went on:

> Our whole history is treason; our blood was attainted before we were born; our creeds are infidelity to the mother church; our constitution, treason to our fatherland. What of that? Though all the governors in the world bid us commit treason against man, and set the example, let us never submit.

Those who would impose upon us a new concept of loyalty not only assume that this is possible, but have the presumption to believe that they are competent to write the definition. We are reminded of Whitman's defiance of the "never-ending audacity of elected persons." Who are those who would set the standards of loyalty? They are Rankins and Bilbos, officials of the DAR and the Legion and the NAM, Hearsts and McCormicks. May we not say of Rankin's harangues on loyalty what Emerson said of Webster at the time of the Seventh of March speech: "The word honor in the mouth of Mr. Webster is like the word love in the mouth of a whore."

What do men know of loyalty who make a mockery of the Declaration of Independence and the Bill of Rights, whose energies are dedicated to stirring up race and class hatreds, who would straitjacket the American spirit? What indeed do they know of America—the America of Sam Adams and Tom Paine, of Jackson's defiance of the Court and Lincoln's celebration of labor, of Thoreau's essay on Civil Disobedience and Emerson's championship of John Brown, of the America of the Fourierists and the Come-Outers, of cranks and fanatics, of socialists and anarchists? Who among American heroes could meet their tests, who would be cleared by their committees? Not Washington, who was a rebel. Not Jefferson, who wrote that all men are created equal and whose motto was "rebellion to tyrants is obedience to God." Not Garrison, who publicly burned the Constitution; or Wendell Phillips, who spoke for the underprivileged everywhere and counted himself a philosophical anarchist; not Seward of the Higher Law or Sumner of racial equality. Not Lincoln, who admonished us to have malice toward none, charity for all; or Wilson, who warned that our flag was "a flag of liberty of opinion as well as of political liberty;" or Justice Holmes, who said that our Constitution is an experiment and that while that experiment is being made "we should be eternally vigilant against attempts to check the expression of opinions that we loathe and believe to be fraught with death."

There are further and more practical objections against the imposition of fixed concepts of loyalty or tests of disloyalty. The effort is itself a confession of fear, a declaration of insolvency. Those who are sure of themselves do not need reassurance, and those who have confidence in the strength and the virtue of America do not need to fear either criticism or competition. The effort is bound to miscarry. It will not apprehend those who are really disloyal, it will not even frighten them; it will affect only those who can be labeled "radical." It is sobering to recall that though the Japanese relocation program, carried through at such incalculable cost in misery and tragedy, was justified to us on the ground that the Japanese were potentially disloyal, the record does not disclose a single case of Japanese disloyalty or sabotage during the whole war. The warning sounded by the Supreme Court in the Barnette flag-salute case is a timely one:

Ultimate futility of such attempts to compel obedience is the lesson of every such effort from the Roman drive to stamp out Christianity as a disturber of pagan unity, the Inquisition as a means to religious and dynamic unity, the Siberian exiles as a means to Russian unity, down to the fast-failing efforts of our present totalitarian enemies.

Those who begin coercive elimination of dissent soon find themselves exterminating dissenters. Compulsory unification of opinion achieves only the unanimity of the graveyard.

Nor are we left to idle conjecture in this matter; we have had experience enough. Let us limit ourselves to a single example, one that is wonderfully relevant. Back in 1943 the House Un-American Activities Committee, deeply disturbed by alleged disloyalty among government employees, wrote a definition of subversive activities and proceeded to apply it. The definition was admirable, and no one could challenge its logic or its symmetry:

> Subversive activity derives from conduct intentionally destructive of or inimical to the Government of the United States—that which seeks to undermine its institutions, or to distort its functions, or to impede its projects, or to lessen its efforts, the ultimate end being to overturn it all.

Surely anyone guilty of activities so defined deserved not only dismissal but punishment. But how was the test applied? It was applied to two distinguished scholars, Robert Morss Lovett and Goodwin Watson, and to one able young historian, William E. Dodd, Jr., son of our former Ambassador to Germany. Of almost three million persons employed by the government, these were the three whose subversive activities were deemed the most pernicious, and the House cut them off the payroll. The sequel is familiar. The Senate concurred only to save a wartime appropriation; the President signed the bill under protest for the same reason. The Supreme Court declared the whole business a "bill of attainder" and therefore unconstitutional. Who was it, in the end, who engaged in "subversive activities"—Lovett, Dodd, and Watson, or the Congress which flagrantly violated Article One of the Constitution?

Finally, disloyalty tests are not only futile in application, they are pernicious in their consequences. They distract attention from activities that are really disloyal, and silence criticism inspired by true loyalty. That there are disloyal elements in America will not be denied, but there is no reason to suppose that any of the tests now formulated will ever be applied to them.

It is relevant to remember that when Rankin was asked why his Committee did not investigate the Ku Klux Klan he replied that the Klan was not un-American, it was American!

Who are those who are really disloyal? Those who inflame racial hatreds, who sow religious and class dissensions. Those who subvert the Constitution by violating the freedom of the ballot box. Those who make a mockery of majority rule by the use of the filibuster. Those who impair democracy by denying equal educational facilities. Those who frustrate justice by lynch law or by making farce of jury trials. Those who deny freedom of speech and of the press and of assembly. Those who press for special favors against the interest of the commonwealth. Those who regard public office as a source of private gain. Those who would exalt the military over the civil. Those who for selfish and private purposes stir up national antagonisms and expose the world to the ruin of war.

Will the House Committee on Un-American Activities interfere with the activities of these? Will Mr. Truman's disloyalty proclamation reach these? Will the current campaigns for Americanism convert these? If past experience is any guide, they will not. What they will do, if they are successful, is to silence criticism, stamp out dissent—or drive it underground. But if our democracy is to flourish it must have criticism, if our government is to function it must have dissent. Only totalitarian governments insist upon conformity and they—as we know—do so at their peril. Without criticism abuses will go unrebuked; without dissent our dynamic system will become static. The American people have a stake in the maintenance of the most thorough-going inquisition into American institutions. They have a stake in nonconformity, for they know that the American genius is nonconformist. They have a stake in experimentation of the most radical character, for they know that only those who prove all things can hold fast that which is good.

It is easier to say what loyalty is not than to say what it is. It is not conformity. It is not passive acquiescence in the status quo. It is not preference for everything American over everything foreign. It is not an ostrich-like ignorance of other countries and other institutions. It is not the indulgence in ceremony—a flag salute, an oath of allegiance, a fervid verbal declaration. It is not a particular creed, a particular version of history, a particular body of economic practices, a particular philosophy.

It is a tradition, an ideal, and a principle. It is a willingness to subordinate every private advantage for the larger good. It is an appreciation of the rich and diverse contributions that can come from the most varied sources. It is allegiance to the traditions that have guided our greatest statesmen and inspired our most eloquent poets—the traditions of freedom, equality, democracy, tolerance, the tradition of the higher law, of experimentation, cooperation, and pluralism. It is a realization that America was born of revolt, flourished on dissent, became great through experimentation.

Independence was an act of revolution; republicanism was something new under the sun; the federal system was a vast experimental laboratory. Physically Americans were pioneers; in the realm of social and economic institutions, too, their tradition has been one of pioneering. From the beginning, intellectual and spiritual diversity have been as characteristic of America as racial and linguistic. The most distinctively American philosophies have been transcendentalism—which is the philosophy of the Higher Law—and pragmatism—which is the philosophy of experimentation and pluralism. These two principles are the very core of Americanism: the principle of the Higher Law, or of obedience to the dictates of conscience rather than of statutes, and the principle of pragmatism, or the rejection of a single good and of the notion of a finished universe. From the beginning Americans have known that there were new worlds to conquer, new truths to be discovered. Every effort to confine Americanism to a single pattern, to constrain it to a single formula, is disloyalty to everything that is valid in Americanism.

SEDITIOUS SPEECH AND LOYALTY PROBES [2]

In view of what the *Washington Post* calls "The commiephobia now epidemic in the United States," and the activities

[2] By Judson King, Director, National Popular Government League. Bulletin no. 230. 16p. National Popular Government League, Washington, D.C. March 12, 1948.

of federal and state governments in connection therewith, let us consider the following:

President Conant of Harvard University appears before a joint committee of the Massachusetts Legislature and voices "determined opposition" to a bill to institute loyalty tests for teachers in all public and private schools and make trustees and board members criminally responsible for their employment. "I doubt," said he, "if there are many such people in the Commonwealth in any form of employment and I know of none anywhere on our teaching staffs."

President Hutchins of Chicago University queried by distinguished newsman, Colonel Robert S. Allen, states that in view of what is happening in loyalty probes he could not blame any member of his faculty for declining the risk to his reputation in accepting service in the Federal Government.

Twenty-two members of the Yale Law faculty address a protest to President Truman saying that "We need not create a police state to escape a police state," charging that "High officials of the National Government are today acting in disregard and defiance of American traditions of civil liberties and, in our considered judgment, in violation of the Constitution of the United States."

Addressing the New York State Bar Association, John Lord O'Brian, Assistant to Attorney General Gregory in the First World War and in charge of administering the Espionage Act, likewise gave warning that constitutional safeguards of freedom are being set aside and his remarks were approved and applauded.

Henry S. Commager, Professor of History at Columbia University, writes for *Harper's Magazine* an article titled "Who Is Loyal to America?" and demonstrated the disloyalty of those who persist in un-American practices.

The *New York Herald Tribune* runs a series of articles by Bert Andrews, able head of its Washington Bureau, describing the star chamber methods by which several employees of the State Department have been dismissed and editorials denouncing these tactics follow.

The conservative *Washington Post* in articles, editorials and the brilliant cartoons of Herblock has for months been exposing and criticising the fashion in which the anti-Communist crusade is being conducted.

Various religious organizations and distinguished churchmen have added their protests and warnings. Lastly, scientific associations are coming to the defense of accused Dr. Condon, Director of the Bureau of Standards.

I respectfully submit that these alarums thus sounded by conservative men of the highest responsibility and character should give pause to puzzled or indifferent Americans who have been disposed to take with a grain of salt the warnings of Roger Baldwin and his American Civil Liberties Union, labor and liberal organizations and leaders in these matters for fear some red or pink fringe might be found on their undershirts.

Without question, the tactics of Moscow present to the American Government, and people and to all governments and peoples, a tough nut to crack. The question is, can we crack it without sacrificing our traditional liberties of thought, speech and action and establishing an American Gestapo?

Whether you believe ethical principles to have originated with the tables handed to Moses on the Mount, or as the result of millenniums of evolution, it has, at least, taken humanity a long time to learn that for individuals, social classes, nations, or United Nations, the Good Life cannot be achieved by lying, deceit, double-dealing, murder, suppression of thought, and enslavement of others.

Therefore, when the Bolsheviks broke away from peaceable, parliamentary, European Socialists and set up the Third International advocating bloody revolution, adopting the Machiavellian doctrine that "the end justifies the means," and set out to create their particular pattern of the Kingdom of Heaven on earth by force and fraud, they committed one of the most criminal blunders in the history of humanity.

It is no answer to cite the fact that ancient slave monarchies, serf supported feudalism and capitalist democracies, to a greater or less degree, have employed force and fraud to exploit the masses and cement their power to rule and strut. Any civilization or any economic system, including communism, which in practice flouts the ethics of the Golden Rule and toleration as visionary and impractical "carries within itself the seeds of its own destruction," as Karl Marx said of capitalism. Arnold Toynbee's list of twenty dead and dying civilizations noted in his recent book, *A Study of History,* would seem to have some bearing on this point.

There are three main types of individuals beholden to Moscow with whom we have to deal. They are:

1. Military spies and informers, aliens or citizens.

2. Provocative agents who join labor and liberal organizations, create disunity, and bring them into disrepute or disruption.

3. Propagandists of mouth and pen.

Is the United States in any such danger from these people as to justify the present alarms? Is the United States Criminal Code strong enough to cope with any peril from this source without making the Bill of Rights a scrap of paper?

Both conservative and progressive legal and historical authorities in the highest brackets say we are not in danger and we are strong enough. They point to the Criminal Code which makes it a crime for even two people to conspire to set going a revolution of force and violence and they point to the investigating agents of the Civil Service Commission and the military bureaus, plus the great organization of the FBI, captained by Mr. J. Edgar Hoover, a veteran administrator of great ability in running down criminals, spies and dangerous characters. They hold that this can be done without endangering freedom of thought and expression of American citizens in respect of domestic, economic and political issues.

Conservative political and industrial spokesmen ignoring the Criminal Code say we are in danger. Their point of view was recently voiced by Speaker Martin, reported in the press to have said . . . "Your legislators will persevere until we have on the statute books adequate laws to deal effectively with traitors." Further, in a radio broadcast on Lincoln's birthday he said: "The New Deal Administration knew full well the intentions of the Kremlin. We Republicans warned of the march of communism for ten or twelve years. We told the nation the Communists were sneaking into high government places. Now it is going to take a Republican administration to clean out the fifth columnists and traitors from the government structure. Those who insisted for years in keeping them there will never do the job."

On the other side of the political fence, Attorney General Tom Clark urges more sedition law "with teeth in it."

Concerning Speaker Martin's speech, radio commentator Elmer Davis who was Director of the Office of War Information during the late war, in his broadcast of February 13 [1948], said:

> We are not going to get a Republican administration for at least eleven months—unless Mr. Truman should happen to die and Speaker Martin succeeded to the presidency. Does the Speaker think it is safe to let these traitors stay in the government for eleven months, unidentified and unexposed? He can get them out now, if he wants to; all he need do is to name names and offer some facts in proof. What are we to think of a public official who evidently knows all about them, but is willing to let them continue their pernicious activities for almost a year longer? What a great many people are likely to think is that the Speaker does *not* know, that he has no facts in evidence, that he is willing to undermine public confidence in the integrity and loyalty of government, merely to gain a political advantage.

Such use is not new to our history. We had a French Jacobin scare in 1798 which produced the famous Alien and Sedition Laws of the Federalist party, actually aimed at Jeffersonism. Also a Russian Bolshevik scare in 1920 manifestly nurtured by Attorney General Palmer as a stepping stone to the presidency. . . .

The penal codes and imperial decrees of all European monarchies placed in the hands of prosecutors and courts legal power . . . to place their construction of treasonable intent upon written and spoken words alone. It halted intellectual and social progress for centuries, and sent untold thousands of innocent men to torture, to prison, to exile and to death. Monarchs employed it as a convenient method of smothering free speech and murdering men who merely opposed their policies. That is the reason why the Philadelphia Convention put Section 3 of Article III in the Constitution which reads in part: "No person shall be convicted of treason unless on the testimony of two witnesses to the same overt act or on confession in open court."

But that was not enough, and the demand came for a Bill of Rights containing a constitutional provision whereby freedom of speech also, not accompanied by overt acts, could not be construed as seditious or as "constructive treason."

A masterly statement of the origin of this amendment was made by the late Alfred Bettman, prominent Cincinnati lawyer, before a literary club in his home city in February of 1920 when the peacetime sedition bills were pending. His subject was "Freedom of Speech and the Press." He spoke with authority since he and John Lord O'Brian as Special Assistant Attorney Generals were in charge of the enforcement during the First World War of the Espionage Act of 1917 which expired at the close of the war. He had made a profound study of the subject and was an influential foe of peacetime sedition laws.

He recounted the history of the fight in Great Britain for freedom of thought, and suppression from the star chamber methods of Charles I to the sedition trials of George III when men were accused of treasonable intent to destroy the Constitution and overthrow the government and jailed and deported when their only offense was to advocate universal suffrage and reform of the "rotten borough" system of elections. He then comes to Charles James Fox's famous Libel Law of 1792 which overthrew the doctrine of Lord Chief Justice Mansfield that the judge, not the jury, was to decide whether a publication was seditious: Says Mr. Bettman:

> Fox's law was adopted about one year after the adoption of the First Amendment, but it had been introduced and discussed before that adoption and, beyond any question, the First Amendment at the very least, was designed to incorporate the provisions of that statute into our constitutional law.

The French Revolution was then in progress and Bettman gives an illustration of the fashion in which the hysteria over it was utilized by the Tory party in power to block domestic reforms at home, urged by the Whigs.

> In a private conversation in a coffee house in 1793 one John Frost gave voice to some opinions on universal suffrage. He was prosecuted for seditious libel and to give an aspect of danger and sedition to words that might intrinsically seem of slight importance the government attorney, in addressing the jury, gave an extended review of the history of the French Revolution.

Although defended by the famous Thomas Erskine, afterwards Lord Chancellor of England, Frost, a reputable attorney, was found guilty, sentenced to six months imprisonment, to stand in the pillory, and was deprived of his right to practice law.

I trust this will help make clear what Chief Justice Hughes was driving at in the classic statement quoted above which recognizes that the requirement of overt acts, to establish seditious or treasonable intent, is the deadline between a thousand years of old world suppression and, at that time, one hundred and thirty years of American freedom of conscience, thought, and expression of ideas, absolutely basic to democracy of any kind.

During the first World War Attorney General Gregory, a Texan, was keenly aware of the danger to civil liberties from war hysteria, and under him, with O'Brian and Bettman in charge, these rights for both aliens and citizens were scrupulously protected. But on March 4, 1919, A. Mitchell Palmer became Attorney General, organized his "Red Raids," and in February of 1920 went before the House Judiciary Committee and declared: "There is a condition of revolutionary intent in the country, on the part of both aliens and citizens, which is of sufficiently widespread a character to merit the serious consideration of the Congress. This is manifest chiefly by the threats, both written and spoken, on the part of such persons to injure, destroy or overthrow the government by physical force or violence." He urged "legislation of a simple character carefully guarding the guaranties of the Bill of Rights but filling what I may call the hiatus which exists at present in the statutory law."

In fact, he was seeking to abolish the "overt act" requirement so that he and his agents could punish aliens or American citizens for making speeches, or writing or circulating articles alleged to be of revolutionary or seditious intent without any overt acts to prove the charge. That is, to punish words not deeds through a peacetime sedition law.

Palmer was a Democrat, but Republican Senator Sterling had already gotten the Senate to adopt by voice vote, and little debate, a similar bill, and Republican Chairman of the House Judiciary Committee, Representative Graham, had another still worse which his committee substituted for the Sterling bill and the next day

asked the Rules Committee for an order for immediate consideration and passage. Both the Sterling and the Graham bills elim-
inated the "overt act" requirement, and added drastic restrictions
on free speech and publication, giving the Postmaster General,
for example, plenary rights to deny the mails to any publication
he considered seditious. Had the rule been granted, there is no
doubt that the bill would have passed the House with a whooping
viva voce vote, as in the Senate.

It is merely a part of the story to relate that at this critical
juncture the National Popular Government League, of which this
writer was then director, took up the fight, obtained a hearing,
warned the country and organized the defense. The distinguished
lawyer, Jackson H. Ralston, led the defense at the hearing presided over by Chairman Phil Campbell of Kansas.

The unconstitutionality and utter folly of the Sterling, Graham and Palmer bills were demonstrated to the committee by
such authorities as Alfred Bettman, by Captain Swinburne Hale,
of the Military Intelligence Service during the war; by Professor
Zechariah Chafee, Jr., of the Harvard School of Law; by Professor J. Allen Smith of Swarthmore College; by Samuel Gom-
pers, president of the American Federation of Labor, and others.
No Reds or even Pinks here!

The committee received 250 telegrams and letters of protest
from great daily newspapers, organizations and citizens. Hostile
at first, seemingly, the Rules Committee became suddenly aware
of the real attempt in these bills to shelve American constitutional
law and practice. The rule was denied. The bill never reached
the floor of the House. Peacetime sedition legislation was ended
for that session, and we all thought forever—at least for our generation. But we were mistaken.

At the time Palmer testified for his bill the notorious "Red
Raids" were then in full swing. Thousands of aliens and citizens, individually or assembled en masse at public meetings or
dance halls, were arrested, without warrant, and charged with be-
longing to a Communist or revolutionary organization, for deportation to Russia, leaving their families here to shift for
themselves.

Under the law these cases had to be turned over to the
Department of Labor for final action. Here Assistant Secretary

Louis F. Post, lawyer and famous editor, was in charge. He was a stout hearted, level headed man who respected American principles and the laws he was administering. Applying the laws strictly, he deported some 700 aliens and cancelled about 2,700 warrants of persons against whom nothing illegal or unworthy was shown.

Palmer and reactionaries in both political parties, enraged at Post, started out to "get him" for this and other reasons. He was known nationally as a progressive, fundamental democrat, editor of the then well-known magazine *The Public* and since the death of Henry George, intellectual leader of the Single Tax movement. Newspapers raved at him during the following months. An impeachment resolution was introduced in the House which was promptly sent to the Committee on Rules for instant action.

When the hearing was held the committee got from Mr. Post the same sort of elementary education on laws governing aliens as it had gotten at the hearing on sedition laws when considering the Palmer-Graham-Sterling sedition bills. After discussion, be it said to its credit, the Rules Committee pigeon-holed the matter and the impeachment proceedings collapsed. An attempt by the American Legion to force his dismissal from office likewise collapsed and he filled out his term.

Again the story requires me to be personal. While the "raids" were still in progress, believing as Justice Charles E. Hughes then said that "It is Americanism not socialism that is at stake," I called a meeting of officers and members of this League to consider the situation. Present were Senators Norris and Owen; Frank P. Walsh; Frederic C. Howe; Jackson H. Ralston; Edward Keating; Amos Pinchot, and several others of like standing.

It was decided to appoint a committee of outstanding lawyers to investigate. Their findings, titled, "Report upon the Illegal Practices of the U. S. Department of Justice," and addressed to the American people was published by this League in May 1920, and was given front-page publicity from coast to coast. It was signed by [a dozen] attorneys whose "loyalty" could not be questioned. . . .

The report concluded with, "There is no danger of revolution so great as that created by suppression, by ruthlessness and the deliberate violation of the simple rules of American law and American decency. . . . Here is no vague and threatened menace but a present assault upon the most sacred principles of our constitutional liberty."

The report of the twelve lawyers had a profound effect upon the American Bar and public opinion, and by common consent did more than any other one thing to end the delirium and the high-handed activities of the Department of Justice and its agents. There were no more Red Raids.

But there was an important sequel. Senator Thomas J. Walsh of Montana, Democrat, admittedly one of the ablest constitutional lawyers in the Congress, rose on the Senate floor the following December (1920) and demanded an investigation of the Report of the Twelve Lawyers. It was referred to the Judiciary Committee, of which Knute Nelson, Republican, was the chairman, who appointed a subcommittee headed by Sterling (he of the Sedition Bill) to make the inquiry. Hearings were held from January to March 1921, the transcript of which makes a volume of 800 pages.

The subcommittee split. Walsh was for finding Palmer guilty. Sterling was determined to whitewash him. Both made reports to the full Judiciary Committee, but it declined to act! The matter dragged for months, until finally in disgust, Senator Walsh in February 1923, had the findings of himself and Sterling printed in the *Congressional Record,* and the Judiciary Committee discharged from further consideration of the matter. Palmer, Sterling and others did not get their much desired whitewashing, nor did Walsh get his desired condemnation. But he won the moral victory. The concluding sentences of his report read:

It is only in such times [of war hysteria] that the guaranties of the Constitution as to personal rights are of any practical value. In seasons of calm no one thinks of denying them; they are accorded as a matter of course. It is rare except when the public mind is stirred by some overwhelming catastrophe or is aghast at some hideous crime,

or otherwise overwrought, that one is required to appeal to his constitutional rights. If, in such times, the Constitution is not a shield,
the encomiums which statesmen and jurists have paid it are fustian.

Finally in 1923 Assistant Secretary of Labor Post, then re-
tired, published a remarkable book in which he proved from the
official records that the alleged gigantic "conspiracy to overthrow the Government of the United States by force and violence" was "a stupendous and cruel hoax." . . .

The 1920 delirium died down. Nevertheless, in the 21-year
period between the two World Wars the term "Bolshevist" and
later "Communist" were hurled against every progressive man or
measure, national or state, designed to curb the abuses of monopoly, to improve the lot of wage workers or the underprivileged, to restrain land monopoly or what not. After 1933 the
terms were employed with especial bitterness against all New
Deal legislation, the Tennessee Valley Authority, the Holding
Company Act and the Wagner Act as examples.

The rapid growth of AF of L craft unions, the rise of the
CIO industrial unions, the establishment of the legal right of
collective bargaining, the spectacular growth of consumer and
producer and other cooperatives, brought violent opposition
from vested interests. Labor unrest and practically every major
strike were charged to be the work of "alien Communists" or
"fellow travelers seeking to overthrow our form of government."
Without doubt a few "borers from within" Communist leaders
had that ultimate purpose.

But the stern truth is that 99 per cent of American workers
and trade unionists were and are no more "Commies" than
small town grocers, heavy industry directors or bank presidents.
It is also true that 99 per cent of "labor troubles" originated
with American working men seeking to improve their lot by
lawful American methods.

But during this period the development of Russia into a
world power and the rise of fascism in Italy and nazism in
Germany, gave further concern to all loyal Americans. . . .
But by the summer of that year [1939] our Congress had become apprehensive—some members said "panicky"—over the
danger from fifth columnists and aliens within our borders or

seeking admission. Two pieces of legislation were inaugurated especially affecting the subject of this bulletin and in this atmosphere was passed the Alien Registration Act of 1940, the title of which read:

> A bill to make unlawful attempts to interfere with the discipline of the Army, the Navy, and the Coast Guard; to require the deportation of certain classes of aliens; to require the fingerprinting of aliens seeking to enter the United States; and for other purposes.

Get the picture. War was on! We might become involved; Anyhow, we proposed to spot and fingerprint any German, Jap, Russian or other alien who might be trying to spread disloyalty among our armed forces. So far, good and wise precaution. And that was what the nation was informed was the purpose of the act.

But what the nation, the American Bar, editors, historians and critical scholars did not generally know, or what even a majority of the Congress did not seem to realize was, that a major part of this act applied to American citizens and insofar as Congress is concerned in effect abolished the "overt act" protection to freedom of speech and swept away the legal principle that guilt must be personal and not by association—two bulwarks of liberty so firmly fixed in our judicial practices as to be expected to last till the Day of Judgment.

Do not take my layman's word for it. Writes Professor Zechariah Chafee, Jr., unquestionably our leading authority on free speech legislation:

> Not until months later did I for one realize that the statute contains the most drastic restrictions on freedom of speech ever enacted in the United States during peace. It is no more limited to the registration of aliens than the Espionage Act of 1917 was limited to spying. Most of the Alien Registration Act is not concerned with registration, and the very first part of it has nothing particular to do with aliens. Just as the 1917 act gave us a wartime sedition law, so the 1940 act gives us a peacetime sedition law—for everybody, especially United States citizens. . . . A. Mitchell Palmer is dead, but the Federal Sedition Act he so eagerly desired is at last on the statute books. . . .

Note now that the absence of proof of personal guilt was why the U. S. Supreme Court refused to approve the deportations of Schneiderman, admittedly a Communist, and of Harry

Bridges charged with being one. Said Justice Murphy in deciding the Bridges case:

> The doctrine of personal guilt is one of the most fundamental principles of our jurisprudence. It partakes of the very essence of the concept of freedom and due process of law, and . . . prevents the prosecution of the innocent for beliefs and actions of others.

Even accused Nazi criminals, with our own Justice Robert H. Jackson as prosecutor, were afforded that protection as an example to the whole world of the fairness of American and English judicial processes in rebuke to totalitarian methods. Says Dr. Walter Gellhorn of the Columbia Law School:

> A recent and highly significant instance of refusal to impute to one man the wrongdoings or beliefs of another is the judgment of the International Tribunal in the Nuremberg Trial. That distinguished tribunal rejected the notion that an individual's participation in the Nazi conspiracy could be proved merely by evidence of his having been a member of a Nazi organization. Prosecution and punishment were made to turn upon individual guilt rather than upon guilt by association.

Shall we refuse to protect Americans as we protected Nazis? Peacetime sedition laws have been used notoriously not merely to punish treason or sedition but as a weapon against economic, political and social reforms opposed by administrations in power. That is why they are so loosely drawn.

Honorable Jerry Voorhis in his new book [*Confessions of a Congressman*] relates incidents which show how either investigations or statutes may be diverted from their ostensible purpose and the public misled thereby. . . . He tells, for example, how Chairman Dies without consulting the Committee released to the newspapers a report giving the impression "that attempts on the part of consumer organizations or government agencies to insist upon honesty in advertising was part and parcel of a Communist program," and "Communist-dominated." Again in 1942 by a similar tactic a *Special Report on Subversive Activities Aimed at Destroying our Representative Form of Government*, was directed against an organization actually non-Communist which published the records of and advised defeat at the polls of certain Congressmen. . . .

Such abuse of power is undoubtedly the reason why, only two weeks before the Alien Registration Act was passed by the

Senate, Senators Norris of Nebraska and Wheeler of Montana made a determined fight against this transfer [of the Immigration and Naturalization Service from the Department of Labor to the Department of Justice]. They held that experience had shown the Department of Justice with its FBI was not the proper agency to administer the service. In an extended speech Norris described the "Red Raids" of Palmer and read to the Senate the charges in the "Report" of the twelve lawyers "Upon the Illegal Practices of the U.S. Department of Justice." Wheeler reminded the Senate of FBI activities when even Senator La Follette, Sr., and other Senators were shadowed by FBI agents and had their offices searched.

Both emphasized the danger to loyal American citizens and organizations from lawless investigations by department detectives and agents for expressions of opinion and activities of a wholly non-seditious character and simply concerned with domestic social reforms. Both read from statements made in 1920-23, before their appointment to the United States Supreme Court, of Justices Charles E. Hughes and Harlan F. Stone warning against the exercise of such powers by administrative agents without proper court review and recommending legislation to prevent such abuses. . . .

The sort of thing for which Section 2 in the Sedition section of the Alien Registration Act opens the door in peacetime, and many times multiplied in times of emergency, is illustrated by the methods employed in the current probe of employees of the Federal Government—that of secrecy.

The late Chief Justice Stone when Dean of the Columbia University Law School in 1920, shocked as was Dean Pound of Harvard at Palmer's ruthless illegalities, pointed out the dangers from such loose legislation in a letter presented to the investigating subcommittee of the Senate above noted, which concluded:

It is inevitable that any system which confers upon administrative officers power to restrain the liberty of individuals, without safeguards substantially like those which exist in criminal cases and without adequate authority for judicial review of the action of such administrative officers will result in abuse of power and in intolerable injustice and cruelty to individuals.

Let us recall at this point that just four years after this statement was made and publicized, President Coolidge on April 7, 1924, appointed Dean Stone Attorney General of the United States to fumigate the odorous mess in which Harry Daugherty had left the Department of Justice; and that Mr. Stone at once put an end to the secret investigations of American citizens which had been carried on by the FBI under Attorney General Daugherty's direction.

And what are the "safeguards in criminal cases" referred to by Dean Stone? Their legal foundation is found in the Bill of Rights put there because the American people well knew the dangers from secrecy in government and were determined that nothing savoring of medieval star chamber methods should ever be practiced in America, even if they had to reject the Constitution, and it is common knowledge that the Constitution would have been rejected had the Bill of Rights not been agreed to in advance. It reads, in case you have forgotten:

Amendment VI. In all criminal prosecutions, the accused shall enjoy the right to a speedy and public trial, by an impartial jury of the state and district wherein the crime shall have been committed, which district shall have been previously ascertained by law, and to be informed of the nature and cause of the accusation; to be confronted with the witnesses against him; to have compulsory process for obtaining witnesses in his favor, and to have the assistance of counsel for his defense.

The foregoing is but a brief summary of a part of the governing high points relating to our subject, omitting mention of germaine Supreme Court decisions and historical data which would fill many bulletins. But putting them together, the following conclusions emerge:

1. The 1920 attempt of Attorney General Palmer, Democrat, and Senator Sterling and Representative Graham, Republicans, and others, to enact a peacetime sedition bill (the wartime Espionage Act was expiring) undermining freedom of speech failed; and Palmer's illegal Red raids were halted, because the courageous exposure of their significance by outstanding American lawyers, educators and editors aroused American public opinion.

2. The pre-World War II peacetime sedition enactment of 1940 caused no special outcry because under the title "and other purposes" it was slipped into the bill dealing with enemy aliens when the world conflict was in full swing and so went unnoticed, in those days of great tension.

However, its repeal is now urged by another outstanding group of educators, lawyers and businessmen aware of its menace. I refer to the Commission on Freedom of the Press established in 1943 and whose work is financed by a grant to the University of Chicago by the magazine *Time* and the *Encyclopaedia Britannica* whom nobody yet has accused of being either Communist or fellow traveller.

One of their reports published as a supplement to *Fortune* magazine for April 1947, and titled "A Free and Responsible Press," reads at p. 18:

> We recommend the repeal of legislation prohibiting expressions in favor of revolutionary changes in our institutions where there is no clear and present danger that violence will result from the expressions.
>
> The Supreme Court has held that expressions urging the overthrow of the government by force are within the protection of the First Amendment unless there is a clear and present danger that these expressions will lead to violence. We believe that this sound principle is violated by the peacetime sedition clauses of the Alien Registration Act of 1940 and by the various state syndicalism acts which make it a crime to advocate the overthrow of the government by force, irrespective of the probable effect of the statements. The really dangerous persons within the scope of these laws can be reached by the conspiracy statutes and the general criminal law. As applied to other persons, which is most likely to be the case, these laws are of dubious constitutionality and unwise. Yet only a few of the agitators who are prosecuted can succeed in getting before the Supreme Court. Consequently, so long as this legislation remains on the statute books, its intimidating effect is capable of stifling political and economic discussion. These acts ought to be repealed.

3. The difference between the two periods is in this: We have had as yet no such disgraceful and illegal mass arrests with shocking cruelties which all could see that characterized the Palmer raids. Just now espionage is carried on quietly and the Departments assure us wholly within the law with care taken not to injure the reputations of innocent persons.

Yet, John Lord O'Brian, today one of the most distinguished members of the bar and whose patriotism none questions, just last January read a paper before the New York Bar Association, titled "Loyalty Tests and National Unity," above noted, in which the constitutionality and practical wisdom of these investigations as conducted is called in question by an authority who knows from official experience what they mean.

4. To repeat, three safeguards of the liberties of American citizens have now been negated either by act of Congress or administrative edict, namely, (1) the Overt Act protection of freedom of speech; (2) that guilt is personal and not by association; (3) the right to a fair, open trial. If ever extreme reaction gains control these legal tools are there—ready for use.

5. Even if it be granted that the Criminal Code needed strengthening, the question arises why the proponents of these measures, in Congress and out, habitually charge patently loyal Americans promoting domestic reforms with treasonable or seditious intent.

6. In this evident effort to mold the mind of America Congress should oblige us with definitions of what communism and fascism are and what they are not. Senators and Congressmen, scores of times, have denounced TVA as "communistic" or even pure "communism." Is it? And what of fascism in the United States? In Europe it was an alliance of politics with monopoly cartels, feudal land holders, and the military.

7. Lastly, are we prepared to pay the inevitable price for this? That great statesman, Edward Livingston, later Andrew Jackson's Secretary of State but who as a young member of Congress fought the Alien and Sedition bills of 1798, predicted what happened. Said he:

The country will swarm with informers, spies, delators, and all the odious reptile tribe that breed in the sunshine of despotic power. The hours of the most unsuspected confidence, the intimacies of friendship, or the recesses of domestic retirement afford no security.

Mr. O'Brian in more moderate language forewarns of like results in our day both as to individuals and organizations. He pleads:

Finally, may we not agree that in the battle of ideas, in which we are now engaged, our great task is to strengthen the faith of our own people, and the people in foreign lands in our standards of justice and fair play? This is the great problem. In importance it overshadows all others. The real danger to our nation lies in these measures to which attention has been drawn, in the mental climate in which they originated and in the apparent indifference to their significance.

8. Clearly, it is now up to the American people and the United States Supreme Court as soon as cases arise whether this trend shall continue.

THE CONSTITUTIONAL RIGHT TO ADVOCATE POLITICAL, SOCIAL AND ECONOMIC CHANGE [3]

Limitations of space do not permit here an extensive discussion of the history of political parties in the decades which preceded and followed the Civil War. Mention, however, of the Liberty, or Abolition, party of 1840; the Free Soil party of 1848; the Greenback party of 1878; the Populist party of 1894; the Farmer-Labor party of 1920 and 1922 should remind us that all of these political groups were in the main directed against a triumphant industrialism whose growth had adversely affected the economic well-being of farmers and wage earners, and whose struggles finally eventuated in the absorption of many of their tenets into the platform of the major political parties.

Nor can we engage in a review of the second period in our history when political rights of citizens were ruthlessly violated and denied. The denial to thirteen million Negro citizens of civil, social, political and economic rights possessed by all other Americans is such a commonplace that we too often forget the enormity of the constitutional violation which this represents.

It was not until the period of 1917-1920 that serious attempts were again made to bar political parties and their members from public life. On the federal scene, this manifested itself not so much in a legislative attack, but in a ruthless assault upon the right of the people by the executive department of the government. The infamous "Palmer Raids" are a part of the archives for all Americans to read and ponder. We would point, however,

[3] From article by the National Lawyers Guild. *Lawyers Guild Review.* 7:57-79. March-April 1947. Reprinted by permission.

to the historic document issued in 1920 by twelve outstanding lawyers whose report upon the illegal practices of the United States Department of Justice did much to bring to an end that deplorable period in American history. . . .

It is significant that Attorney General Palmer subsequently urged and Congress introduced some seventy peacetime sedition bills, none of which were passed.

In the same period, state repressive action was more extensive. Criminal syndicalism laws were enacted. Radical utterances were penalized. Teachers were subjected to loyalty oaths. This wave of restrictive measures was founded upon a desire to punish organizations and its members who opposed America's entry into the war, and out of fear of the impact of the Russian Revolution upon a restive labor movement impatient with recalcitrant monopolies unwilling to disgorge their immense profits in the form of wage increases. In the State of New York, the Lusk Legislative Committee reported on the dangers of "revolutionary radicalism" and caused the enactment of legislation directed against liberal teachers in the school systems, and the ouster of five Socialist Assemblymen duly elected by the people. The conduct of the Lusk Committee met with uniform condemnation.

In 1923, one of the first acts of Governor Alfred E. Smith was to sign a repealer of the Lusk Laws:

I am satisfied that they should not remain upon the statute books of this state because they are repugnant to the fundamentals of American democracy. Under the laws repealed teachers, in order to exercise their honorable calling, were in effect compelled to hold opinions as to governmental matters deemed by a state officer consistent with loyalty; . . . Freedom of opinion and freedom of speech were by those laws unduly shackled. . . . In signing these bills, I firmly believe that I am vindicating the principle that, within the limits of the penal law, every citizen may speak and teach what he believes.

More than a decade later, Governor Herbert H. Lehman, in vetoing an act intended to bar from the classified civil service all persons advocating the overthrow of government by force or violence stated:

I am profoundly convinced that any statute which directly or indirectly limits opportunity for free public discussion undermines the very foundation of constitutional government. . . . The threat to democracy lies, in my opinion, not so much in revolutionary change achieved by force or violence. Its greatest danger comes through gradual invasion of constitutional rights with the acquiescence of an inert people; through failure to discern that constitutional government cannot survive where the rights guaranteed by the constitution are not safe-guarded even to those citizens with whose political and social views the majority may not agree . . . . Were we of this great liberal state to approve this bill today, we might readily find tomorrow that we had opened flood gates of oppressive legislation in the nation against re-ligious, social, labor and other minority groups.

The Supreme Court of the United States, interpreter of the fundamental law, has with firmness and clarity enunciated the purpose and meaning of the Bill of Rights. . . .

For a legislature to declare an American political party un-lawful by a "finding" that the party's tenets are inconsistent with the legislature's ideas of proper political doctrines, and to punish therefor, constitutes, in effect, a legislative trial with-out any judicial safeguard provided by the fundamental law. It is a usurpation of the powers of one of the government, the judiciary, by another arm of the government, the legislative. "When our Constitution and Bill of Rights were written, our ancestors had ample reason to know that legislative trials and punishments were too dangerous to liberty to exist in the nation of free men they envisioned. And so they proscribed bills of attainder."

Nor, indeed, can statutes or presidential orders which con-tain such vague phrases as "subversive" or "disloyal" or "un-American" be enacted for the purpose of proscribing free op-portunity of discussion or depriving American citizens of equal opportunity of employment. "A statute which upon its face, and as authoritatively construed, is so vague and indefinite as to permit the punishment of the fair use of this opportunity is repugnant to the guarantee of liberty contained in the Fourteenth Amendment."

The "clear and present danger" rule enunciated by the Supreme Court constitutes a restriction of limited scope upon the broad right of free discussion guaranteed by the Constitution.

The rule is a "working principle" to determine "where the individual's freedom ends and the state's power begins." One may not falsely cry fire in a crowded theater, nor counsel murder. But "in balancing the two ends against each other, always begin at the free speech end." "It is therefore in our tradition to allow the widest room for discussion, the narrowest range for its restriction."

Here is the clear and present danger rule:

The question in every case is whether the words used are used in such circumstances and are of such a nature as to create a clear and present danger that they will bring about the substantive evils that Congress has a right to prevent. It is a question of proximity and degree.

How carefully the rule must be applied is exemplified in the decisions which followed the enunciation of the "clear and present danger" rule. In *Frohwerk* v. *U.S., Debs* v. *U.S., Abrams* v. *U.S., Schaefer* v. *U.S., Pierce* v. *U.S.,* and *Gitlow* v. *New York,* the majority of the Court appeared to overlook the rule and Holmes, who had written for the majority in the *Schenck* case soon found himself dissented with Brandeis from the Court's decisions. Perhaps the reason for this situation may be found in one of the dissenting opinions of Justice Brandeis:

Like many other rules for human conduct, it can be applied correctly only by the exercise of good judgment; and in the exercise of good judgment calmness is, in times of deep feeling and on subjects which excite passion, as essential as fearlessness and honesty.

Indeed, as late as 1927, the Court had not yet "fixed the standard by which to determine when a danger shall be deemed clear; how remote the danger may be and yet be deemed present; and what degree of evil shall be deemed sufficiently substantial to justify resort to abridgment of free speech and assembly as the means of protection."

It was not until the sweep of events which followed the inauguration of Franklin D. Roosevelt in the 1930's, that the Supreme Court, under the guidance and leadership of Chief Justice Hughes "began at the free speech end."

Stromberg v. *California,* had already set the stage by invalidating a statute in part, which by its broad and vague language punished the unfurling of a red flag as a symbol of peaceful opposition to organized government. In *De Jonge* v. *Oregon*, the right of persons to assemble at a public meeting held under the auspices of the Communist party, and freely to discuss social and political changes was upheld. In *Herndon* v. *Lowry*, a statute which, as authoritatively construed, denied a Communist the right to solicit membership in the Communist party was held invalid." ". . . The penalizing even of utterances of a defined character must find its justification in a reasonable apprehension of danger to organized government. The judgment of the legislature is not unfettered." In *Hague* v. *CIO*, and *Thornhill* v. *Alabama*, the "dissemination of information concerning the facts of a labor dispute" was included within the area of free discussion guaranteed by the Constitution. "Every expression of opinion on matters that are important," stated the Court, "has the potentiality of inducing action in the interests of one rather than another group in society. But the group in power at any moment may not impose penal sanctions on peaceful and truthful discussion of matters of public interest merely on a showing that others may thereby be persuaded to take action inconsistent with its interests. Abridgement of the liberty of such discussion can be justified only where the clear danger of substantive evils arises under circumstances affording no opportunity to test the merits of ideas by competition for acceptance in the market of public opinion."

In *Bridges* v. *California*, the doctrine began to take on true meaning. "What finally emerges from the 'clear and present danger' cases is a working principle that the substantive evil must be extremely serious and the degree of imminence extremely high before utterances can be punished. These cases do not purport to mark the furthermost constitutional boundaries of protected expression, nor do we here." In *Schneiderman* v. *U. S.*, advocacy of the platform and program of the Communist party was again before the Supreme Court. In this case, the government contended that a person who believed in and advocated the principles of that party was not entitled to retain citizenship. The Supreme Court rejected that contention and held that advocacy of social, political and economic doctrines were protected by the Bill of Rights.

In *Thomas* v. *Collins,* the right of labor to organize the unorganized was involved. In holding invalid a statute which required a labor organizer, among other things, to register with officials of government as a condition to speaking to workers, the Court stated: "Accordingly, whatever occasion would restrain orderly discussion and persuasion, at appropriate time and place, must have clear support in public danger, actual or impending." Finally, in *Bridges* v. *Wixon,* the Court stated: "Proof that the Communist party advocates the theoretical or ultimate overthrow of the government by force was demonstrated by resort to some rather ancient party documents, certain other general Communist literature and oral corroborating testimony of government witnesses. Not the slightest evidence was introduced to show that either Bridges or the Communist party seriously and imminently threatens to uproot the government by force or violence."

The Communist party has been submitting itself to the franchise of the American people for the last twenty-eight years, and some of its members have been elected to public office. In the few cases in which one of its members has been tried for advocating force and violence, the evidence has not been about anything they have done, nor about their party program, but about the writings of earlier Communists, the documents of the Communist International, and in particular the implication drawn from these by the prosecution.

The Communist answer concerning the place of force and violence in social change is that it is a forecast of what may happen, not advocacy of what they want. The Supreme Court in the Schneiderman case held that no immediate danger to our institutions existed in the free discussion and advocacy by the Communist party of the nationalization of means of production and the expropriation of property with or without compensation. It found that the "concept of the dictatorship of the proletariat is one loosely used," and that "it does not appear that it would necessarily mean the end of representative government in the federal system." It rejected arguments of the government that historical documents issued by Marxist philosophers in the nineteenth century justified a conclusion that the Communist party advocated the overthrow of government by force and violence. "A tenable conclusion from the foregoing is that the party in 1927 desired to achieve its purpose by peaceful and democratic means."

The Constitution of the Communist party adopted at a convention held on July 28, 1945, provides in its preamble:

The Communist party upholds the achievements of American democracy and defends the United States Constitution and its Bill of Rights against its reactionary enemies who would destroy democracy and popular liberties.

The purpose of the organization are described as follows:

The purposes of this organization are to promote the best interests and welfare of the working class and the people of the United States, to defend and extend the democracy of our country, to prevent the rise of fascism, and to advance the cause of progress and peace with the ultimate aim of ridding our country of the scourge of economic crises, unemployment insecurity, poverty and war, through the realization of the historic aim of the working class—the establishment of socialism by the free choice of the majority of the American people.

The argument is made that these provisions of the Constitution are only a smoke screen behind which a situation is to be brought about in which the overthrow of democratic government will be violently accomplished. The contention is that democratic forms are to be used to accomplish the destruction of democracy.

The charges of deceit belong in heresy trials, not in political procedures. The test is action, not the dubious ground of belief about motives. "Fear of serious injury cannot alone justify suppression of free speech and assembly. Men feared witches and burnt women." "We have passed beyond that stage in political development when heresy-hunting is a permitted sport."

The fact is that the validity of political principles must be determined only on the basis of action and deeds; and deeds can be punished under law. Principles can only be proscribed by the judgment of the people in the market place of ideas. There are plenty of available statutes now on the books to punish conspiracies against the government, or any other criminal conduct of whatsoever form or nature. The only purpose which the proposed bills now pending in the House would seem to have is the creation of the crime of political heresy, establishing their sponsors' own tests of opinion and belief. "If there is any fixed star in our constitutional constellation, it is that no official, high or petty, can prescribe what shall be orthodox in politics, nationalism, religion, or other matters of opinion or force citizens to confess by word or act their faith therein."

The proposed legislation herein seeks, first, to outlaw the Communist party, to proscribe its beliefs, and to penalize its members and sympathizers. Secondly, the bills seek to exclude members of the Communist party and all sympathizers from all public employment. The President's Loyalty Order attempts this objective by executive fiat.

Clearly, in the light of this report, all of the proposed measures and presidential decree do violence to our fundamental law and our democratic way of life. We would add the following consideration concerning the President's order. It is a dangerous doctrine, fraught with the direst consequences, for the Executive Department of government to exercise the power of determining the subversiveness or disloyalty of every organization in the entire nation, political, civic or religious. Nowhere in the Constitution is such power vested in the President or Congress. Further, to impute doctrines of an organization, so illegally determined, to its members with resultant dismissal from employment, constitutes heresy hunting of the worst kind.

The only thing "we have to fear is fear itself," said Franklin D. Roosevelt. And, to the Daughters of the American Revolution, the great architect of the Four Freedoms and the Economic Bill of Rights significantly stated: "Remember, remember always that all of us, and you and I especially, are descendants from immigrants and revolutionists."

One of the stated purposes of the United Nations Charter to which the American government is a signatory is "promoting and encouraging respect for human rights and for the fundamental freedoms for all without distinction as to race, sex, language or religion." Clearly, we cannot deny to our own citizens the basic democratic rights which the peoples of all the world including America are entitled to enjoy by virtue of the provisions of the Charter. Professions of faith in democracy, when such restraints exist, are meaningless.

History is not without its examples of the familiar techniques employed by entrenched groups to destroy the liberties of the people. The formula attempted by the Federalists in 1798 to destroy the opposition of the people to a war against France was to vigorously, and falsely, characterize the opposition as an "alien and seditious menace." Under the guise of attacking "Bolsheviks and anarchists," the agents of Attorney General Palmer and J. Edgar Hoover in 1920 broke into the homes and meeting halls of respectable men and women without warrant and arrested trade union leaders, workers, socialists, civic leaders—many of whom had manifested opposition either to America's entrance into World War I or to the burdensome effects of unbridled monopolies. From 1933 on, Hitler purportedly fought the "Communist menace" while he destroyed every vestige of political, religious and economic liberty in Germany.

Discussing the technique of the Fascists, President Kenny in his address to the 1946 Convention of the National Lawyers Guild, stated:

> The instigators of fascism understood well that if their design were to succeed it had to be concealed in a thick fog of falsehood. An integral part of the Fascist ideology therefore, a part without which the rest could never come into being, was that the people of the world must be deliberately confused as to its real nature, that it must be shielded by what its chief exponent himself called "the big lie."
>
> This lie which set the people of the world groping in the dark, separate and alone, powerless to defend their liberty, their freedom, their very lives, is now as familiar as it is monstrous. It is simply that facts shall not be described for what they are, leaving to the people to pass judgment upon them, but that they shall be labeled as communism; and that all the evils committed by fascism were necessary to ward off the menace of communism. Once this basic notion was accepted, it was easily embellished. The fight for peace was a Communist plan. Therefore it had to be suppressed. The exercise of labor's rights was a Marxist notion. Therefore it had to be eliminated. Insistence upon democracy was a Red slogan. Those who uttered it had to be destroyed. International cooperation was a foundation of Communist theory. Therefore it could not be tolerated.
>
> This lie so embellished was dinned into the ears of the multitude. To accomplish this purpose the most tremendous propaganda barrage

in all history was unleashed. Its propagators denied to the people anything else. They so distorted the capacity of the people to understand
what was actually happening that the people were intellectually and
emotionally disarmed for the defense of their liberty.

Nor should the bond between political despotism and the
cartelization of German economy be ignored. In April 1933,
Gustav Krupp von Bohlen submitted to Hitler on behalf of the
Reich Association of German Industry a plan for the reorganization of German industry, which he stated was characterized by
the desire "to coordinate economic measures and political necessity." The testimony of the accused Nazi leaders, as well as the
reports of Justice Jackson and other American observers make
abundantly clear the role which large German industrial and
financial interests played in the destruction of the political freedom of the people of that country, which was the method for
stifling the protests of the millions of Germans who no longer
could find a stake in Germany's economic future. As Krupp
stated in 1933: "the turn of political events is in line with the
wishes which I myself and the board of directors have cherished
for a long time."

We are now in the midst of a critical period in our history.
Sober warnings have emanated from the President of the United
States and his economic advisers that our domestic economy will
be on the brink of chaos if inflation continues unabated and the
purchasing power of the people rapidly dwindles. The concentration and control of wealth into the hands of a few large
monopolies has assumed alarming proportions. While profits
show a steady increase, the protests and demands of the people
for a larger stake in the products of their labor in order to maintain a minimum standard of living remain unanswered. More
than that—there is a startling similarity to the Hitlerian technique in the activities of the representatives of large business
interests in their demand for such legislation as is under discussion herein, and in their statements from the forum of the
"Un-American Activities" Committee, successor to the notorious
Dies Committee. By the use of the label "anti-communism" and
the epithets "Communist," "disloyal" and "subversive," these
large business interests and their Congressional mouthpieces seek

to inoculate American public opinion with the notion that "Americanism" consists in the defense of the status quo; "Un-Americanism" consists in any criticism of or suggestion to change it.

The Thomas Committee, and its progenitor, the Dies Committee, have consistently followed one formula: under the guise of attacking "communism," they have attacked progressive persons and ideas in the field of politics and economics. The label of "disloyalty" has been pinned on all persons who belonged to any society or organization which sought any social advance. Such well known public figures as Henry Wallace, Frank Murphy, Felix Frankfurter, Archibald MacLeish, John Dewey, Bishop Francis J. McConnell, Professor Harlow Shapley, Chester Bowles, David Lilienthal, Edgar Warren and countless others have been smeared as disloyal and subversive. Liberal radio commentators are attacked; and Army Orientation Fact Sheet No. 64 describing the nature of native fascism is dubbed a "Communist propaganda sheet"; trade union leaders, clergymen, scientists, scholars, public officials, teachers, actors, artists—persons from all walks of life are vilified and depicted as guilty of subversive activities, because they advocate social policies with which the members of the Committee disagree. The pleas of these citizens for public housing and public health measures, for increased wages, for anti-lynching bills are deemed "communist." Liberals and progressives are to be swept from the service, thus paralyzing the enforcement of existing social and labor legislation. And all of this, under the guise of a drive against communism.

The significance of this concerted attack upon the fabric of American life should not be underestimated. It is not only the rights of a political party which are here involved; it is the freedom of the American people which is endangered. The opportunity to learn the truth concerning our society from the interplay of ideas in a free and unfettered arena is being denied to all of us. For the American people encompass the vast trade unions, the farmers, the diverse political parties, the Negroes, the foreign born, the large aggregations of public spirited citizens joined in organizations concerned with problems of religion, science, education, social service, economic welfare and the millions of men and women who seek progress and social advance. At different stages in our history, one or the other of these groups have been more vulnerable to attack by the enemies of civil liberties. But if the history of civilization teaches us anything, it is this: no whole people are free if any part of them is slave. . . .

We cannot afford to take liberties with our liberty. Complacency is not justified upon the assumption that these proposed repressive measures, even if enacted, will have only temporary life—that they are bound to fall and their proponents meet the disgrace which was the fate of the Federalists in 1801 and of Attorney General Palmer more than a hundred years later. History, it is true, often repeats itself, but not always in the same way. Anti-Semitism broke out sporadically in Germany as some despotic king succeeded some benevolent ruler. From 1933 on, however, anti-Semitism assumed a different form and six million persons were destroyed, a fate surely not envisioned by the civilized world before it transpired as a possible sequence to "trivial" anti-Semitic outbreaks.

The lynching of Negro citizens, the practice of Jim Crow segregation, discrimination in education and employment have long been looked upon by many merely as regrettable incidents which time and the Supreme Court would one day eliminate. But the Thirteenth, Fourteenth and Fifteenth Amendments were adopted more than seventy-five years ago. The violation of civil rights has denied not only to Negroes the social, economic and political advantages to which they have the right, but has retarded the development and expansion of our whole country, outstandingly in the South. And the horrible lynchings in Monroe, Georgia, and elsewhere, the repression of Negro veterans since the close of the war, must give pause to those who believe that recent decisions of the courts or views of enlightened statesmen have closed the door to widespread violations of the Constitution.

We must be alert to recognize the manifold forms in which attacks upon civil liberties appear. The very ruthlessness and lawlessness of the Palmer raids made it less difficult for the American people to recognize the plain attempt to subvert freedoms guaranteed by the Constitution. The attacks upon civil liberties can come also under the guise of "lawfulness." We have the best example of this in the conduct of a Congressional committee and in the Loyalty Order issued by the Executive. The

American people must be on guard against these so-called legal and orderly attempts to deprive them of their basic civil rights. It must be always remembered that the Bill of Rights was not adopted to defend a minority. It was enacted by the demand of the whole people as a defense against those who control government power.

Nor can there be any assurance that the courts, especially the trial courts, will act as a bulwark in defense of constitutional guarantees. . . .

Civil liberties are the medium through which a democratic people assure the betterment of their ways of life. When the rights of assembly and free speech are denied to workers by depriving them of the right to strike, to picket or to belong to a union of their own choosing, the well-being and the material conditions of the workers are endangered. When the basic civil rights of the Negro people are flagrantly disregarded, lynchings, segregation and the varied forms of discrimination result. When restrictions upon the franchise and political opinion are indulged, a hostile and arbitrary government eventuates.

The way to progress lies through the free exchange of ideas. Those who advocate social change and criticize the existing order must be as free to express their views as those who advocate the status quo. That is the real essence of democracy. Those who would deny the American people the right to learn the truth, by repressing all opposition to our existing institutions, subvert the democratic process and place the lid upon man's progress to a better world.

We were once a brave new country, in which "free enterprise" meant not only the uncontrolled exchange of goods but the untrammeled interchange of social ideas. We were once unafraid of new ideas. The advance of our geographic frontiers across the vast areas of our country carried with them advanced ideas of freedom and the rights of man. The country prospered because it was not afraid to meet the challenge of new and radical ideas, which were born in the minds of men out of the seeds of life's experiences. Many of these once considered radical and alien have come to be universally accepted and are today the laws of the land.

Today our ambassadors abroad use the language of democracy in the capitals where they represent our government. Yet at home our government denies to its own citizens the essence of democracy. Abroad the people are shedding the old and adopting new ideas and ways of life. At home our citizens are denied the right to advocate fundamental social, economic and political changes which they believe would advance the horizons of freedom in America.

The people know that this country has the capacity to produce all that mankind needs to provide freedom from want; yet we suffer from poverty in the midst of plenty. Our laws command equality for all; yet we suffer from discrimination and denial of equal rights. Science has discovered the secret of atomic energy which can release mankind from a life of drudgery; yet we suffer the dread of mass annihilation through the atom bomb.

These are the conditions which present a challenge to Americans. They have the duty to meet that challenge. Intolerance and force kill human beings but they can never exterminate ideas. Americans have the right to explore everywhere in the realm of new ideas, to propagate their discoveries, however radical; to advocate social change, however revolutionary.

Only through the free conflict of ideas can we hope to solve the great riddles of mankind, the elimination of poverty, insecurity, discrimination, and war. Those who resist such freedom of inquiry are enemies of the people for they doom our land to endless cycles of economic crises and poverty, of war and annihilation, of bigotry and spiritual degradation. And they must fail as enemies of progress have failed through the ages.

SHOULD THE COMMUNIST PARTY BE OUTLAWED? [4]

[Mr. Stassen] asked me four questions:

1. Do you agree that the Communist organizations in the world today are under the direction of the Kremlin in Moscow? Certainly.

[4] By Thomas E. Dewey, Governor of New York. From radio debate with Harold E. Stassen, delivered at Portland, Oregon, May 17, 1948. *Vital Speeches of the Day.* 14:484-7. June 1, 1948. For Mr. Stassen's speech see p.145-54.

2. Do you agree that the world Communist organization is a threat to world peace? Certainly.

3. Do you agree that the objectives of these Communist organizations is to destroy the liberties of other men? Certainly.

Finally, fourthly, if you agree to these things, under what provisions of the Constitution—as I glance at my quick notes here—and what legal action, are you against outlawing them when we are drafting young men in time of peace to build up the defenses against Communist aggression?

The last question, of course, entirely begs the question. The question is not whether any one is interested in helping any Communist preserve his liberties. No one in America has the slightest interest in the Communists. My interest is in preserving this country from being destroyed by the development of an underground organization which would grow so closely in strength, were it outlawed, that it might easily destroy our country and cause us to draft all of the young men in the nation.

Now I find that the difficulty here tonight is that Mr. Stassen has not adhered to his subject or his statements. He says he is for the Mundt bill because, says Mr. Stassen, it outlaws the Communist party. But the fact of the matter is, he is in grievous error. The only authority he quotes is the head of the Communist party, which is not exactly a very good authority for seeking the truth. Usually, if a Communist says it does this, you know it does the opposite. So let's find out whether the Mundt bill does outlaw the Communist party. That is the first job. If the Mundt bill did outlaw the Communist party, then we would be able to debate here.

Here's what Mr. Mundt says on May 14, 1948: "This bill does not outlaw the Communist party."

On February 5, 1948, Congressman Mundt said: "I have been one of those who have not looked with favor upon proposals to outlaw the Communist party or to declare its activities illegal because I fear such action on the part of Congress would only tend to drive further underground the forces which are already largely concealed from public view."

"What I want to do," said Mr. Mundt, "is to drive the Communist functionaries out of the ground, into the open, where patriotic Americans of every walk of life can come to learn their identity and understand their objectives."

Now, we have the head of the Communist party saying that it does outlaw it, and Mr. Stassen says so. Mr. Mundt, whose bill it is, says his bill does not outlaw the Communist party.

So, as between that debate, let us now see what the committee says. After all, here is a committee bill, and the committee presumably knows what its bill does. In short—I have studied the bill—what it says is that it shall be a crime to endeavor to teach, to advocate or to conspire to establish in the United States a dictatorship under the control of a foreign government.

Well, if that isn't a crime now, then I have greatly misread all the sections of the laws as they now are. But, before going to that—that's No. 1 in the Mundt bill. That certainly does not outlaw the Communist party. That simply says it is a crime to try to overthrow the government of the United States and establish a dictatorship under the control of a foreign power. And if that isn't good sound doctrine, I don't know good sound doctrine. But it doesn't outlaw the party. It says the Communists can't hold public office. Well, theoretically they are not supposed to hold them now. It says they can't get passports, and they can't get them now.

Does that outlaw the Communist party? Mr. Foster, the head of the Communist party, and Mr. Stassen says it does. Mr. Mundt says it doesn't. So, what does the committee say. The committee report—and this is the report of the congressional Committee on Un-American Activities, whose bill this is —this committee has been widely criticized in our country because it has been called a red-baiting committee. As a matter of fact, it has been doing a fine, solid, good American job for a great many months. It has done a fine job of exposing Communists and bringing them out in the open, where they belong. Here is what the committee says about the Mundt bill, April 10, 1948: "Too often a cursory study on this problem leads one to believe that the answer is very simple, that all we have to do is outlaw the Communist party or pass a law requiring its members to register and the problem will solve itself. This is not the case. The Communist party in its operations present a problem which is something new under the sun. It changes its spots, its tactics, its strategy without conscience." I am continuing to quote the report.

"Several bills before the committee attempt to approach this problem by outlawing the Communist movement as a political party. The subcommittee has found it necessary," and mark you, this, "to reject this approach." It seems perfectly clear that this bill does not outlaw the Communist party, and Mr. Mundt in the committee says it doesn't, but just to complete it, let me give you the rest of this point so there can be no possible misunderstanding that Mr. Stassen and Mr. Foster, the head of the Communist party, are wrong.

The report of the committee and the Mundt bill continues: "The committee gave serious consideration to the many well-intentioned proposals which attempted to meet the problem by outlawing the Communist party." Now I am skipping a little —no, I will read it. "Opponents of this approach differed as to what they desired. To bar the Communist party from the ballot, others would have made Communist party illegal per se political. Several advanced an argument against compelling that approach." And then it gives them:

1. Illegalization of the party might drive the Communist movement further underground.

2. Illegalization has not proved effective in Canada and other countries which tried it.

3. We cannot consistently (and this is of the greatest importance) we cannot consistently criticize the Communists of Europe for spreading opposition to political parties if we resort to this same totalitarian method here.

4. If the present Communist party severs the puppet strings by which it is manipulated from abroad, if it gives up its undercover methods, there is no reason for denying it advocating its beliefs in the way other political parties advocate theirs.

It is absolutely clear that the Mundt bill does not outlaw the Communist party, was not intended to, and that is the exact opposite of what the Mundt bill has intended to accomplish and does accomplish. So let's get back to the debate.

Mr. Stassen, here in Oregon on April 27, said: "I hold that the Communist party organization should be promptly outlawed

in America and in all freedom-loving countries of the world."
And he repeated this in many states all the way from New Jersey
to Oregon. That is the issue—not the Mundt bill. The issue
is, shall we pass a law outlawing the Communist party. Now,
I suppose, if you say, "Let's outlaw the Communist party and
preserve our liberties." And if you say it fast enough and don't
think, it seems to make sense. But my friends, it makes no sense.
You cannot do both, and no nation in all the history of the
world ever succeeded in doing it.

The question before us is shall the Communist party be outlawed? The only way I know that could be done is to declare
by law that people calling themselves Communists would be
denied a place on the ballot and that anyone who is a member
of that party, after it, the passage of the law, should be tried,
convicted, and sentenced to prison for a crime. I believe in keeping the Communist party everlastingly out in the open so we can
defeat it and all it stands for.

Now, this outlawing idea is not new. It is as old as government. For thousands of years despots have shot, imprisoned,
and exiled their people, and their governments have always
fallen into the dust. This outlawing idea is as old as communism
itself. It is the fact, and I might again refer just to get our history straight, to the report of the House Committee on Un-
American Activities. I quote from page eleven, no, page thirteen of the report dated—well, I can't find the date. It is the
report of the hearing before the subcommittee on legislation activities of the Eightieth Congress on H. R. 4422 and H. R. 4480.
I quote from page thirteen: "The Communist party was illegal
and outlawed in Russia when it took over control of the Soviet
Union."

The fact is that the czars of Russia were the first people in
the world to follow this idea of outlawing the Communist party.
They whipped them and they drove them to Siberia, they shot
them, and they outlawed them. In the year 1917 Lenin and
Trotsky were exiled. What was the result? This outlawing
gave them such colossal following, such enormous popularity,
such great loyalty on the part of the people that they were able
to seize control of all Russia with its 180 million people, and

the first nation to outlaw Communists became the first Communist nation.

That is what I do not want to happen to the United States of America. For twenty-five years Mussolini outlawed communism, and they grew and flourished underground despite their punishment and their killing and their shooting. As a result, four weeks ago the Communists and their allies polled more than 30 per cent of the vote in the recent Italian election.

In all of Nazi Europe the Communists were underground and they emerged at the end of the war so strong that they were so popular the French Maquis and others almost seized power in the governments of Europe at the end of this war because of the enormous strength that came to them from the underground.

And Czechoslovakia is another example, and I am grateful to Mr. Stassen for bringing it up. For seven years in Czechoslovakia the Communists were forced underground by the Nazi tyranny, and in those seven years they developed such enormous strength that they were able shortly after the liberation of Czechoslovakia, which we could have done, but our troops were pulled back and the Russian troops were allowed to go into Prague, they were able, before long, to take over the whole nation because they had flourished in the dark, underground.

Here is an issue of the highest moral principle. In the present issue the people in this country are being asked to outlaw communism. That means this: shall we in America, in order to defeat the totalitarian system which we detest, voluntarily adopt the method of that system?

I want the people of the United States to know exactly where I stand on this proposal because it goes to the very heart of the qualification of any candidate for office, and to the inner nature of the kind of country we want to live in. I am unalterably, wholeheartedly, and unswervingly against any scheme to write laws outlawing people because of their religious, political, or social or economic ideas.

I am against it because it is a violation of the Constitution of the United States and of the Bill of Rights, and clearly so. I am against it because it is immoral and nothing but totalitarianism itself. I am against it because I know from a great many years' experience in the enforcement of the law that the proposal wouldn't work, and instead it would rapidly advance the cause of communism in the United States and all over the world.

Now, let's look at this thing. It is a war of ideas in the world, and we are in it. It is also a war of nerves. The conflict between two wholly different ways of life—system of human freedom and the brutal system of the police state. On one side of this great world struggle are ranged all those who believe in the most priceless right in the world—human freedom. We believe that every man and woman has a right to worship as he pleases, the freedom of speech, assembly and the press. We believe that every man and woman has an absolute right to belong to the political party of his choice. We believe, in short, that human beings are individuals and that they do and should differ among themselves. We know that each of us has within himself a portion of error and we believe that each of us has within himself a touch of God.

On the other side of this struggle are the advocates of the all-powerful totalitarian state. They believe human beings are cogs in a machine, God-less creatures, born to slave through life with every thought and every act directed by an overpowering, all-powerful government. Everywhere, these two conflicting schemes of life, the free system and the police state, are struggling for the soul of mankind. The free world looks to us for hope, for leadership, and most of all for a demonstration of our invincible faith. The free way of life will triumph so long as we keep it free.

Now, as in all the days of our past, let us hold the flag of freedom high. I have watched this proposal, this easy panacea of getting rid of ideas by passing laws, I have been increasingly shocked. To outlaw the Communist party would be recognized every place on earth as a surrender of the great United States to the methods of totalitarianism. Stripped to its naked essentials, this is nothing but the method of Hitler and Stalin. It is the control borrowed from the Japanese war leadership. It is an attempt to beat down ideas with a club, the surrender of everything we believe in.

There is an American way to do this job, a perfectly simple American way. We have now twenty-seven laws on the books, and I have the whole list of them in front of me, outlawing every conceivable act of subversion against the United States. I spent eleven years of my life as a prosecutor in New York. That was in the days when they said nobody could clean up the organized underworld. They said we had to use the methods of dictators, that we had to go out and string them up. I had judges and even men in high places tell me that. A group of young men took it on, and week after week, month after month, year after year, they worked and they delivered the City of New York from the control of organized crime, and they did it by constitutional means and under the Bill of Rights.

We can do that in this country. All we need is a government which believes in enforcing the law, a government which believes wholeheartedly in human freedom, and the administration of our government which will go ahead and do the job. I have no objection to the strengthening of the law. In fact, I have spent a good many years of my life endeavoring to strengthen the criminal laws of our country. And they should be strengthened. But let us remember for all time to come in these United States, we should prosecute men for the crimes they commit but never for the ideas that they have.

Now, times are too grave to try any expedients and fail. This expedient has failed, this expedient of outlawing has failed in Russia. It failed in Europe, it failed in Italy, it failed in Canada. And let me point out that in Canada they tried it once and the Communist party grew so powerful and dangerous that they repealed the law in 1936, and in 1940 they tried it again and the Communist party came right up with a dozen new false faces exactly as it would do if you passed the ludicrous law to outlaw them here. They would come up under forty new fronts. They would then say, "we are not Communists any more," exactly as they did in Canada—"we are just good Canadians working to support our government." And what happened. What happened in Canada is exactly what would happen here. They became so strong that during the war, in the face of a law which says it is illegal to belong to the Communist party, they developed the greatest atomic bomb spy ring in history, and Canada had to repeal the law.

Let us not make such a terrific blunder in the United States, that we build up these dangerous venomous subversive people with the power to overthrow our government. Let us never make the blunders that have been made throughout the history of the world. Let us go forward as free Americans. Let us have the courage to be free.

SURREBUTTAL

I gather from Mr. Stassen's statement that he has completely surrendered. The Mundt bill obviously does not outlaw the Communist party. Mr. Stassen in these words has from Oregon to New Jersey and back again gone before audiences, the American people, demanding in these words that the Communist party be outlawed in the United States and in the other free nations of the world.

The Mundt bill does not outlaw the Communist party. The only authorities Mr. Stassen cites for the fact that—for his claim that—it does, are the present head of the Communist party and a former Communist, whereas I point out very clearly that the author of the bill, Mr. Mundt, and the committee which sponsored it, both say in the official records of the Congress of the United States that the bill does not outlaw the Communist party.

Now, if Mr. Stassen says that that is all he wants, then he has completely surrendered, because he admits that he didn't mean it when he has been demanding from one end of this country to the other that the Communist party be outlawed, and he is willing to settle now when confronted with the facts for a law which the author, and the committees say does not outlaw the party, which, of course, it doesn't.

As a matter of fact, there are—I made a mistake a while ago, there are not seventeen laws, there are twenty-seven laws in this United States on this subject. There is the 1938 act requiring all agents of foreign governments to register under penalty of five years imprisonment and $10,000 fine. The Voorhis act of 1940 requiring registration of all subversive political organizations. The Smith act, which makes it unlawful to teach or advise the desirability of overthrowing the government of the United States by force, or to publish any literature teaching, advising, suggesting or to conspire to do so, all under penalty of ten years imprisonment and $10,000 fine—all of the things of which Mr. Stassen has spoken are covered by the Smith act, by the Treason bill, the misprision of treason, inciting rebellion, insurrection, correspondence with a foreign government—I am reading a few of the titles—criminal sedition, conspiracy, subversive activities, sabotage, broad conspiracy, inciting desertion, sabotage, nonmailable matter, inciting mutiny, espionage, mutiny, sedition, conspire to commit espionage or sedition—that's about it—the list is endless.

The Mundt bill is perfectly harmless, probably. I have some doubts about its constitutionality. It supplements these bills in a very small way. It doesn't outlaw the Communist party. It may have the virtue of helping to keep them out in the open, because its main provisions are that the Communists must register all their members and keep them everlastingly out in the open. That is a very good provision of law. The other parts of it, if they are constitutional, they are swell.

Now, let's get on to the rest of the subject. Mr. Stassen has surrendered. He is no longer in favor of outlawing the Communist party. He is now willing to be content with a bill which simply says what is practically already in the law and which all people in the Congress say does not outlaw the party. This is so dangerous, this idea. It is so fundamental to American liberties that I should like to enlarge upon it just a little.

Mr. Stassen has spoken of New York. He has spoken of our history. Let me give you just a bit of history. One hundred and fifty years ago the French were the Bolsheviks of the world. They had a violent revolution and they beheaded their nobility just as the Communists did in Russia. First, they had purges of the old government and then they had purges among themselves, and then they started rattling their swords for world conquest. It is just like the movie we have been through, and this is where we came in. We see the same thing now, 150 years later. Many people in the infant America were trembling in their boots just the same as Americans are now trembling in their boots. They were afraid for the cause of free government.

Let me quote from Chaffee, one of the great American historians. He writes: "In 1798 the impending war with the French, the threat of revolutionary doctrines by foreigners in our midst, and the spectacle of the disastrous operation of these doctrines abroad"—I am still quoting—"facts, all of which," says Mr. Chaffee, "have a familiar sound today, led to the enactment of the alien sedition laws."

These laws punished false and malicious writings, if they were intended to incite the heat of people, or to aid any philosophy design of any foreign nation against the United States. The act created such a furor and opposition that the whole country was in turmoil. The only Federalist leader who dared speak out for the Bill of Rights was John Marshall, who later became the great Chief Justice of the Supreme Court.

Soon every person who was prosecuted, however violent the language he used, was treated as a martyr and a hero. Adopting what the historians Charles and Mary Beard described in their *Basic History of the United States* as underground political tactics, Thomas Jefferson wrote an indictment of the laws and persuaded the State of Kentucky to declare them null and void. At the next election Thomas Jefferson was elected President of the United States, and the Federalist party was utterly wrecked. Jefferson pardoned all the victims of these laws, Congress later refunded all the fines, and Thomas Jefferson's party held uninterrupted office in the United States for twenty years. That was the result of an early American attempt to shoot an idea with the law. You can't do it. And now that Mr. Stassen has surrendered in his outlawing idea, let's nail this thing down so hard no American will ever again seek to give the slightest impression to our people that it can be done. It can't. It is self-destructive. Even in the midst of the Civil War, General Burnside tried to suppress the newspapers that were hostile to our government. General Burnside put them out of business and Lincoln gave him orders to quit, saying in strong language: "It is better that the people hear what they have to say than fear what they might say if they were suppressed."

Now, we have a lot of Communists in New York; we have a great many of them, and they cause us great trouble. But we lick them. The number in the country is down from 100,000 two years ago to 70,000 last year, to 68,000 this year. In New York their influence is at the lowest ebb in their history. They ganged up with the Democrats, the American Labor party, the mis-called "Liberal party," and the PAC to beat us two years ago. The Communists labeled me as their public enemy Number One, and we licked them by the biggest majority in history. Why? Because we kept them out in the open; because we everlastingly believe in the Bill of Rights; because we know that if, in this country, we will always keep every idea that's bad out in the open, we will lick it. It will never get any place in the United States.

THE GREAT TEACHER THAT TEACHES NOTHING [5]

Some of the frequently repeated lessons of history lie in the field of ideas—ideas considered dangerous because they challenge accepted institutions and beliefs. In the face of such a challenge the response of established authority is always the same: Suppress these ideas. Hunt down the scandalous persons who hold them. Warn the public. Drive the wolves from the flock. The public becomes terrified, and the hunt is on.

Ideas are like a nonfilterable virus: they divide and conquer. At first known only to a few, they soon are on everybody's lips. The hue and cry has attracted wide attention to them. If it lasts long enough they may be driven underground, but they emerge later, possibly in changed form, but no less dangerous. Sometimes by relentless pressure an area has been kept uninfected for a long period, but in the atmosphere engendered by persecution no ideas can grow, and the region remains sterile, an enclave of backwardness.

The pattern is today taking the shape of the Red Menace. The popular mood has been thus appraised: "The consensus in the country today is that we can no longer afford to let people

[5] By Louise Fargo Brown, Professor Emeritus of History, Vassar College. *Survey Graphic*. 37:366-7. August 1948.

think as they choose." In other words, we are so afraid of communism that we abandon our tradition of freedom.

Those who preach this peril are afraid of a set of ideas—just as were those who tried to wipe out the early Christians, the Waldenses, the Lollards, the Anabaptists, Roman Catholics, Mormons, Abolitionists. Each of these groups in its day was stigmatized as a threat to society. Most were accused of immoral practices; all held ideas—usually ideas about property—which, if carried out, threatened to change some accepted ways of life. All these groups survived persecution; none is considered today to have caused the injuries so much dreaded.

Now it is the Communists who are enemies of society. Like some of those earlier groups, the Communists hold out the possibility of a world in which none will be poor and all will be free. Their notions about how this brave new world could be built are tied up in such a web of Marxian dogma that they can make no progress except in a society where standards of living are depressed below anything conceivable to Americans.

They do not and cannot carry conviction in this country. Even among our most extreme depressed group, the Negroes, their campaign has been a notable failure. Fear of communism here has no basis in fact, unless it is tied up with fear that Soviet Russia will try to force its system upon us by armed might.

After the war, Americans recognized that Russia must have either security guaranteed by the United Nations or security through arrangements with its neighbors. Its terrible toll of war casualties and the devastation of its territory evoked great sympathy.

Even after the first moves in the game of power politics with Russia, it was widely realized that such a game could be ended peaceably only if played in an atmosphere reasonably free from fear and suspicion. What forces suddenly fogged the atmosphere with suspicion and fear?

It is more complicated to do business with Communist than with capitalist states, but Americans have been trading successfully with the USSR for almost thirty years. Anti-Communist agitation here began with the Bolshevik Revolution. It was rooted in fear for the capitalist system; in the belief (recently embodied in the Taft-Hartley Act) that unions would be more responsible if there were no Communist leaders in the labor movement. These sentiments were not at an inflamed level, and there was little attention paid to Cassandras like W. C. Bullitt, W. L. White, Eugene Lyons, George H. Earle. There was a widespread revulsion of horror at the reckless suggestion that we had better embark on a "preventive war" while we alone had atomic bombs.

One key to the change of sentiment is to be found in communism's habit of becoming a creed, and absorbing the faith and loyalty usually reserved for religion. Although Soviet Russia has changed her official policy from suppression to toleration, and reliable witnesses have testified that this is the policy of Communist Yugoslavia, the fact remains that Communist governments give to religion only toleration, not support. Something like a crusade against communism has been launched by the Roman Catholic Church, and it has spilled over into non-Catholic circles. Naturally Russia is the chief target. . . .

We need to analyze the anti-communism crusade. When the Knights of Columbus publish advertisements attacking communism we can evaluate them, but when a radio commentator day after day rails against the USSR it is not so easy to discover whether he speaks from conviction or as an unthinking participant in a crusade against ideas. If the American tradition of the right of the individual to make his own decisions is to survive— and it is as dear to the thoughtful Catholic as to anyone—it must be remembered that the tradition grew out of the struggle for political, as well as religious, freedom.

We are told that the "heresy" of discussing controversial issues—political, economic, social, historic—has spread to the schools, and that the Communists are to blame. Many school systems are being stampeded into suppressive action; school-boards and college officials are banning lecturers, books, magazines, and are revising teachers' training courses.

The question now is whether we can afford the price of heresy-hunting.

The price is higher than we think. Techniques have changed since history's earlier lessons in this grim fact. We are not invited to the spectacle of a Communist being burned at the stake in Union Square, or thrown to the lions. Instead, we are asked to look on while individuals suspected of association with Communists are deprived of their means of livelihood and their possibilities of usefulness to society. The Taft-Hartley and Smith Acts and the Mundt-Nixon bill embody not only the doctrine of guilt by association but the doctrine that citizens may be deprived of important rights as a penalty for holding certain opinions. We have seen official investigators persuade the movie industry to "purge" itself of men whose sole offenses was to refuse to answer questions as to their political affiliations.

The price of heresy-hunting is the creation of intellectual vacuums which fear and hatred hasten to fill. In the atmosphere of persecution, speculation which might be fruitful dies unuttered on the tongue. The United States is one of the great powers today partly because of its natural resources but chiefly because the American tradition of freedom has allowed everyone to contribute his ideas to the common store. Some of the most useful Americans come from families that left Europe to escape death or persecution because of their revolutionary opinions. When flurries of fear have led to efforts to suppress ideas, we have always been brought to our senses by the efforts of citizens true to the tradition of freedom.

Today, we have reached one of these danger spots. Men who hold to the principle of authority, who in their hearts fear the democratic tradition, have the public ear. And these men insist that "nonsense" about freedom from want and freedom from fear must be swept out as so much rubbish. There is a red tinge about such ideas. The old bogey of the Russian with the bomb which frightened earlier generations has been invoked, only now the beard has been replaced by a handle-bar mustache. The FBI investigators inquire at colleges and universities whether men and women applying for government positions belonged to radical organizations when they were students perhaps twenty years ago. We seem to be preparing to demonstrate that one of history's greatest lessons is still unlearned, perhaps the most tragic demonstration ever made. That is the sense in which we are in danger.

The current efforts to suppress communism—if history is a guide—will not succeed. In this country it may be forced underground, where its activities cannot be followed and estimated. Persecution's usual effects on intellectual activity are already observable. The government is finding it difficult to persuade competent scientists to fill essential positions in view of the number of men and women who have been dropped on evidence supplied by the FBI. Conformity and mediocrity are valued above vision.

The threat of world chaos demands the mobilization of American intellectual resources as well as material resources. This is not the time to embark on a witch hunt which will serve to seal the lips and blind the eyes of any American who can see beyond the mists of partisanship and through the fog of prejudice. It is the time to shake off the dread of creeping bogeys and face our destiny. It is not in our tradition to walk with fear.

IT'S NOT ONLY COMMUNISTS' RIGHTS! [6]

Soviet expansion, Communist infiltration, and the fear of another war are responsible for growing threats to civil liberties far beyond the Communists aimed at. Already under pressure of anti-Communist hysteria the Federal Government has (1) Adopted a sweeping program of testing the loyalty of all federal employees to weed out suspected Communists; (2) Held for deportation a score of long-resident Communist aliens solely for their associations; (3) Imposed unreasonable restrictions on foreign journalists and others coming to United Nations conferences or international gatherings, solely because of admitted or suspected Communist affiliations; (4) Through the Un-American Activities Committee of the House conducted a veritable witch-hunt for Communists in the movie industry, in government service and private associations; (5) Through bills in Congress considered outlawing the Communist party as advocates of violence or registering Communists as foreign agents; (6)

[6] American Civil Liberties Union, New York. April 1948. p. 2-7.

Required trade union officers to declare they are not Communists to get access to the National Labor Relations Board.

None of these activities squares with our professions of democratic rights and freedom of opinion and propaganda up to the point of "clear and present danger" of illegal acts. All are aimed at penalizing opinions or associations. Freedom of speech, press and organization are endangered by such restrictions on Communists. They do not stop with Communists. Many extend beyond Communists to those who may knowingly or innocently associate with Communists, to unions in which Communists like others are legitimately members, and to any movement which Communists take part in or support.

But it will be argued that such freedom for Communist propaganda opens the door to infiltration in critical agencies, such as the communications industries, trade unions, professional associations, and political and civil organizations, thus establishing bases for concealed minority power manipulating democratic machinery.

The answer to that contention is that the only way to combat such tactics is to oppose them by stronger democratic force, and machinery that cannot be manipulated by a minority. Vigorous public exposure of concealed Communist agencies is always an effective antidote.

While Communists should have the same rights as others to be elected to public office, the voters can be trusted to reject those opposed to American concepts of democracy. In appointments to public office, officials can be generally trusted to select employees of unquestioned loyalty in posts where divided loyalties are a danger, and where in exceptional cases such persons may be found, to transfer them.

The American Civil Liberties Union is wholly opposed to all restrictions on opinion or association aimed at Communists or any others. It is opposed on principle, not because of any sympathy with communism. The Union by formal resolution excludes from its committees and staff all persons supporting any anti-democratic movements in the United States or abroad, and specifies Communists and their fellow travelers among them.

It is not therefore as special pleaders, but as defenders of civil liberties for all without distinction, that we oppose restrictions on Communists for their opinions and legal activities.

While the ACLU defends the rights of Communists, as of all others, it does not join in the many "front" agencies in that defense. Its part is played by independent briefs in the courts, representations to public officials and public declarations. . . .

Proposals are before Congress (1) to bar the Communist party from the ballot in the states as a national defense measure against a party which Congress will state as a fact advocates the overthrow of government by force, (2) to register Communists as agents of a foreign government and to extend registration to "Communist front" organizations, with restrictions on the rights of their members. Similar bills frequently are presented to state legislatures.

Neither democratic principles nor practical expediency can justify these proposals. They are clearly unconstitutional. These laws impose penalties upon opinion. They propose that Congress make a finding of fact which properly belongs to the courts. They probably exceed the powers of Congress over elections. If the Communist party, as alleged, advocates violence or acts as a foreign agent, criminal statutes can be invoked. That they have not been indicates that there is no such case to be made. Any machinery to deny political rights to Communists inevitably would restrict the rights of all political minorities.

Further, outlawing the Communist party would not work in practice. The party could evade the law by changing its name, as it has in other countries where attempts have been made to outlaw it. Severe measures of repression would simply drive Communists underground into a conspiracy more difficult to combat. Repression might well foster its growth. All such proposals should be opposed. . . .

Public employees must of course be loyal to the United States and to their oaths of office. No superior loyalty should be tolerated. But that principle does not justify the wholesale tests of loyalty of all federal employees undertaken by the President's order of March 1947. The results demonstrate its futility. After checking half of the two million federal employees, the FBI found no cases for action by loyalty boards and only a few hundred for further inquiry. Such an inquisition inevitably intimidates public servants and makes them far more hesitant in taking forthright positions in the discharge of their duties or in their activities as citizens.

While conceding the right of the government to require loyalty, the Union is opposed to the system under which the tests now operate.

The following reforms are essential:

1. Four departments of the government excluded as "sensitive areas," and with the right to discharge without hearing, should be brought under the system of appeals to the Loyalty Review Board. Most of the discharges to date have taken place in these four departments—Army, Navy, State and Atomic Energy Commission.

2. Accused employees should have the right to know the nature of the charges against them, to have them established by witnesses and to cross-examine them. Under the rules adopted by the Loyalty Review Board, not even the Board itself may go behind the FBI reports to determine sources and witnesses. No right of confrontation or cross examination of witnesses is provided.

3. The black list of organizations published by the Attorney General as subversive should be subject to tests by open hearings. While membership in such organizations is only one factor in determining disloyalty, mere public blacklisting is unjust without findings based upon fair hearings.

4. The words "totalitarian," "fascist," "communist," and "subversive" used in the order should be clearly defined. These vague words mean too many different things to different people.

The Union futhermore holds that whatever justifications may be found for federal loyalty tests, their application to state or municipal employees should be opposed both as unnecessary and as an interference with an essentially federal matter. . . .

For a decade the House Un-American Activities Committee has been engaged in a veritable witch-hunt, chiefly for Communists. They appear, in the minds of the Committee, to be the only real "Un-Americans." The procedures of the Committee have been so arbitrary and prejudiced as to call forth widespread condemnation. Whether under Democratic or Republican leadership, the record has been the same.

The search for Communist influence has gone far afield, smearing genuine liberals, New Dealers and labor leaders in an endeavor to enforce conformity to conservative prejudices.

A fair appraisal of the Committee's past performance holds no hope for future improvement. Nothing has been so un-American as the Committee's own activities. There can be no compromise with the conclusion that the Committee should be wholly abolished. Its danger to freedom of opinion has been proved to the hilt. At the very least, its unfair procedures should be checked by a code of rights for witnesses and persons attacked. Though abolition is politically impracticable at the moment, mounting opposition may achieve ultimate results. . . .

Under the law the government can bar from entry or deport those aliens who advocate the overthrow of government by force. The lower courts have held that Communists do so. But there is no controlling Supreme Court decision to that effect and a test is therefore necessary to establish policy. Acting on the decision of the lower courts, the government is engaged in a crusade (1) to deport long-resident alien Communist leaders; (2) to bar entry or to impose restrictions on alien Communists, admitted or suspected, who seek to attend sessions of the United Nations or conferences of international agencies associated with it.

The Civil Liberties Union is opposed to all deportations for opinion and association. It is equally opposed to barring the entry of foreigners because of their political views or associations. It is opposed to imposing restrictions on such foreign visitors beyond fixing the length of their stay and, where national security is involved, the area of their travel. It is opposed to these restrictions which would deny foreign visitors alleged to be Communists, freedom of speech and press and reasonable freedom of movement in connection with their legitimate international missions. The responsible American or United Nations sponsors of such visitors should be sufficient guarantee of their conduct. . . .

SHOULD WE OUTLAW THE COMMUNIST PARTY? [1]

Boiled down, the mass of argument of current proposals to outlaw the Communist party in the United States involves two considerations: principle and expediency. Does the dominant, temporary majority in a democracy have the moral right to suppress any fraction of its political opposition? And if it has, can Marxist activities in the United States be effectively controlled by the simple method of making its political expression illegal?

It is unfortunate that some irresponsible organs of the press in conjunction with certain demagogues in and out of Congress have so whipped up fear and hatred of Soviet Russia that many normally cautious Americans are almost ready to scrap some of our most cherished constitutional liberties in order to get back at the Communists. It is an unhappy situation because so much more than the rights of the relatively few acknowledged Communists are at stake. The fact that Congress is seriously proposing such legislation advertises to the world that we are no longer so sure of the vitality of democracy and its superiority to other political forms. In order to combat the threat of a totalitarian philosophy, we are asked to buttress democracy by adopting a totalitarian measure.

Perhaps this last statement sins in its simplicity. It is true that some politicians now proposing that the Communist party be banned from the ballot do so, not because its members are Marxists, but because they consider Communists as agents of a potential war enemy. Sincere leaders of this belief should consider, however, whether better means lie at the government's disposal for suppressing espionage or treason.

Others who advocate outlawing the Communist party are not so disinterested. They are employing the Communist scare—well or ill grounded as it may be—to alter the free American political system for their own advantage. Such persons are as subversive as those whom they seek to outlaw, and probably much more

[1] By Max Knepper, author, journalist. *Forum*. 107:497-501. June 1947.

dangerous, since they already possess considerable power whereas the Communists have comparatively little power.

The power to defend itself is inherent in any state. In the totalitarian nation the government's rights of self-defense are unlimited. Suppression of all opposition parties is usually the first step, followed by curbs on speech, press, assembly. Thought control, enforced by arbitrary police power, is the ultimate refinement in the state's battle against change or overthrow.

The democratic state also has the right of self-preservation, but its rights are limited both in scope and methods. Assassination of public officials is punished as severely in the United States as in Russia. Acts of violence or civil disobedience are suppressed by force and their perpetrators are punished. In a democratic state, however, change is not prohibited. The organic law prescribes how such changes may occur, and as long as individuals or minorities agitate for modifications within this framework, their position is legal. After all, the Constitution itself may be legally amended out of existence.

Most of us are familiar with these facts, but when we become annoyed with opposition, particularly if we hold public office, we find ourselves castigating opponents and calling for their suppression as enemies of public order, the American system, the Constitution, or all three.

Communists, in their role as a political party, enjoy the privilege of any other party in offering platforms and candidates to the voters, regardless of the fact that their program is offensive to the great majority of Americans who, of course, never vote for it. Theoretically, however, the Communists might convert a majority to their viewpoint, in which case, by all democratic rules, the Communists would be entitled to power. If, to prevent such a contingency, the present government employs the authority of the state to outlaw the Communist party, it is taking from the American people the right to make a free choice from among the various political philosophies offered in the election market place. Once such a precedent is established, there is nothing to inhibit further suppression, until the party in power remains the only legal party. Let us not forget that many ultra-conservatives made no distinction between the New Deal and communism, or at least they professed not to. Yet the New Deal was overwhelmingly supported at the polls three times.

It is quite possible that in a showdown between Soviet Russia and the United States many members of the Communist party—possibly most—would sympathize with Russia and, therefore, may be considered potential traitors. But the open political activity of the Communist party and its declared preference for the Russian social system is not, *per se,* treason.

The Founding Fathers, alert to the tendency of entrenched office holders to label their opponents "traitors," defined treason in the Constitution as follows: "Treason against the United States shall consist *only* (my italics) in levying war against them, or in adhering to their enemies, giving them aid and comfort."

Although the Soviet Union is currently feared or disliked by most Americans, we are not officially at war with that state. In a strict sense, therefore, speeches or articles upholding the Soviets are not treason and cannot be prosecuted. Why, then, outlaw a party for advocating something which is not illegal?

In this connection, it is pertinent to remind careless politicians and intellectually honest industrialists and publishers that the capitalist system is not recognized by the Constitution as an established, integral part of the political order. Many Americans have been led to believe, however, that the profit system is a part of the basic law of the land. This, of course, is a fallacy. Capitalism can exist in either a democracy or dictatorship, and so can socialism. The confusing of capitalism with democracy may in the future do the latter a great disservice.

American citizens should observe that the British Labor party, which is a socialist party, did not replace Parliament by a labor dictatorship when it came to power.

This slight excursion into economics serves to remind readers that the economic tenets of the Communist party, no matter how unpopular, do not constitute a valid reason for outlawing the organization. There is only one point on which proponents of such action have a case. That is the revolutionary feature of the party and its advocacy of a dictatorship of the poletariat. The question might well be asked whether a party with a revolutionary program has a place in a democratic system. The answer, of course, is whether the revolutionary program is *economic* or *political*. If political, then all parties adhering to strictly constitutional changes might justifiably unite in the decision that an organization advocating revolution should not be tolerated as a political party.

If the Communist party is recruiting members for the purpose of overthrowing rather than electing a government, then its leaders should be prosecuted for inciting rebellion. If inadquate legislation exists for such prosecution, then government leaders are justified in asking Congress to outlaw the party.

But the Communists deny violent intentions and profess observance of constitutional methods. While Communist participation in democratic governments abroad has not been reassuring, we cannot definitely declare at this time that the American Communist party is plotting violent overthrow of the democratic system.

However, suppose that principle is sacrificed to expediency, as customary in wartime. Will illegalizing the Communist party serve a practical purpose?

There are approximately 74,000 acknowledged Marxists in the United States including Trotskyites and other heretical Communist sects. Everyone knows, though, that this is only the visible part of the iceberg. If one included all members of "front" organizations, ultra left-wing unions, subscribers to pro-Communist publications, and various protest groups, the number of "Reds" would run into millions, although such a method of computation is scarcely to be recommended for its accuracy. There is no reliable measure, since most Communists do not register their convictions for obvious reasons. On the basis of local and national elections, one might approximate the number at something less than a million. And incidentally, this is one argument for retaining the Communist party on the ballot. It offers a barometer for measuring economic and social discontent.

In the fact that there may be nearly a million Communists of which but 75,000 have registered as such, we have one answer to the feasibility of outlawing the party. Economic repression of Communists has existed for some time. Private employers understandably will not hire persons who are declared enemies of the profit system. Since 1940 the Federal Government has carefully screened Communists from employment, and many states and political subdivisions have legislation barring them from civil service. Thus in the practical sphere of economics communism has been outlawed for years, and the result has been the usual reward of repression. Communists have merely concealed their politics, so that only one tenth or less of their numbers can be identified by registration. Now legislation is proposed to submerge the other tenth! But surely nobody is naive enough to believe that such legislation will force Communists to abandon their creed. If a simple statute is enacted prohibiting the existence of the party, what is to prevent its members from evading the law simply by changing their title? A rose by any other name—!

To be effective, a law suppressing communism would have to be exceedingly general. Unless sponsors of this legislation are only indulging in a little worthless demagogy, or perhaps needling Soviet Russia, they will have to put teeth in their measure by prohibiting, not simply membership in the Communist party, but in any group which advocates replacement or modification of the existing social system. Thought and attitude tests will have to be provided. The police power will have to be expanded tremendously, and, concomitantly, civil liberties restricted.

Naturally all this has extremely forbidding implications. If it becomes illegal to criticize features of the economic system, which parties and which political philosophies will remain within the law? The answer to this question is definitely beyond the $64 class.

The objective spectator is led to wonder whether some forces in the nation are less interested in outlawing the Communist party as an end than as a means for getting at non-Communist, left-wing organizations, particularly unions. Once the Communist party is outlawed, the pattern for legal harassment of union leaders, progressive politicians, and just ordinary critics of current abuses is clear. Investigations, indictments, detainments, and prosecutions would be the order of the day. Since in times of depression, strikes and elections, charges of "Red" are hurled with more liberality than accuracy, repressive legislation would invite wide abuse. Even though the courts, which generally show an appreciation for civil rights, might freely dismiss charges, unscrupulous prosecutors could all but crush unions by accusing their leaders of communism.

As for the Communists themselves they would thrive under the impetus of martyrdom. At present they have no moral justification for their charge that democratic capitalism is a fraud. They have enjoyed for years the legal right to present their platform and candidates to the American people. But if this right is withdrawn, it will vindicate their argument that capitalist democracy, as soon as it feels itself challenged, throws off its mask and reveals its dictatorial might.

Those who sincerely believe that communism is a real and present menace to American democracy will raise the question whether our state is to remain defenseless against a group which, if it came to power, would destroy the civil rights of liberals and conservatives alike.

The answer is that the democratic state is not defenseless against conspiracy to overthrow it from within or without. Its first defense is its superior attraction as the guarantor of liberty. The people must be made aware that democracy offers invaluable rights to be cherished regardless of the economic system in vogue, and that it need not be dismantled in order to reform the present social system.

Secondly, a democratic government has a moral right, as well as the legal right, to enact stringent laws for punishment of treasonable or rebellious acts. The United States already has statutes severely punishing treason, sabotage, and rebellion. If necessary, these laws should be supplemented to control intercourse with foreign agents or governments. Giving of information vital to the defense or welfare of the United States to foreign countries is already a crime. If additional FBI and intelligence officers are required to enforce this legislation, they should immediately be provided.

If the Communist party, defeated at the polls, should attempt to seize the government by armed force, each and every member participating in such action should be (and probably would be) punished. After all, it is not in its role as a constitutional political party that the Communist party is objectionable, but in its alleged role of a conspiratorial organization carrying out the mandates of a foreign government. These activities would be only enhanced and morally justified by denying the Communist party the same privileges enjoyed by others.

American democracy is not so degenerate that it must prop itself up by totalitarian devices. Its situation is not so precarious that it must deny its opponents a hearing. But neither does it have to allow an undemocratic minority to hack away at its foundations. By reasonable laws, equally applicable to all groups, it can control the behavior of all citizens to insure that exercise of civil rights is not translated into destructive acts.

SHALL WE OUTLAW THE COMMUNIST PARTY? [8]

There are many ways of how not to fight communism. The history of the struggle against various forms of totalitarianism is replete with boomerangs, with cases of fanatical opponents unwittingly promoting the very forces they set out to combat. We have had anti-Nazis who in their zeal seized upon the weapons of exaggeration and untruth only to give impetus to the Nazi ideology. We all know anti-Fascists who have fallen for their own totalitarian idols and who thereby foster Fascist reaction. And now, perhaps more than ever, we are being driven by emotional anti-Communists who would adopt methods sure to consolidate the sinister Communist ranks in our midst.

Those of us who have devoted decades to the crusade against the original totalitarian phenomenon in the world, the Soviet-Communist power, can with justice cry out these days, "Save us from our friends and we shall take care of our enemies!" Among these "friends" who are clamoring for measures to outlaw the Communist party are many "summer soldiers" of the fight against communism who but yesterday hailed one or another form of dictatorship as the wave of the future. Char-

[8] Editorial, *Plain Talk*. 1:3-4. April 1947.

acterizing them all is the abysmal ignorance of the nature of communism and of the Fascist-Nazi offspring it had spawned.

Experience over nearly thirty years has shown that there are three ways of grappling with the Communist problem.

First, there is the bloody and ruthless method adopted by Kemal Pasha in Turkey and by Chiang Kai-shek in China in the twenties. The creator of modern Turkey laid the foundations for a quarter of a century of good neighbor relations with Russia by unceremoniously stringing up on gibbets the Communist leaders of his country, for which he was rewarded by the Kremlin with the first foreign loan ever advanced by the Soviet Government. Acting upon far greater and more onerous provocation, Generalissimo Chiang followed Ataturk's example by exterminating large numbers of Chinese Communist rebels and would-be quislings. Stalin would respect us more if we aped these tactics, but they are contrary to every American and Western concept, and are indeed subversive of democracy itself.

Second, there is the recent experience of Canada, and before the war, that of Finland and Switzerland. Small, compact and homogeneous, Finland and Switzerland, under the conditions prevailing in the thirties, successfully coped with the problem by outlawing their Communist parties. For Finland it was especially easy, as nearly all the Finnish Reds were marked men, having fled to Russia after their abortive attempt to seize and hold power.

Far more appropriate for American purposes is the lesson provided by Canada where, after the party had been banned, it was reconstituted under a new name, the Labor Progressive party. It was a leader of that party, and a member of the Dominion Parliament, Fred Rose, who was exposed as the ringleader of the great Canadian spy network operating in the service of the Soviet Government. And let it not be forgotten that this exposure came not as a result of the vigilance or the efforts of the Canadian authorities or the Canadian press, but as the casual by-product of a Soviet official's decision to attain freedom for himself and his family.

The experience of Canada proves that the outlawing of the Communist party would only lead to (1) its reemergence under a new name, (2) its secret and espionage branches being driven deeper underground, (3) the establishment in America of a Gestapo or an OGPU to ferret out the armor-plated conspiracy, and (4) the cry of martyrdom being raised by Communists which would rally to their support considerable groups of misguided citizens. Many are still laboring under the obsolete notion that the Communist party, in reality an agency of a foreign power, is a normal political party and as such entitled to the protection of the Bill of Rights and other constitutional provisions.

Third, there is the American way of dealing with the problem, under our fundamental laws and consistent with our matchless strength which warrants no hysteria or fear. Within this framework we can adopt a series of effective measures such as the following to cope with Red and other totalitarianism:

a. An act requiring all political parties to have their membership rolls open at any time to public inspection.

b. A legislative ban on dual membership in political parties, under which no member of the Communist party, for instance, could simultaneously belong to the American Labor party or the Democratic party or the Republican party.

c. A requirement that all political bodies affiliated with any foreign bodies, governmental or otherwise, shall file or publish full statements of their finances, their membership, their affiliates and other relevant activities.

d. The barring from government service of members of Communist or Fascist organizations, or of members of such "fronts" as can be reasonably shown to be transmission belts for totalitarian forces.

e. The denial of the privilege of granting passports or visas to members of totalitarian organizations.

f. The changing of our existing libel laws so as to insure effective punishment for the defamatory and smearing tactics so far pursued by the Communist and Fascist press with flagrant impunity.

g. The imposition of severe penalties for the refusal by subpoenaed witnesses to testify before the Congress on matters relating to totalitarian activities.

Pitiless exposure is the best remedy for the darkness in which the Communist party operates. All conspirators know how to evade the law. Few of them can function in open daylight.

Passing a law outlawing the Communist party would lull the country into a false sense of security and compel the outlaws to construct a complete underground movement. Moreover, as William Green, President of the American Federation of Labor, put it, such legislation would be "tantamount to a declaration of voluntary bankruptcy of the ideas and ideals of American democracy."

THE COMMUNIST CREED [9]

The basis of Communist action in the world, whether in the United States or any other country, is the Communist creed, which is a belief that there will be no peace on earth until all the nations of the world are Communist. This is a very genuine belief which is held by a large number of people, and in the furtherance of that belief they have developed the doctrine that the end justifies the means, and that any means, even the most foul, are justifiable in order to achieve this domination of the world by communism. . . .

I should consider the Communist party of the United States composed, in the first place, of potential traitors, since certainly if the United States were in war with the Soviet Union the members of the American Communist party would do all they could to help the Soviet Union and to injure their own country. In the second place, I should consider it a conspiracy to commit murder on a mass scale.

That, I think, confronts us with a very practical question of what to do under the present circumstances. The United States, without question, today is in danger, as President Truman very clearly brought out in his statement asking for support for Greece and Turkey. He said that "the national security of the United States was involved." . . . The safety of the United States is involved because the gradual taking over of countries,

[9] From statement of William C. Bullitt, former United States Ambassador to Russia and France, before the House Committee on Un-American Activities, Washington, D.C., March 24, 1947. *Vital Speeches of the Day.* 13:460-3. May 15, 1947.

the gradual taking over of areas, while possible future victims are lulled into a false sense of security is the essence of the Soviet tactics, just as it was the essence of Hitler's tactics. . . .

The existence in the United States of an enormous fifth column of the national Communist dictator is an even greater threat to the United States than was ever the fifth column of the National Socialist dictatorship of Hitler, and, therefore, I think that you have brought up this question at an extremely appropriate moment. Nevertheless, I should like to say that I am not at all sure that it is wise, in the public interest of the people of the United States, to declare it a crime, at the present time, to belong to the American Communist party, for the following reasons:

We know that the Communist party in this country is organized as follows: There are the dues-paying members, who have party books, and so on. Those are the more or less public members of the party. There is then the underground organization of the party. That is a series of small groups, of three or five persons, organized secretly in a secret organization, which even if the party should be suppressed by law, could continue to function. In the third place, there is that extraordinary group, usually very able men, men who are so important to the Soviet Union and to the Communist party that they are not allowed to admit that they are members, because it may get them into trouble. That is a very important group, although not large.

If we should make it a crime to belong to the Communist party, I do not believe that today we have sufficient information with regard to all these groups to put our hands on them effectively, nor do I believe that if we did put our hands on them effectively we would actually go through with any punishment of them.

For example, when I was Ambassador to Moscow, one of the minor tasks I had was to ask the Soviet Government to accept again into the Soviet Union a number of its subjects who were illegally in the United States. We tried to deport these persons to their country of origin and the Soviet Government refused to receive them, just wouldn't take them back. Well, what are you going to do with them? You get out a deportation order against a man who is obviously an undesirable citizen of any country, and his country of origin refuses to receive him? Well, you may keep him under arrest pending deportation for a given period, but you can't keep him very long, and you just have to turn him loose again. We do not shoot people whom we dislike, as they do in the Soviet Union.

Now, in the Communist party in the United States, according to such information as I have, approximately 60 per cent of the members are of alien origin. Sixty per cent of the members, I believe, are men and women who have come to the United States, and after being here a given length of time have sworn to uphold the Constitution of the United States. It seems to me that one of the things that we should look into is perhaps this: That we should make, perhaps, membership in the Communist party on the part of a naturalized citizen prima facie evidence that his citizenship was fraudulently acquired and that the immigrant in taking the oath of allegiance to support the Constitution of the United States committed perjury. That, I think, might hit 60 per cent of the party.

There is a good precedent for that. We did exactly that with the German Bund, as you know, and deported from the United States—I have forgotten how many thousands of German Bundists—and I fail to see why we might not try to do that with Communists of alien origin. But when we consider doing that, let's also consider the fact that the Soviet Government will refuse to have these people sent back, and let us then try to think, before we pass any such law, what we are going to do with them.

These are some practical considerations that I am just bringing up as suggestions.

Another point which I should like to suggest to you is this: We have a requirement of the election laws that all campaign contributions made to the Democratic and Republican parties —to all political parties—should be reported. The major parties all make returns of the names of their contributors. The Communist party, I believe, under that law should be required to list all its contributors and dues paying members—because the payment of dues is just as much a contribution to a political party as the making of a campaign contribution once every four years, or whatever the period may be.

That is another suggestion which I should like to make, which probably will be ineffectual, but nevertheless it seems to me to point in a direction that might be useful.

And third, I should like to say this: I am perfectly certain that a time will come, and it may be close at hand, when it will be essential to our national safety to break up this criminal conspiracy, which is worldwide, break it up as far as we can in the United States.

In other words, that we shall have to take extremely severe action against the Communists, both those who are openly members of the party and those who are secretly organized in the underground, and those who are the, so to speak, unparty members, because they are too important to be jeopardized.

We will have to take action against them. The only basis upon which we can take action is the basis of knowledge, and I believe that at this moment the first thing we ought to do toward insuring the safety of the United States at a moment which may not be very far off, is greatly to increase the appropriation of the FBI for handling precisely this problem of Communists in the United States.

I know that the FBI has done excellent work on this line. They have proved what they could do in the case of the German Bund, but in the case of the Communist party you have many, many more, thousands and thousands more dangerous persons than you had in the German Bund; and I believe that the FBI should be given sufficient funds so that when the crisis comes it can seize all the members of the Communist party who have any importance, just as effectively as it seized the members of the Bund.

I do think, therefore, that at the present time we are not equipped to face this issue by passing legislation making it a crime to be a member of the Communist party. I do not believe that the people of this country are quite sufficiently aware of the danger to them involved in the existence of the party and the determination of the Soviet Union to conquer the United States, to face up to the penalties involved. The last thing we want to do is to make martyrs of anybody. The last thing we want to do is to throw away one iota of our Bill of Rights contained in the first ten amendments to the Constitution. Our glory in the world and, indeed, our great strength, is in the fact that we stand for freedom. The Soviet Government today, in the world where it is really known, stands for just one thing, which is slavery.

It is a very old fight, an extremely old fight, which has gone on for twenty-five hundred years at least, between the idea of freedom, exemplified at the time by the Athenian democracy, and the idea of tyranny, exemplified at that time by the great kings of Persia. This fight is on today, and the great explosive idea which we have to offer to the peoples of eastern Europe who are under the heel of the Soviet Government, to all the peoples of the world, even the peoples of the Soviet Union who are under the heel of the Soviet Government, is the idea of freedom; and in my belief while we have to devise with the utmost care a method of handling this criminal conspiracy, I think it has to be done so as to avoid, meticulously, touching one iota of our Bill of Rights and our personal freedoms.

THE COMMUNIST PARTY AND THE BALLOT [10]

The legislative season of the winter of 1941 was characterized by the number of bills introduced with the intent of abridging civil rights. Prominent among these were bills to outlaw and bar from the ballot the Communist party, the German-American Bund, and any group or person advocating the overthrow of the government by force and violence, or affiliated with any party or group which advocates force or violence, sabotage, sedition or treason, or is directly or indirectly affiliated with any foreign government or agency. Such bills were introduced in twenty-seven out of the forty-three state legislatures which were in session. . . .

The two points . . . most common to all this legislation are foreign affiliation or control, and advocacy of the overthrow

[10] From article by Harry F. Ward, Professor, Union Theological Seminary. *Bill of Rights Review*. 1, no. 4:286-92. Summer 1941.

of the government. This penalizing of political advocacy of force and violence is an extension of the same attempt in the field of industrial disputes. The core of the criminal syndicalism statutes passed in a number of states just after the [first] World War was the prohibition of the advocacy of force and violence. These bills were so nearly identical in language that they plainly followed a model statute sent out by an organization of employers. . . .

The current attempt to prevent political movements by legislation was preceded by severe interference with the rights of political minorities in the recent national election. In that campaign the Communist party was ruled off the ballot either by executive decision or court action in fifteen states, and in some cases this action extended to other radical minority groups. In several of those states many persons were indicted for exercising their legal right to sign a nominating petition. In some cases this action was preceded by intimidating publication of the names of petition signers, and by terroristic pressure of organized groups. . . .

In . . . an emotional atmosphere laws containing such vague terms as "force and violence," "subversive," "foreign control" permit latitude of interpretation and disregard of fact. The record of the use of criminal syndicalism statutes makes clear what will happen. In not a single prosecution under them was an overt act proved. They were used to abridge the right of labor to organize, and to prevent radical political utterances. On the other hand the direct advocacy of acts of force and violence by employers and politicians was never prosecuted. The Civil Liberties Union has collected a number of such incitements in its pamphlets, "Who Advocates Force and Violence?"

The Jeffersonian doctrine of free speech tolerates advocacy of the overthrow of government and of force and violence so long as it is unaccompanied by any overt act or direct incitement to overt acts. It was clearly expressed in his inaugural address of 1801. . . . A modern putting of it was voiced by Justice Cuthbert W. Pound of the New York Supreme Court, dissenting in the case of *Benjamin Gitlow* under the New York Criminal Anarchy Act, 1925: "Although the defendant may be the worst of men; although left-wing socialism is a menace to organized government; the rights of the best of men are secure only as the rights of the vilest and most abhorrent are protected."

This doctrine of free speech concerning political change has never been realized in times of strain. . . . The essence of the limitation upon the Jeffersonian doctrine, and the free speech guarantee of the Bill of Rights, is that Congress may punish utterances if there is a "clear and present danger" that they will result in action harmful to the state, particularly by bring-about something which Congress has forbidden, e.g., interference with conscription. The difficulties that lie in the interpretation of what is a "clear and present danger" are shown by the fact that in most of the cases that came before the Supreme Court after the rule was laid down, Justice Holmes found himself in dissent from the judgment of the majority.

This fact in the *Gitlow* case led to one of his most pungent utterances which is directly applicable to the present laws forbidding the ballot to certain minority groups. His words are:

If what I think the correct test is applied, it is manifest that there was no present danger of an attempt to overthrow the government by force on the part of the admittedly small minority who shared the defendant's views. It is said that this manifesto was more than a theory, that it was an incitement. Every idea is an incitement. It offers itself for belief, and if believed it is acted on unless some other belief outweighs it, or some failure of energy stifles the movement at birth. The only difference between the expression of an opinion, and an incitement in the narrower sense, is the speaker's enthusiasm for the result. Eloquence may set fire to reason. But whatever may be thought of the redundant discourse before us, it had no chance of starting a present conflagration. If in the long run the beliefs expressed in proletarian dictatorship are destined to be accepted by the dominant forces of the community, the only meaning of free speech is that they should be given their chance and have their way.

The Supreme Court has also established the precedent that the states may punish speech presumed to be dangerous to the state, such as advocacy of methods of violence. This is a limitation of the "clear and present danger" rule. From this position to penalizing, not the method of political and economic change, but advocacy of change itself, is only a step, and that step has already been taken by a loudly vocal minority. Congressman Dies has defined attempts to change our form of government as un-American, and the phrase "advocating a change in the form of government" occurs again and again in anti-sabotage and anti-alien bills introduced both in state legislatures and Congress during the present lesgislative season.

Since the first objective of all this repressive legislation is the Communist party, the question of fact before the courts is whether the Communist party does advocate the overthrow of the government by force and violence. Several lower courts have so held, with one decision to the contrary. But when that case reached the Supreme Court it was decided on another point . . . . The Communist party has been submitting itself to the franchise of the American people for twenty years. In the few cases in which one of its members have been tried for advocating force and violence, the evidence has not been about anything they have done, nor about the party program, but about the writings of earlier Communists, the documents of the Communist International, and in particular the implications drawn from these by the prosecution. This has now become a standard procedure. . . .

The Communist answer on this point of their historic doctrine concerning the place of force and violence in social change, is that it is prophecy of what will happen, not advocacy of what they want. They contend that force and violence will attend a change from capitalist to socialist society because [those] opposed to that change will use any means to prevent it, including the overthrow of democratic government. Professor Harold Chapman Brown, of the University of California, in summarizing this doctrine before Judge Landis at the Bridges' trial in 1939, thus expressed the core of it:

Where the Communists differ from other believers in the ultimate victory of the working class, is that they do not believe that the victory will be achieved until a very much more severe struggle than is ordinarily contemplated. They believe that the ruling class will use every means, political, economic, and military, to defend its privileges, and that the final decision will not be reached without open civil war. In support of this they quote evidence to show the readiness of the ruling class in many countries to fling constitutional considerations to the wind when their privileges are in danger.

He pointed out that communism differs from

other revolutionary philosophies which proclaim the right of the "militant minority" to endeavor to change society. The glorification of the minority, or the coup d'etat really belongs to the Blanquist school, which was always vigorously opposed by Marxism. . . .

The Constitution of the Communist party, U.S.A., adopted by the Tenth National Convention, May 27-31, 1938, and amended by the Special Convention, November 16-17, 1940, is very specific. The preamble declares among other things that the Communist party

upholds the achievements of democracy, the right of "life, liberty, and the pursuit of happiness," and defends the United States Constitution against its reactionary enemies who would destroy democracy and all popular liberties. . . .

Section 1 of Article VI. The Party: Rights and Duties of Members, reads as follows:

The Communist party of the U.S.A. upholds the democratic achievements of the American people. It opposes with all its power any clique, group, circle, faction or party which conspires or acts to subvert, undermine, weaken, or overthrow any or all institutions of American democracy whereby the majority of the American people have obtained power to determine their own destiny in any degree. It condemns and opposes all policies and acts of sabotage, espionage, and all other forms of fifth column activity. The Communist party of the U.S.A., standing unqualifiedly for the right of the majority to direct the destinies of our country, will fight with all its strength against any and every effort, whether it comes from abroad or from within, to impose upon our people the arbitrary will of any selfish minority group, or party, or clique, or conspiracy. . . .

The final argument of those who seek to outlaw the Communist party, is that these provisions of its constitution are only a smoke screen behind which a situation is to be brought about in which the overthrow of democratic government will be violently accomplished. The contention is that democratic forms are to be used to accomplish the destruction of democracy. But this is a position which makes democratic action impossible. The democratic grant of political rights to minorities, no matter how unpopular, presupposes good faith on both sides. Its test is actions, not the dubious ground of belief about motives. This charge of deceit, like the vague phrases of recent repressive legislation, belongs in heresy trials, not in political procedures.

The question of deceit is not to be determined by arguments about doctrines and their implications, it is subject to concrete determination. The American way of determining the legality of any political party is solely its program of action and its deeds, not the implications of theoretical writings. There are plenty of laws to stop any acts against the government, or any conspiracies for such acts, and officials certainly have sufficient willingness to use these laws in time. When investigating committees and legislative bodies, as they are now doing, create the crime of political heresy by setting up tests of opinion and belief, they themselves are destroying the democratic process.

The record of history is clear enough concerning the consequences of attempts to suppress political heretics. To make illegal groups proposing radical social change is simply to drive them underground and to force the issue from the arena of discussion to the field of direct action. If any political party, no matter how radical its proposals, can be debarred from appeal to the franchise of our people, the first step in the path that leads to the totalitarian state has been taken. The right of the people to hear, to think, and to organize for political action, cannot be abridged without making it impossible for them to govern themselves in ways of their own choosing. For the majority to deny any unpopular minority the right to express itself and to appeal to the franchise, is to deny democracy itself any possibility of advance. That such action is a step toward the overthrow of the American system of government, is shown clearly by the records of the nations in Europe which took it. In our own nation the attack upon the constitutional right of Communists has been followed by a general assault upon the rights of labor, upon progressive legislation, upon academic freedom. It is clear that if the wave of reaction is to be stopped it must be checked when it attacks the most unpopular political party. Otherwise when the Left is smashed, the Center is then destroyed and there remains only the Right. Our traditional democratic rights, and our constitutional guarantees, must be kept open for all if in the future they are to be available for any.

In this time of strain we may well take as our guide the words of Justice Holmes, dissenting in the case of *Abrams et al.* v. *United States*:

> But when men have realized that time has upset many fighting faiths, they may come to believe even more than they believe the very foundations of their own conduct, that the ultimate good desired is better reached by free trade in ideas—that the best test of truth is the power of the thought to get itself accepted in the competition of the market, and that truth is the only ground upon which their wishes can be safely carried out. That, at any rate, is the theory of our Constitution. It is an experiment, as all life is an experiment. Every year, if not every day, we have to wager our salvation upon some prophecy based upon imperfect knowledge. While that experiment is part of our system, I think that we should be eternally vigilant against attempts to check the expression of opinions that we loathe and believe to be fraught with death, unless they imminently threaten immediate interference with the pressing purposes of the law [so] that an immediate check is required to save the country.

LIBERALS AND THE COMMUNIST TRIAL [11]

My friend and colleague, Morris Ernst, raises a novel point, but it is hard to see what it has to do with the present trial of the twelve Communist leaders.

They are not being tried for a secret conspiracy. They are being tried for openly advocating the Communist program and objectives. Even if they were tried for secret advocacies, the doctrine that secret utterances which may have an illegal object are in themselves criminal establishes a concept unknown in American law. While the Civil Liberties Union adheres to its settled position that only a "clear and present danger" of unlawful acts justifies prosecution, it is giving Ernst's proposal a thorough examination.

The government's indictment in the current case makes precisely the sort of charges which Ernst says should be resisted. There is no indication yet that a secret conspiracy, apart from the

[11] By Roger Baldwin, Director, American Civil Liberties Union. *New Republic.* 120:8. January 31, 1948.

vociferous Communist propaganda, is involved. The indictment alleges conspiracy to "teach and advocate" "the Marxist-Leninist principles of the overthrow and destruction of the government of the United States by force and violence." There is no allegation of secrecy. There is no allegation of overt act. The prosecution rests solely on the utterances and publications of the Communist party.

It has always been American public policy—and this has been embodied in many court decisions—that no language, publication or propaganda should be punished unless it constitutes, in Justice Holmes's language quoted above, a clear and present danger of unlawful acts. The Supreme Court has held that there must be great danger and the prospect of immediate action to justify penalties which infringe freedom of speech and press. Nothing in the indictment suggests any such danger.

If the government knows of secret conspiratorial acts by the Communists, why did it not indict them for such acts? It could have done so, for example, under the General Conspiracy Statute, instead of the questionable Smith Act, which has been condemned in principle by such an authority on free speech as Professor Zechariah Chafee of Harvard University.

Many people believe, and there seems to be compelling evidence, that the American Communist party is under the control of the Russian government, either directly or through a third group such as the Communist party of France. If the United States Government has evidence to support this charge, why does it not indict the Communists for failing to register as the agents of a foreign principal?

I hope I don't need to say, at this late date, that the American Civil Liberties Union has no sympathy with communism, or with any other totalitarian doctrine. We would not oppose a federal indictment based upon overt acts by the Communists tending toward the violent overthrow of the government. But we do oppose action by any governmental body in this country which seeks to punish people for their beliefs and the mere expression of their beliefs. We opposed the application of the Smith Act against the Minnesota Trotskyites, at a time when the Communist party was gleefully supporting the prosecution. We also opposed its only other use, the trial of alleged pro-Nazis in the District of Columbia.

There are some who would say that certain ideas are so dangerous, so abhorrent, that the effort to spread them must be suppressed even though no connection with overt acts is shown. (This, of course, is not Morris Ernst's view.) Such a notion seems to me dangerous in the extreme. Powerful influences will always tend to say that unpopular ideas are of this character and that advocating them is an illegal conspiracy.

As for a distinction between what is private, or secret, and what is public, here, too, we enter a shadowland where clear-cut applications of Morris Ernst's principle are difficult. In the first place, "private" is not the same as "secret." All sorts of discussions are held by all sorts of people which are private without being secret. The top groups in many organizations discuss problems tentatively without wishing these views made known generally. But that is not illegal. The attempt to decide what is actually private or secret and what is public is too difficult to be entrusted to run-of-the-mill public officials. There has never been a Supreme Court ruling on the question of secret versus public debate.

In spite of Morris Ernst's novel principle, the only fair acid test I can conceive would continue to be the "clear and present danger." Ideas alone should not be punished as incitements in the absence of acts or the immediate danger of them. As Holmes once said: "Every idea is an incitement."

Nor is Ernst's parallel with Quisling in Norway an apt one. Quisling was guilty of the overt acts of aiding a foreign power to seize and govern his country. He didn't just talk about what he might do, at some future time, like the Communists; he did it.

The only safe rule is not to prohibit utterances or publications dealing with public questions unless they are, first, direct incitements to unlawful acts shown to have been either attempted or actually committed, or, second, advocacies of actions which immediately threaten great danger.

If there is any evidence that the Communists now on trial have engaged in such activities, the indictment does not say so and the case appears to rest on the dangerously shaky ground of making long-tolerated propaganda criminal. A conviction would in effect outlaw the Communist party, and drive it underground, a result I am sure Morris Ernst does not desire and one which the recent debate over the Mundt-Nixon bill in Congress shows the country does not desire.

EXCERPTS

I would call a halt to all schemes, formulated in hysteria, for the outlawing of the Communist party in the United States. You may have inferred, and correctly, that I do not like either the American Communists or their political party. It is one thing to dislike a movement profoundly, even to regard it as potentially revolutionary and correspondingly dangerous, and quite another thing to deal with it by the statutory ban of outlawry. The latter is the course, in my judgment, of men of little imagination. So long as it is humanly possible, and as much as possible, I would keep the Communists out in the open. I would have them make their silly speeches and shout their distorted doctrines from the stump and not in caves or cellars. It will be time enough to talk of driving them underground when their activities above ground or below have actually become a present danger. The merits of any doctrine, however foolhardy, are best determined in the competition of the market place. I believe in the Bill of Rights for those whose opinions I abhor no less than for those whose opinions I approve. Nor is there anything particularly idealistic about all this. It is just plain old fashioned common sense. If you would multiply the breed, persecute them. If you would frustrate their faith, let them talk. Their ultimate frustration must be accomplished by removing the conditions in which they appear to thrive. In letting them talk, we may even learn something from time to time about their leadership or concerning the latest gyrations of their "party line."—*Edwin D. Dickinson, Dean, School of Jurisprudence, University of California. Association of the Bar of the City of New York. Record. D. '47. p.360.*

There are in the English-speaking countries and in those of Western Europe large numbers of people who favor what they think communism to be, who look on far-away Russia through a haze of rose-colored romance and wish that what they regard as a system of well ordered, sagely planned, equally shared benefits and responsibilities could be introduced in their lands too. It is a curious thing this deeply rooted, unshakable faith in the Russian utopia. It has no basis in fact. The evidence against it is tragically strong. The evidence in its favor is weak. It is a faith that springs from failure and from the bitterness that comes from failure in communities which allow free competition and initiative, or it is the product of ambition and the craving for power which besets some men and women. It is not by any means confined to the uneducated element in the population.

Not many of these believers have been to Russia. Not many of them seem anxious to go, even if it were possible. History as a rule is not their strong point. Otherwise they might ask themselves whether it is probable that a nation like the Russians, with only thirty years between them and the later Middle Ages, should suddenly have found the secret of happiness, efficiency, and prosperity. They might also wonder why Russia is so unwilling to allow observers to travel in her territories or to trust press correspondents to send out uncensored reports, photographs, and all the customary information which a normal country is glad to allow to be published.

The most effective method of dealing with this type of communism does not appear to be suppression by legal enactment and police prosecution. There may be Communists who are so malevolent towards existing institutions in their own country that they must be forcibly repressed, but for the average Communist an almost certain cure is a reasonable degree of prosperity and well-being. It is a rare thing to find a man with a home of his own, a balance in the bank, and a congenial mode of livelihood who favors communism, unless indeed he is consumed with the cancer of ambition. Especially is a sound system of land ownership and housing vital to the maintenance of a contented people. Oppressive landlordism and slums do more to foster the creed of communism than all the writings and the speeches of agitators. Agrarian discontent is written large into the history of revolution. The factory system of the industrial era has produced the labor extremist.

If the faith of the Western Communist in an invisible, idealized Russia is surprising, so also is the faith of the average anti-Communist in private enterprise as the dominating type of human activity. It does not seem to strike these extremists in either camp that a well-balanced community must include institutions of all kinds. The defense forces of a nation are essentially communistic in character. The law courts and police, the schools, the post office, the roads are socialistic. The homes of the people are their private domains. All three forms of ownership and control existing side by side together form a civilized society, aiming at what may be defined as the ideal of civilization—the greatest amount of personal liberty which can be combined with the utmost extent of united effort. Like all ideals this one can never be reached. It can only be approached through progressive stages, but the nearer any society comes to the ideal, the less will be the internal friction, and the more enlightened will be its functioning, leaving exclusive despotism, communism, and individualism behind it to wither and die in the limbo of oblivion.—*H. G. Scott, lecturer, author of From Storm to Storm. International Journal. Winter '48-'49. p.50-1. 230 Bloor St. W. Toronto, Canada.*

What shall we do about our domestic conspirators? Shall we allow ourselves to get hysterial about them? Shall we outlaw the Communist party? Shall we forbid or break up peaceful meetings devoted to the discussion of theories which most of us consider false? Shall we censor or suppress publications which advocate measures—short of violence—which most of us oppose? Shall we engage in witch hunts? Shall we pin the label of Communist or fellow traveler on every one whose social views we do not like? Shall we deprive men of their reputations or their livelihoods on the strength of biased and sensational testimony which would instantly be rejected by any court of law? Shall we make culprits of the few misguided but well-meaning young people who may be temporarily seduced by doctrines which most of us abhor?

If we have any sense, we shall do none of these things. No evil is ever exorcised by outlawing it. It lives on and burrows, unseen by the eye of the law. Censorship never stopped the spread of any doctrine in which its adherents ardently believed. On the contrary, censorship creates an added curiosity concerning the forbidden material. The authors of the first amendment of the Constitution of the United States were not thinking merely of meetings devoted to causes of which they approved when they guaranteed the right of peaceable assembly. And surely by now we ought to know about the futility of witch hunts. We have experimented with them at intervals since the middle of the seventeenth century, to our shame be it spoken. For every so-called witch that was ever caught scores of innocent persons have suffered cruel and unjust persecution.

None of these methods of suppression accords with the principles on which American society is based and in which we profess to believe. American democracy is not strengthened by resort to action which violates these principles. On the contrary, it is weakened. The case of the conspirators is strengthened, for they can claim to be the victims of injustice. The surest defense of American democracy is the faith of American citizens in its superiority to other forms of social organization and their insistence that under no provocation shall its integrity be compromised or impaired.

The truly American way of dealing with any hostile and hidden movement is to show it up. We need no more laws than we have already to take care of any direct attacks upon our institutions. To meet the indirect attacks we need only to be vigilant—and vocal; vigilant to detect the party line in the publications and utterances of those who plot the overthrow of the American system, vigilant in examining the multitude of false fronts which the plotters erect to conceal their intent; and vocal in public and private discussion. Communism should be talked about. We should never treat it as a kind of unmentionable disease toward which we pursue a hush-hush policy, lest perchance it corrupt somebody. We should drag it into the open, see what it is and how it works. And wherever possible we should drag individual Communists into the open, see what sort of people they are and what they are trying to do. Communism is instantly robbed of all power to damage the American system as soon as its carriers are identified and their purposes are made clear. Like many another germ that flourishes in darkness, it cannot live when exposed to the sunlight.

American democracy, on the other hand, seeks no concealment. It can afford to be fully known. It challenges the world to produce the record of any other system which has insured to the population on so wide a scale economic opportunity, justice, and freedom. At any rate, America's full record, the failures as well as the triumphs, is open for the whole world to inspect. America gladly abides the arbitrament of the truth.

And not for itself alone. Fate has cast America in the role of leader in the worldwide struggle to restore the ideal of the truth to the judgment seat before which the causes of men and of nations are brought to trial. The role is congenial to America's history and aspirations. On the success of American effort depends the future of human freedom everywhere, the future of honor and decency and compassion. Once more America is "the last, best hope of the earth." May we who are its citizens keep our nation worthy of this high mission.—*Samuel P. Capen, Chancellor, University of Buffalo. School and Society. S. 6, '47. p.181-2.*

BIBLIOGRAPHY

An asterisk (*) preceding a reference indicates that the article or a part of it has been reprinted in this book.

BIBLIOGRAPHIES

Bibliographic Index, 1937-1942. Communism. p. 348-9. H. W. Wilson Co. New York. '45.

Bibliographic Index, 1943-1946. Communism. p. 160. H. W. Wilson Co. New York. '48.

Chamber of Commerce of the United States. Annotated bibliography. *In* Communist infiltration in the United States. p. 38-40. The Chamber. Washington 6, D.C. '46.

Chamber of Commerce of the United States. Annotated bibliography. *In* Communists within the labor movement. p. 53-4. The Chamber. Washington 6, D.C. '47.

Chamber of Commerce of the United States. Bibliography on communism. *In* Program for community and anti-Communist action. p. 48-56. The Chamber. Washington 6, D.C. '48.

Peters, Clarence A. comp. Bibliography. *In his* American capitalism vs. Russian communism. (Reference Shelf. Vol. 18, no. 7) p. 289-305. H. W. Wilson Co. New York. My. '46.

United States. House. Committee on Un-American Activities. Index II to publications of Special Committee on Un-American Activities (Dies Committee), and the Committee on Un-American Activities (1942-1947, inclusive) (supplement to 1942 index): October 21, 1947. 221p. 80th Congress, 2d session. Supt. of Docs. Washington, D. C. '48.

BOOKS, PAMPHLETS AND DOCUMENTS

Allen, Raymond B. Communism and education; an open letter to friends of the University of Washington. 11p. The University. Seattle. O. 7, '48.

*American Civil Liberties Union. It's not only Communists' rights! 8p. The Union. 170 5th Ave. New York 10. Ap. '48.

American Federation of Labor. American Federation of Labor vs. Communism; action of 65th A.F. of L. convention, October 16, 1946. 8p. The Federation. Washington 1, D.C. '46.

American Jewish League Against Communism. Jews against communism. 9p. The League. 220 W. 42d St. New York 18. '49.

Andrews, Bert. Washington witch hunt. 218p. Random House. New York. '48.

Ascoli, Max. Shadow of communism. *In his* Power of freedom. p. 3-12. Farrar, Straus & Co. New York. '49.

Avery, Andrew. Communist fifth column; what's the truth about it and what isn't. 47p. Chicago Journal of Commerce. Chicago. '46.
Reprint of articles appearing in the Chicago Journal of Commerce between June 24 and July 11, 1946.

Avery, Andrew. Communist power in U. S. industry. 61p. Chicago Journal of Commerce. Chicago. '47.
Reprint of articles appearing in the Chicago Journal of Commerce between January 13 and 31, 1947.

Baarslag, Karl. Communist trade union trickery exposed; a handbook of Communist tactics and techniques. rev. & enl. 81p. Argus Publishing Co. 55 E. Washington St. Chicago 2. '49.

Bachrach, Marion. You are on trial. 18p. New Century Pubs. New York. Ja. '49.

Becker, Carl L. Freedom and responsibility in the American way of life. 122p. Alfred A. Knopf. New York. '45.

Beloff, Max. Communism: its strength and its future. (Behind the headlines. Vol. 8, no. 4) 25p. Canadian Institute of International Affairs. 230 Bloor St. W. Toronto 5, Ont. S. '48.

Boarman, Patrick M. Communist infiltration in Christian service agencies. (Economic Council papers. Vol. 4, no. 6) 4p. National Economic Council. Empire State Bldg. New York 1. F. '48.

Boyer, Richard O. If this be treason. 31p. New Century Pubs. New York. D. '48.

Browder, Earl. World communism and U. S. foreign policy. 55p. The Author. 55 W. 42d St. New York 18. '48.

Budenz, Louis F. This is my story. 379p. Whittlesey House. New York. '47.

Bullitt, William C. Great globe itself; a preface to world affairs. 310p. Charles Scribner's Sons. New York. '46.

Burnham, James. Struggle for the world. 248p. John Day Co. New York. '47.
Abridged. Life. 22:59-62+. Mr. 31, '47.

Burns, Emile. Triumph of communism; Communist manifesto centenary speech. 15p. Communist Party. 16 King St. London WC2. Universal Distributors Co. 38 Union Sq. New York 3. '48.

California. Legislature. Joint Fact-Finding Committee on Un-American Activities. Third report. 403p. Sacramento. '47.

California. Legislature. Senate Daily Journal. p. 1145-1545. Report of the Joint Fact-Finding Committee on Un-American Activities in California to California State Legislature. Sacramento. Ap. 9, '43.

California. Legislature. Senate Fact-Finding Committee on Un-American Activities. Fourth report; Communist front organizations. 448p. Sacramento. '48.

Canadian Chamber of Commerce. Communist threat to Canada. 40p. The Chamber. 530 Board of Trade Building. Montreal. '47.

Cannon, James P. American Stalinism and anti-Stalinism. 48p. Pioneer Pubs. New York. '47.

Chamber of Commerce of the United States. Program for community anti-Communist action. 56p. Economic Research Department. The Chamber. Washington 6, D.C. '48.

Chamber of Commerce of the United States. Committee on Socialism and Communism. Communism within the government; the facts and a program. 57p. The Chamber. Washington 6, D.C. Ja. '47.

Chamber of Commerce of the United States. Committee on Socialism and Communism. Communist infiltration in the United States: its nature and how to combat it. 40p. The Chamber. Washington 6, D.C. '46.

Chamber of Commerce of the United States. Committee on Socialism and Communism. Communists within the labor movement; a handbook on the facts and counter-measures. 54p. Economic Research Department. The Chamber. Washington 6, D.C. '47.
Same. 60p. '47.

Cherdron, Otto P. Erroneous philosophies that always have led humanity into chaos. 31p. The Author. 1901 9th East St. Salt Lake City, Utah. '48.

*Childs, John L. and Counts, George S. America, Russia, and the Communist party in the postwar world. 92p. John Day Co. New York. '43.

Civil Rights Congress. America's thought police; record of the Un-American Activities Committee. 46p. The Congress. 205 E. 42d St. New York 17. O. '47.

Civil Rights Congress. Description and analysis of the Mundt police state bill (H.R. 5852) 6p. mim. The Congress. 205 E. 42d St. New York 17. '48.

Civil Rights Congress. What are the facts in the case of the twelve indicted Communist leaders. 8p. mim. The Congress. 205 E. 42d St. New York 17. N. '48.

Clark, John M. Guideposts in time of change. 210p. Harper & Bros. New York. '49.

Cole, G. D. H. World in transition; a guide to the shifting political and economic forces of our time. 646p. Oxford University Press. New York. '49.

Communist manifesto and the last hundred years. 92p. World Socialist Party of the United States. 27 Dock Sq. Boston 8. '48.

Communist Party. National Educational Department. Campaign against the frameup of the Communist leaders; speaker's notes. 23p. The Party. 35 E. 12th St. New York 3. '48.

Communist Party. National Educational Department. Theory and practice of the Communist party; first course. (Marxist study series 1) 48p. New Century Publishers. New York. Je. '47.

Conant, James B.   Laws vs. Communists in schools and colleges; statement before a committee of the Massachusetts legislature, February
9, 1948. 6p. American Civil Liberties Union. 170 5th Ave. New
York 10. '48.

Crofts, Alfred.   May Day reflections; is there a genuine internal Communist menace in the United States? (Journeys behind the news.
Vol. 9, no. 34) 7p. mim. Social Science Foundation. University
of Denver. Denver. My. 3, '47.

Crofts, Alfred.   Un-American follies; the danger of leaving Americanism
to the definition of a partial and uninformed political committee.
(Journeys behind the news. Vol. 10, no. 10) 7p. mim. Social
Science Foundation. University of Denver. Denver. N. 24, '47.

Cronin, John F.   Communism, a world menace. 31p. National Catholic
Welfare Conference. 1312 Massachusetts Ave. Washington 5, D.C.
'47.

Cushman, Robert E.   New threats to American freedoms. (Public Affairs
pamphlet no. 143) 32p. Public Affairs Committee. 22 E. 38th St.
New York 16. S. '48.

Dallin, David J.   Real Soviet Russia. tr. by J. Shaplen. rev. & enl.
325p. Yale University Press. New Haven. '47.

Davies, A. Powell.   Liberalism versus communism. 12p. Federal Union.
700 9th St. Washington 1, D.C. '47.

DeMille, Cecil B.   While Rome burns; address before Economic Club of
Detroit, April 19, 1948. 14p. Economic Club of Detroit. 321 W.
Lafayette Ave. Detroit 26. '48.

Dennis, Eugene.   Dangerous thoughts; the case of the indicted twelve.
15p. New Century Pubs. New York. O. '48.

Dennis, Eugene.   Is communism un-American? 9 questions about the
Communist party. 15p. New Century Pubs. New York. Mr. '47.

Dennis, Eugene.   Let the people know. 32p. New Century Pubs. New
York. Ap '47.

Dennis, Eugene.   Red-baiters menace America. 11p. New Century Pubs.
New York. O. '46.

Derry, George H.   How the reds get that way; (some big words to
discuss). 20p. Knights of Columbus, Supreme Council. New
Haven, Conn. '48.

Dies, Martin.   Trojan horse in America. 366p. Dodd, Mead & Co.
New York. '40.

Duranty, Walter.   Stalin & Co.; the politburo—the men who run Russia. 261p. William Sloane Associates. New York. '49.

Ebon, Martin.   World communism today. 536p. Whittlesey House.
McGraw-Hill Book Co. New York. '48.

Fischer, Ruth.   Stalin and German communism; a study in the origins
of the state party. 687p. Harvard University Press. Cambridge.
'48.

Flynn, Elizabeth G. Meet the Communists. 23p. Communist Party, U.S.A. 35 East 12th St. New York 3. My. '46.

Flynn, Elizabeth G. Twelve and you; what happens to democracy is your business, too! 23p. New Century Pubs. New York. S. '48.

Foster, William Z. Meaning of the 9-party Communist conference. 23p. New Century Pubs. New York. '47.

Foster, William Z. New York Herald Tribune's 23 questions about the Communist party answered. 31p. New Century Pubs. New York 3. '48.

Foster, William Z. Our country needs a strong Communist party. 23p. New Century Pubs. New York. F. '46.

Foster, William Z. and others. Marxism-Leninism vs. revisionism. 111p. New Century Pubs. New York. F. '46.

Fourth International. Only victorious socialist revolutions can prevent the third World War! manifesto of the Fourth International to the workers, the exploited and the oppressed peoples of the entire world, April 1946. 31p. Pioneer Pubs. 116 University Place. New York 3. '46.

Gitlow, Benjamin. I confess; the truth about American communism. 611p. E. P. Dutton & Co. New York. '40.

Gitlow, Benjamin. Whole of their lives; communism in America—a personal history and intimate portrayal of its leaders. 387p. Charles Scribner's Sons. New York. '48.

Gouzenko, Igor. Iron curtain. 279p. E. P. Dutton & Co. New York. '48.

Greer, Thomas H. Radical efforts since World War I. In his American social reform movements; their pattern since 1865, p. 177-212. Prentice-Hall. New York. '49.

Hart, Merwin K. No wonder they squawk! (Council letter no. 179) 4p. National Economic Council. Empire State Bldg. New York 1. N. 15, '47.

*Hoover, J. Edgar. Communism in the United States. (Confidential—from Washington. No 47) 4p. George Washington Victory Council. George Washington University. Washington, D.C. Je. '48.

Hoyt, Palmer, Jr. Communism—how it operates. 8p. mim. Social Science Foundation. University of Denver. Denver 10, Colo. O. 18, '48.

Hoyt, Palmer, Jr. Middle way. 10p. mim. Social Science Foundation. University of Denver. Denver 10, Colo. N. 1, '48.

Johnson, Hewlett. Soviet success. 285p. Hutchinson & Co. London; New York. '47.

Johnston, Clem D. Communist infiltration in the United States. 10p. mim. Chamber of Commerce of the United States. 1615 H. St. Washington 6, D.C. Mr. 11, '47.

*Johnston, Eric. Ideology for democracy. 11p. Motion Picture Association of America. 1600 Eye St. Washington 6, D.C. N. 5, '48.
Same. Commercial and Financial Chronicle. 168:2612+. D. 23, '48; Abridged. Midland Schools. 63:10-11. D. '48.

Josephson, Emanuel M. America's Communist conspiracy; address, Madison Square Garden, January 10, 1946. 8p. Chedney Press. 127 E. 69th St. New York. '46.

Kahn, Gordon. Hollywood on trial; the story of the 10 who were indicted. 229p. Boni & Gaer. New York. '48.

Kamp, Joseph P. Strikes and the Communists behind them. 65p. Constitutional Educational League. 342 Madison Ave. New York 17. '47.

Kelsen, Hans. Political theory of Bolshevism; a critical analysis. (Publications in political science. Vol. 2, no. 1) 60p. University of California Press. Berkeley and Los Angeles. S. '48.

*King, Judson. Seditious speech and loyalty probes; a comparison between the periods of World War I and World War II. (Bulletin no. 230) 16p. mim. National Popular Government League. 23 Columbia Ave, Takoma Park. Washington 12, D.C. Mr. 12, '48.

Kirkpatrick, T. C. Communism: how it works and what you can do about it. 18p. Economic and Business Foundation. New Wilmington, Pa. O. 21, '48.

Koestler, Arthur. Yogi and the commissar, and other essays. p. 131-217. Macmillan Co. New York. '45.

Kravchenko, Victor A. I chose freedom; the personal and political life of a Soviet official. 496p. Charles Scribner's Sons. New York. '46.

Laidler, Harry W. Communism. In his Social-economic movements. p. 347-471. Thomas Y. Crowell Co. New York. '44.

Lane, Arthur B. I saw Poland betrayed. 344p. Bobbs-Merrill Co. Indianapolis. '48.

Laski, Harold. Communism. 256p. Henry Holt & Co. New York. '27.

Lehrman, Hal. Russia's Europe. 341p. D. Appleton-Century Co. New York. '47.

Lenin, Nikolai. Selected works. 2 vols. Universal Distributors Co. 38 Union Sq. New York 3. '47.

Lewis, Alfred B. Liberalism and Sovietism. 32p. New Leader Association. 7 E. 15th St. New York 3. '46.

Life and Look show us communism. 40p. Queen's Work. 3115 S. Grand Boulevard. St. Louis 19. '48.
Reprint of Portrait of an American Communist. John McPartland. Life. 24:74-8+. Ja. 5, '48; and Does Communism threaten Christianity? Dorothy Thompson. Look. Ja. 20, '48.

Loucks, William N. and Hoot, J. W. Comparative economic systems. 3d ed. 836p. Harper & Bros. New York. '48.

Lyons, Eugene A. Red decade; the Stalinist penetration of America. 423p. Bobbs-Merrill Co. Indianapolis. '41.

Marx, Karl and Engels, Frederick. Communist manifesto. 75p. New York Labor News Co. 61 Cliff St. New York 8. '48.

Mauriac, François and others. Communism and Christians. tr. from the French by J. F. Scanlon. 294p. Newman Press. Westminster, Md. '49.

*Meiklejohn, Alexander. Free speech and its relation to self-government. 107p. Harper & Bros. New York. '48.

Minor, Robert. How Ben Davis was elected. 24p. New Century Pubs. New York. F. '46.

Morris, George. Red baiting racket and how it works. 39p. New Century Pubs. New York. O. '47.

Murry, John M. Free Society. 292p. Andrew Dakers. London. '48.

Naft, Stephen. Answer please! questions for Communists. 29p. New Leader Association. 7 E. 15th St. New York 3. '48.

Nagy, Ference. Struggle behind the iron curtain. 471p. Macmillan Co. New York. '48.

Nearing, Scott. From capitalism to communism. 23p. World Events Committee. 125 5th St. Washington 2, D.C. '48.

Nomad, Max. Communism. *In* Gross, Feliks, ed. European ideologies; a survey of 20th century political ideas. p. 47-100. Philosophical Library. New York. '48.

Norborg, Christopher. Operation Moscow. 319p. E. P. Dutton & Co. New York. '47.
Excerpt. Communist fellowship. Catholic World. 166:77-8. O. '47.

Oakeshott, Michael. Communism. *In his* Social and political doctrines of contemporary Europe. p. 81-159. Macmillan Co. New York. '42.

Odegard, Peter H. Frontiers of freedom. 22p. Walter H. Shepard Foundation, Ohio State University. Columbus. Ap. 28, '48.

Oneal, James and Werner, G. A. American communism; a critical analysis of its origins, development and programs. new & rev. ed. 416p. E. P. Dutton & Co. New York. '47.

Padelford, Norman J. and Tompkins, F. Pauline, eds. Current readings on international relations. p. 298-307. Problems in peacemaking. Addison-Wesley Press. Cambridge, Mass. '49.

Peters, Clarence A. comp. American capitalism vs. Russian communism. (Reference Shelf. Vol. 18, no. 7) 305p. H. W. Wilson Co. New York. My. '46.

Peters, J. Secrets of the Communist party exposed! the secret Communist party manual on organization (their plan for conquest of the United States and the world). 63p. State Publishing Co. 12 N. 3d St. Columbus 15, Ohio. '47.

Pettingill, Samuel B. and Hays, Arthur G. What do we mean by un-American activities? (Wake up America! Broadcast no. 342) 20p. American Economic Foundation. 295 Madison Ave. New York 17. O. 27, '46.

Roberts, Leslie. Home from the cold wars. 224p. Beacon Press. Boston. '48.

Rosenfarb, Joseph. Freedom and the administrative state. 274p. Harper & Bros. New York. '48.
See especially p. 96-8, 181-2.

Russell, Dean. Bill of rights. (In Brief. Vol. 2, no. 2) 11p. Foundation for Economic Education. Irvington-on-Hudson, N.Y. O. '48.

Sayers, Michael and Kahn, Albert E. Great conspiracy; the secret war against Russia. 433p. Little, Brown & Co. Boston. '46.

Schmidt, Emerson P. Anti-Communist program; testimony before House Committee on Un-American Activities, March 26, 1947. 18p. mim. Chamber of Commerce of the United States. Washington, D.C. '47.

Schuman, Frederick L. Soviet politics at home and abroad. 663p. Alfred A. Knopf. New York. '46.

Schwarzschild, Leopold. Red Prussian; the life and legend of Karl Marx. 422p. Charles Scribner's Sons. New York. '47.

Sheen, Fulton J. Communism and the conscience of the west. 247p. Bobbs-Merrill Co. Indianapolis. '48.

Socialist Party of Great Britain. Communist manifesto and the last hundred years. 92p. World Socialist Party of the United States. 27 Dock Sq. Boston 8. '48.

Somerville, John. Soviet philosophy; a study of theory and practice. 369p. Philosophical Library. New York. '46.

Southworth, Gertrude Van Duyn and Southworth, John Van Duyn. What about communism? a report to the American people. 36p. Iroquois Publishing Co. Syracuse, N.Y. '48.

Spellman, Francis C. Communism is un-American. 17p. Constitutional Educational League. 342 Madison Ave. New York 17.
Reprinted from American Magazine. 142:26-8. Jl. '46.

Spivak, John L. Save the country racket. 63p. New Century Pubs. New York. N. '48.

Stalin, Joseph. Leninism; selected writings. 479p. International Pubs. New York. '42.

Stokes, Jeremiah. Americans' castle of freedom; under Bolshevik fire on our home front, fateful facts all America must know. 84p. Federated Libraries. 36½ W. Second South St. Salt Lake City, Utah. '44.

Summers, Robert E. Federal information controls in wartime. (Reference Shelf. Vol. 20, no. 6). 301p. H. W. Wilson Co. New York. F. '49.

Sweinhart, James. Communist plot exposed! a series of articles published in the Detroit News March and April 1948. 95p. Inland Press. 610 W. Congress St. Detroit 26, Mich. '48.

Taylor, Warren. American and un-American activities. 6p. mim. Publicity Bureau. Oberlin College. Oberlin, Ohio. My. 20, '47.

*Thompson, Dorothy. Truth about communism. 17p. Public Affairs Press. 2153 Florida Ave. Washington 8, D.C. '48.

Trotsky, Leon. Stalin; an appraisal of the man and his influence. tr. by Charles Malamuth. 516p. Harper & Bros. New York. '41.

United States. House. Americanism, communism, and fascism, a comparison; compiled by Coordinator of Information for House of Representatives. 1p. Supt. of Docs. Washington, D.C. '47.

United States. House. Committee on Foreign Affairs. Subcommittee no. 5. National and International Movements. Strategy and tactics of world communism; report; with supplements I and II. 62+238+129p. House document no. 619. 80th Congress, 2d session. Supt. of Docs. Washington, D.C. '48.
Supplement III, separate in 2 parts. 27+36p.

United States. House. Committee on Un-American Activities. Excerpts from hearings regarding investigation of Communist activities in connection with the atomic bomb; hearings, September 9-16, 1948. 79p. 80th Congress, 2d session. Supt. of Docs. Washington, D.C. '48.

United States. House. Committee on Un-American Activities. Hearings on proposed legislation to curb or control the Communist party of the United States; hearings, February 5-20, 1948, on H.R. 4422 and H.R. 4581. 500p. 80th Congress, 2d session. Supt. of Docs. Washington, D.C. '48.

United States. Committee on Un-American Activities. Hearings regarding communism in labor unions in the United States; hearings February 27, July 23-25, 1947. 231p. 80th Congress, 1st session. Supt. of Docs. Washington, D.C. '47.

United States. House. Committee on Un-American Activities. Hearings regarding Communist espionage in the United States government, July 31-September 9, 1948. p. 501-1378. 80th Congress, 2d session. Supt. of Docs. Washington, D.C. '48.

United States. House. Committee on Un-American Activities. Hearings regarding Communist espionage in the United States government, December 7-14, 1948. 1379-1474p. 80th Congress, 2d session. Supt. of Docs. Washington, D.C. '48.

United States. House. Committee on Un-American Activities. Hearings regarding the Communist infiltration of the motion picture industry; hearings, October 20-30, 1947. 549p. 80th Congress, 1st session. Supt. of Docs. Washington, D.C. '47.

United States. House. Committee on Un-American Activities. Interim report on hearings regarding Communist espionage in the United States government, August 28, 1948: investigation of un-American activities in the United States. 15p. 80th Congress, 2d session. Supt. of Docs. Washington, D.C. '48.

United States. House. Committee on Un-American Activities. Investigation of un-American activities and propaganda; report, June 7, 1946, pursuant to H. Res. 5. 73p. 79th Congress, 2d session. Supt. of Docs. Washington, D.C. '46.

United States. House. Committee on Un-American Activities. Investigation of Un-American propaganda activities in the United States; hearings, March 24-28, 1947, on H.R. 1884 and H.R. 2122, bills to curb or outlaw the Communist party of the United States. 340p. 80th Congress, 1st session. Supt. of Docs. Washington, D.C. '47.

United States. House. Committee on Un-American Activities. Investigation of un-American activities in the United States; the Communist party of the United States as an agent of a foreign power. 56p. H. Rept. no. 97. 80th Congress, 1st session. Supt. of Docs. Washington, D.C. Ap. 1, '47.
    Same. Congressional Record. 93:(daily) A1729-45. Ap. 14, '47.

United States. House. Committee on Un-American Activities. Investigation of the Un-American propaganda activities in the United States (regarding Leon Josephson and Samuel Liptzen); hearings March 5, 21, 1947. 86p. 80th Congress, 1st session. Supt. of Docs. Washington, D.C. '47.

United States. House. Committee on Un-American Activities. 100 things you should know about communism and education. 19p. Supt. of Docs. Washington, D.C. '48.

United States. House. Committee on Un-American Activities. 100 things you should know about communism and government. 18p. Supt. of Docs. Washington, D.C. '48.

United States. House. Committee on Un-American Activities. 100 things you should know about communism and labor. 21p. Supt. of Docs. Washington, D.C. '48.

United States. House. Committee on Un-American Activities. 100 things you should know about communism and religion. 16p. Supt. of Docs. Washington, D.C. '48.

United States. House. Committee on Un-American Activities. 100 things you should know about communism in the United States. 30p. Supt. of Docs. Washington, D.C. '48.

United States. House. Committee on Un-American Activities. Protecting the United States against un-American and subversive activities; report, April 30, 1948 (to accompany H.R. 5852) 14p. H. Report no. 1844. 80th Congress, 2d session.. Supt. of Docs. Washington, D.C. '48.

United States. House. Committee on Un-American Activities. Report of the Committee on Un-American Activities to the United States House of Representatives, Eightieth Congress, December 31, 1948: investigation of un-American activities in the United States. 25p. 80th Congress, 2d session. Supt. of Docs. Washington, D.C. '49.

United States. House. Committee on Un-American Activities. Report of the Subcommittee on Legislation of the Committee on Un-American Activities on proposed legislation to control subversive Communist activities in the United States, April 10, 1948: investigation of un-American activities in the United States. 7p. 80th Congress, 2d session. Supt. of Docs. Washington, D.C. '48.

United States. House. Committee on Un-American Activities. Report on Civil Rights Congress as a Communist front organization, September 2, 1947: investigation of un-American activities in the United States. 47p. H. Rept. no. 1115. 80th Congress, 1st session. Supt. of Docs. Washington, D.C. '47.

United States. House. Committee on Un-American Activities. Report on Southern Conference for Human Welfare, June 12, 1947: investigation of un-American activities in the United States. 17p. 80th Congress, 1st session. Supt. of Docs. Washington, D.C. '47.

United States. House. Committee on Un-American Activities. Report on the Communist party of the United States as an advocate of the overthrow of government by force and violence: investigation of un-American activities in the United States. 160p. H. Rept. no. 1920. 80th Congress, 2d session. Supt. of Docs. Washington, D.C. My. 11, '48.

United States. House. Committee on Un-American Activities. Soviet espionage within the United States government; second report. D. 31, '48. 129p. 80th Congress, 2d session. Supt. of Docs. Washington, D.C. '49.

United States. House. Committee on Un-American Activities. Testimony of Victor A. Kravchenko; hearings, July 22, 1947, on H.R. 1884 and H.R. 2122. 30p. 80th Congress 1st session. Supt. of Docs. Washington, D.C. '48.

United States. House. Committee on Un-American Activities. Testimony of Walter S. Steele regarding Communist activities in the United States; hearings, July 21, 1947, on H.R. 1884 and H.R. 2122. 176p. 80th Congress, 1st session. Supt. of Docs. Washington, D.C. '47.

United States. House. Special Committee on Un-American Activities. Special report on subversive activities aimed at destroying our representative form of government. H. Rept, no. 2277. 22p. 77th Congress, 2d session. Supt. of Docs. Washington, D.C. Je. 25, '42.

Vyshinsky, A. Y. Lenin and Stalin, the great organizers of the Soviet state. 74p. Universal Distributors. 38 Union Square. New York 3. '48.

Walker, Jerry. World empire; communism's great challenge. 72p. Cosmos Publishing Co. 475 5th Ave. New York 17. '48.

Ward, Harry F. Soviet spirit. 160p. International Pubs. New York. '44.

Westmeyer, Russell E. Communism in the Soviet Union and elsewhere. *In his* Modern economic and social systems. p. 205-90. Farrar & Rinehart. New York. '40.

What's true and what's false about the Mundt-Nixon bill. 4p. Counterattack. 55 W. 42d St. New York 18. My. 28, '48.
Special supplement with Counterattack. My. 28, '48.

Wilkerson, Doxey A. Why Negroes are joining the Communist party. 15p. Communist Party, U.S.A. 35 E. 12th St. New York 3. '46.

Williams, Aubrey. What is happening to our civil rights? 13p. The Author. c/o Southern Farmer. Montgomery 1, Ala. S. 11, '47.

Wittke, Carl. What shall we do with the Communist party? 4p. mim. Publicity Bureau. Oberlin College. Oberlin, Ohio. Ap. 16, '47.

PERIODICALS

America United. 3, no. 16:1-14. Ap. 20, '47. Radio forum conducted by the American Federation of Labor on Is communism a threat to the United States?

American Affairs. 10:223-5. O. '48. Slanted movie. Jonathan Hasbrouck.

American Bar Association Journal. 32:453-7. Ag. '46. Civil rights: the boundless responsibility of lawyers. T. C. Clark.

American Bar Association Journal. 34:15-17. Ja. '48. Lawyer schools or policy science? Yale law faculty's manifesto stirs debate.

American Bar Association Journal. 34:191-3. Mr. '48. Soviet communism today: a graphic account of what it does to lawyers. W. L. R.

American Bar Association Journal. 34:193-4. Mr. '48. Lawyers' views sought as to laws to curb the Communist party.

American Bar Association Journal. 34:281-2. Ap. '48. Communists in U. S.; registration urged by House of delegates.

*American Bar Association Journal. 34:645-8+. Ag. '48. Communism vs. the constitution: the power to protect our free institutions. F. B. Ober.

American Bar Association Journal. 34:899-901+. O. '48. Communism and Communists: Association votes support of Mundt-Nixon bill.

American Federationist. 46:1330-5. D. '39. I accuse the Communist party. Simon Cohen.

American Federationist. 48:20-1. Jl. '41. Our immediate obligation; Communist invasion of the labor movement.

American Forum of the Air. 8, no. 19:1-15. My. 21, '46. Are communism and democracy mutually antagonistic? C. B. Luce and others.

American Forum of the Air. 9, no. 17:1-15. Ap. 29, '47. Should Congress outlaw the Communist party? Milton Howard and others.

American Forum of the Air. 9, no. 49:1-11. D. 16, '47. Should we outlaw the Communist party? G. H. Taylor and others.

American Forum of the Air. 12, no. 3:1-10. Ja. 18, '49. Should the Un-American Activities Committee be abolished? K. E. Mundt and Emanuel Cellar.

American Magazine. 129:16-17+. Ap. '40. Rebirth of an American; the confessions of a young revolutionist. Howard Rushmore.
   Same abridged. Reader's Digest. 36:57-60. Je. '40.

American Magazine. 142:26-8+. Jl. '46. Communism is un-American. Francis Cardinal Spellman.
   Also contains Communism is a menace. J. E. Hoover.

American Magazine. 143:22-3. Je. '47. Hotbeds of communism; a report and map showing the Communist's own estimate of their strength throughout the world. Robert Crandall.

American Magazine. 143:24-5+. F. '47. Red fascism in the United States today. J. E. Hoover.
   Same. Congressional Record. 93:(daily) A566-8. F. 13, '47.

*American Magazine. 146:19+. Jl. '48. Reds are after your child. H. D. Gideonse.

American Mercury. 53:671-80. D. '41. Stalin's American power. Max Eastman.
   Same abridged. Reader's Digest. 39:39-48. D. '41.

American Mercury. 63:261-9. S. '46. Behind Soviet foreign policy. Max Eastman.

American Mercury. 64:645-56. Je. '47. Can Truman avoid World War III? W. C. Bullitt.
   Same abridged with title Strength of our new foreign policy. Reader's Digest. 50:25-9. Je. '47.

American Mercury. 66:7-16. Ja. '48. World communism has passed its peak. Martin Ebon.

American Mercury. 66:309-16. Mr. '48. Collapse of Czech democracy. Daniel Seligman.

American Mercury. 66:721-8. Je. '48. New Communist internationals; four worldwide organizations.

American Mercury. 67:169-76. Ag. '48. What liberalism means to me. J. T. Flynn.

*American Mercury. 67:389-96. O. '48. Are Communists traitors to America? Roscoe Drummond.

American Mercury. 67:413-21. O. '48. Wallace's Communist-front party. Charles Angoff.
   Discussion. American Mercury. 67:756-7. D. '48.

American Political Science Review. 39:31-41. F. '45. Communist party of the USA; an analysis of a social movement. Barrington Moore, Jr.

American Scholar. 17, no. 1:81-92. [Ja.] '48. American century? V. M. Dean; S. K. Padover.
   Discussion. American Scholar. 17, nos. 2-4:230-6, 359-61, 483-5+. [Ap.-O.] '48.

American Scholar. 17, no. 2:139-49. [Ap.] '48. In defense of American activities. Walter Gellhorn.

American Scholar. 18, no. 1:9-10. [Ja.] '49. Can we live with our enemies? Christian Gauss.

American Teacher. 33:4. D. '48. Teachers and communism.

Annals of the American Academy. 249:54-65. Ja. '47. Civil liberties in the atomic age. R. E. Cushman.

Annals of the American Academy. 257:1-12. My. '48. Persistence of power politics. T. V. Kalijarvi.

Annals of the American Academy. 257:47-56. My. '48. Great powers in the new world order. Robert Strausz-Hupé.

Annals of the American Academy. 258:59-65. Jl. '48. One world versus an iron curtain world. Joseph S. Roucek.

Annals of the American Academy. 259:10-16. S. '48. Why a third party in 1948? H. A. Wallace.

Annals of the American Academy. 259:24-9. S. '48. Do left-wing parties belong to our system? Norman Thomas.

Antioch Notes. 24:1-4. Ja. 15, '47. Freedom to inquire. A. E. Morgan.
    Same. High School Journal. 30:206-7. O. '47.

Association of the Bar of the City of New York. Record. 2:350-61. D. '47. Political subversives: an appraisal of recent experience and forecast of things to come. E. D. Dickinson.

Atlantic Monthly. 181:27-30. My. '48. Stop Russia's subversive war. W. J. Donovan.

Atlantic Monthly. 182:19-23. Ag. '48. Subversive of what? J. P. Boyd.

*Bill of Rights Review. 1:286-92. Summer '41. Communist party and the ballot. H. F. Ward.

Bulletin of the Pan American Union. 82:286. My. '48. Brazil ousts Communist legislators.

Business Week. p. 116. O. 2, '48. Dealing with reds.

California Law Review. 35:336-51. S. '47. Open window and the open door: an inquiry into freedom of association.

Canadian Forum. 28:1+. Ap. '48. Lights go out in Czechoslovakia.

Catholic World. 162:410-17. F. '46. Out of their own mouths. Helen Williams.

Catholic World. 163:461-2. Ag. '46. No compromise. Hamilton Fish.

Catholic World. 164:385-91. F. '47. How Communists get that way. J. M. Gillis.

Catholic World. 165:104-5. My. '47. Taking communism seriously. J. M. Gillis.

Catholic World. 166:11-18. O. '47. Russia's advance in the United States. J. E. Uhler.

Catholic World. 167:122-7. My. '48. Century under the Communist manifesto. M. H. Dohan.

Catholic World. 167:146-9. My. '48. I am a Communist. J. H. Quilligan.

Christian Century. 65:849-51. Ag. 25, '48. Peace with Russia. J. F. Dulles.
Discussion. Christian Century. 65:946. S. 15, '48.

Christian Century. 66:164-5. F. 9, '49. Academic freedom as a cloak.

Christian Science Monitor Magazine Section. p. 2. My. 22, '48. Finland breathes again. Ralph Hewins.

Christian Science Monitor Magazine Section. p. 2. F. 12, '49. Liberty and violence; indictments may outline America's stand on Communists' future in U.S. Mary Hornaday.

Churchman. 162:6. My. 15, '48. You are a Communist! R. W. Searle.

Churchman. 162:4. O. 1, '48. Masons and communism.

City Club Bulletin (Chicago). n.s. 15:45-6. Je. 7, '48. Mundt-Nixon bill.

Collier's. 118:14-15+. Ag. 10, '46. Trouble in paradise. Walter Davenport.

Collier's. 119:22+. F. 8, '47. Turn the light on communism. R. M. LaFollette, Jr.

Collier's. 119:110. My. 24, '47. Outlaw the reds? but why?

Collier's. 122:14-15+. S. 18, '48. How the reds snatched Henry Wallace. L. F. Budenz.

*Collier's. 122:13-14+. O. 23, '48. Red web in U.S. labor. L. F. Budenz.

Collier's. 122:16-17+. N. 20, '48. Red plan for S-Day. L. F. Budenz,

Collier's. 122:28+. N. 27, '48. Capture of the innocents. L. F. Budenz.

Columbia Law Review. 47:416-31. Ap. '47. Constitutional limitations on the Un-American Activities Committee.

Columbia Law Review. 48:589-605. My. '48. Registration of groups tending to influence public opinion.

Commentary. 5:291-6. Ap. '48. Prague: I saw it happen twice; eye-witness account of the Communist coup. C. E. R. Geyde.

*Commentary. 5:423-31. My. '48. Civil liberties and the Communists. Robert Bendiner.

Commentary. 6:253-9. S. '48. Counter-offensive against communism. M. J. Goldbloom.

Commercial and Financial Chronicle. 164:2941. D. 5, '46. Study ordered on U.S. employees loyalty.

Commercial and Financial Chronicle. 164:3207+. D. 19, '46. Enslavement of labor. Matthew Woll.

Commercial and Financial Chronicle. 165:1796+. Ap. 3, '47. Indictment of Soviet policies. L. F. Budenz.

Commercial and Financial Chronicle. 165:1845. Ap. 3, '47. Government employees to have loyalty test.

Commercial and Financial Chronicle. 165:2909+. My. 29, '47. Class
conflict idea; a threat to freedom. W. A. Irwin.

Commercial and Financial Chronicle. 166:209+. Jl. 17, '47. U.S. vs.
communism in one world. H. E. Stassen.

Commercial and Financial Chronicle. 166:919+. S. 4, '47. What do
the Communists really want? Robert Thompson; Eugene Lyons.

Commercial and Financial Chronicle. 167:102+. Ja. 8, '48. Menace
of communism's growth. J. E. LeRossignol.

Commercial and Financial Chronicle. 167:2097+. My. 13, '48. How
to fight the reds. J. F. Dulles.

Commercial and Financial Chronicle. 168:805+. Ag. 26, '48. Communism and world peace. J. F. Dulles.

Commonweal. 45:604. Ap. 4, '47. Communist man-hunt.

Commonweal. 45:631. Ap. 11, '47. 100,000 Communists. C. G.
Paulding.

Commonweal. 48:253-6. Je. 25, '48. Mundt-Nixon bill. Christopher
Emmet.
    Discussion. Commonweal. 48:306-7, 354. Jl. 9, 23, '48.

Commonwealth & Empire Review (London). 82:27-33. Jl. '48. Communist policy in the Commonwealth and empire. Leslie Paul.

Congressional Record. 93:(daily) A543-4. F. 12, '47. Communism
is anti-American. E. F. Hazleton.

Congressional Record. 93:(daily) A1003-4. Mr. 10, '47. Former
editor of Communist Daily Worker reveals In Fact to be a camouflaged organ of the Communist party.

Congressional Record. 93:(daily) 1217-18. Mr. 20, '47. Outlawing
the Communist party. Ed Will.

Congressional Record. 93:(daily) A1233-5. Mr. 20, '47. How to
meet communism. F. J. Sheen.

Congressional Record. 93:(daily) 2824-7. Mr. 27, '47. Protection of
internal security of the nation. Kenneth McKellar.

Congressional Record. 93:(daily) A1409-12. Mr. 28, '47. Statement
before House Committee on Un-American Activities, March 26,
1947. J. E. Hoover.

Congressional Record. 93:(daily) A1425-6. Mr. 28, '47. Communism; statement before House Committee on Un-American Activities, March 27, 1947. Eric Johnston.

Congressional Record. 93:(daily) A1665-7. Ap. 9, '47. Why the
Communist party in America should be restrained. K. E. Mundt.

Congressional Record. 93:(daily) A1670-2. Ap. 9, '47. Communism in Hollywood from testimony of Hon. Eric Johnston.

Congressional Record. 93:(daily) A1776-8. Ap. 15, '47. Break with Communist Russia. J. E. Rankin.

Congressional Record. 93:(daily) A1808-14. Ap. 16, '47. Report on American Youth for Democracy. Committee on Un-American Activities, House of Representatives.

Congressional Record. 93:(daily) A2142-51. My. 1, '47. Evils of communism; testimony before House Committee on Un-American Activities, March 24, 1947. W. C. Bullitt.

Congressional Record. 93:(daily) A4639-42. N. 24, '47. Americanism, communism, and fascism—a comparison. J. F. Richardson. Same. School Life. 30:28-31. F. '48.

Congressional Record. 93:(daily) 11547-50. D. 15, '47. Barring un-American parties from the election ballot. W. C. Cole.

Congressional Record. 95:(daily) A397-9. Ja. 27, '49. Reds delay crisis in West in order to concentrate on Orient in plan of world conquest. G. A. Tokaev.

Congressional Record. 95:(daily) A404-5. Ja. 27, '49. Communist tyranny. R. H. Markham.

Congressional Record. 95:(daily) A441. Ja. 31, '49. Trial of Communist leaders; two articles from Deseret Evening News, Salt Lake City. Vivian Meik.

Congressional Record. 95:(daily) A589-90. F. 7, '49. Two voices of Soviet Russian policy. Julius Epstein.

Congressional Record. 95:(daily) A1091-4. F. 24, '49. International communism: its origin and growth. W. L. Furbershaw.

Congressional Record. 95:(daily) 2008-19. Mr. 8, '49. Control of subversive activities.

Congressional Record. 95:(daily) A1545-6. Mr. 16, '49. Comparison of communism with democracy. W. O. Douglas.

Congressional Record. 95:(daily) A1751-3. Mr. 23, '49. Cultural and Scientific Conference for World Peace arranged by the National Council of the Arts, Science and Professions. J. S. Wood.

Congressional Record. 95:(daily) A1794-8. Mr. 24, '49. So-called rights of Communists and atheists under the constitution of the United States. C. H. Davis.

Contemporary Review. 174:343-8. D. '48. Why has Marxism failed in England? Bernhard Reichenbach.

Contemporary Review. 174:372-9. D. '48. Can the rot be stopped? George Glasgow.

Counterattack; Facts to Combat Communism. Published weekly by American Business Consultants, Inc. 55 W. 42d St. New York 18.

Current History. n.s. 14:1-5. Ja. '48. Cominform. S. B. Fay.

Current History. n.s. 15:213-17. O. '48. Behind the Tito-Stalin feud; difference between Soviet and Yugoslav system. W. S. Vucinich.

Current History. n.s. 15:334-7. D. '48. Waging the cold war. R. G. Cowherd.

Department of State Bulletin. 20:179-83. F. 13, '49. American answer to Chinese Communist propaganda. J. M. Cabot.

Economic Council Letter. No. 185:1-4. F. 15, '48. Danger is real—and near.

Economic Council Letter. No. 205:1-4. D. 15, '48. Treason in Washington? M. K. Hart.

Economic Council Papers. 4:1-4. F. 15, '48. Communist infiltration in Christian service agencies. P. M. Boarman.

Economist (London). 153:760-1. N. 8, '47. Loyalty in technicolor.

Economist (London). 154:441-2. Mr. 20, '48. Can it happen here?

Economist (London). 154:925. Je. 5, '48. Definition of treason.

Economist (London). 155:415-16. S. 11, '48. Zinoviev writes again.

Economist (London). 155:566-7. O. 9, '48. One year of the Cominform.

Economist (London). 155:734-5. N. 6, '48. Almanach de Moscou; directory of leading Communists issued by Committee of House of Representatives.

Editorial Research Reports. 2, no. 20:779-98. N. 13, '46. Communism in America. B. W. Patch.

Editorial Research Reports. 1, no. 5:91-106. F. 5, '47. Investigations of un-Americanism. Kendrick Lee.

Editorial Research Reports. 1, no. 4:53-68. Ja. 28, '48. Individual rights and congressional investigations. F. L. Van Schaick.

Editorial Research Reports. 1, no. 6:91-106. F. 11, '48. Control of communism in the United States. L. B. Wheildon.

Educational Leadership. 6:184+. D. '48. Teachers and world communism. M. E. Cary.

Educational Record. 29:400-9. O. '48. Academic freedom today. C. W. De Kiewiet.

Engineering and Mining Journal. 148:74-81. Jl. '47. Communism menaces the mining industry. R. H. Ramsey.

Factory Management and Maintenance. 104:82-6. Je. '46. You can't laugh off the Reds.

Factory Management and Maintenance. 106:108-12. F. '48. What the Communists have done to French industry. Michael Marsh.

Facts on File; Weekly World Digest. Facts on File, Inc. 516 5th Ave. New York 18.
See current issues and cumulative indexes.

Federal Bar Journal. 9:61-94. O. '47. State control of subversive activities in the United States. S. B. Groner.

Foreign Affairs. 19:737-50. Jl. '41. Narkomindel and Comintern; instruments of world revolution. B. C. Hopper.

Foreign Affairs. 26:421-31. Ap. '48. Foreign policy of the American Communist party. Joseph Barnes.

Foreign Affairs. 27:175-214. Ja. '49. Stalin on revolution. Historicus.

Foreign Affairs. 27:215-31. Ja. '49. No peace, no war. Max Beloff.

Fortune. 33:105-7. Je. '46. Hammer and tongs: new C. P. line.

*Forum. 107:497-501. Je. '47. Should we outlaw the Communist party? Max Knepper.

Forum. 108:198-203. O. '47. Lost American freedom. A. K. Smart.

Forum. 109:65-8, 129-33, 193-7. F.-Ap. '48. American civil rights in a revolutionary age. E. D. Ellis.

Forum. 109:106-11. F. '48. Loyalty board. S. W. Richardson.

Forum. 109:267-70. My. '48. Marshall plan strategy. Adolf Sturmthal.

Friends of the Public Schools. Bulletin. 10:7. My. '48. When will we wake up and outlaw communism? communistic indoctrination in schools.

*Friends of the Public Schools. Bulletin. 11:7-8. Ag. '48. What are we waiting for? outlaw communism now!

Harper's Magazine. 175:133-42. Jl. '37. Professor quits the Communist party. Stuart Browne.

Harper's Magazine. 180:587-97. My. '40. American Communists. Dale Kramer.

Harper's Magazine. 192:528-36. Je. '46. It's tough to be a Communist. Irwin Ross.

Harper's Magazine. 192:536-42. Je. '46. Spectre that haunts the world. Granville Hicks.

Harper's Magazine. 194:412-18. My. '47. Why I broke with the Communists. J. H. Franklin.

*Harper's Magazine. 195:193-9. S. '47. Who is loyal to America? H. S. Commager.

Also separate. 7p. Harper's Magazine. Dept. G. 49 E. 33d St. New York 16; Same abridged. New Statesman and Nation. 34:346-7. N. 1, '47.

Harper's Magazine. 195:438-43. N. '47. How to rid the government of Communists. J. A. Wechsler.

Harvard Law Review. 60:1193-234. O. '47. Report on a report of the House Committee on Un-American Activities. Walter Gellhorn.

Harvard Law Review. 61:592-611. Ap. '48. Loyalty tests and guilt by association. J. L. O'Brien.

*Human Events. 5, no. 13:1-4. March 31, 1948. Techniques of communism. Bertrand de Jouvenel.

Same with title How to seize a country. Reader's Digest. 52:62-3. Je. '48.

Illustrated London News. 212:374. Ap. 3, '48. Principle of loyalty to the state. Cyril Falls.

Infantry Journal. 62:40-8, 34-40; 63:33-7. My.-Jl. '48. Strategy and tactics of world communism.

Abridged from United States. Committee on Foreign Affairs. Report. 62p. House document no. 619. 80th Congress, 2d session. '48.

Information Service (Federal Council of the Churches of Christ in America). 26, no. 39:1-4. N. 29, '47. Loyalty, security, and civil rights.

International Affairs. 24:170-80. Ap. '48. Soviet ideology and propaganda. G. H. Bolsover.

International Affairs. 24:339-49. Jl. '48. Cominform and world communism. Dennis Healey.

International Journal (Toronto). 3:160-4. Spring '48. Strength and aim of communism. Hans Kohn.

International Journal (Toronto). 4:33-46. Winter '48-'49. Techniques of the Communist party in France. L. G. Cowan.

International Journal (Toronto). 4:47-51. Winter '48-'49. Communism as an historical episode. H. G. Scott.

Iron Age. 162:127. S. 2, '48. Red hearings confirm public suspicion of Communists; Gallup poll.

Journal of Politics. 9:355-91. Ag. '47. Communism in eastern and southeastern Europe. Vernon Van Dyke.

Journal of the History of Ideas. 9:259-302. Je. '48. Evolution of the Socialist vocabulary. A. E. Bestor, Jr.

Labors Monthly Survey. 8:1-8. Mr.-Ap. '47. World-wide struggle for individual rights.

Ladies' Home Journal. 65:11-12. Jl. '48. Ends, means and values. Dorothy Thompson.

*Lawyers Guild Review. 7:57-79. Mr.-Ap. '47. Constitutional right to advocate political, social and economic change—an essential of American democracy. National Lawyers Guild.

Lawyers Guild Review. 7:112-21. My. '47. Civil rights for the President's committee. Will Maslow and J. B. Robison.

Lawyers Guild Review. 8:281-4. Ja.-F. '48. Civil rights in a cold-war era. R. W. Kenny.

Life. 21:84-5+. Jl. 29, '46. U.S. Communist party. A. M. Schlesinger, Jr.

Life. 23:137-8+. N. 24, '47. Movie hearings. Sidney Olson.

Life. 24:26. Ja. 12, '48. Is there a witch hunt?

Life. 24:34-5. Mr. 22, '48. Jan Masaryk found one answer. Dorothy Thompson.
     Same abridged. Reader's Digest. 52:122-4. Je. '48.

Life. 24:33-7. Je. 7, '48. Finns resist.

Life. 24:36. Je. 14, '48. Mundt-Nixon bill.

Life. 25:24. S. 6, '48. How red a herring? spy revelations.

Masses & Mainstream. 1:26-34. D. '48. Twelve; a lawyer looks at the case. G. T. Boxley.

Michigan Law Review. 46:521-32. F. '48. Investigatory power of Congress; validity of the Un-American Activities Committee inquiries into professional and political affiliations. C. M. Soller.

Monetary Times. 116:22-4+. Je. '48. How to combat communism: a Monetary Times symposium. D. M. Chisholm and others.

Nation. 164:385-8. Ap. 5, '47. Washington witch-hunt. H. S. Commager.

Nation. 165:223-6. S. 6, '47. Is the Constitution un-American? I. F. Stone.

Nation. 165:492-4. N. 8, '47. Grand inquisition. I. F. Stone.

Nation. 166:519-20. My. 15, '48. What dictatorship?

Nation. 166:594-5. My. 29, '48. Debate of the pigmies.

Nation. 167:117-18. Jl. 31, '48. Communist arrests. Freda Kirchwey.

Nation. 167:247-8. S. 4, '48. How do you separate them, Mr. Wallace?

Nation. 167:255-7. S. 4, '48. Meaning of liberty. F. B. Evans.

Nation. 168:118-19. Ja. 29, '49. Communists on trial. Robert Bendiner.

Nation. 168:121-3. Ja. 29, '49. Full disclosure: dangerous precedent. A. G. Hays.

Nation. 168:151-2. F. 5, '49. Blitz in Los Angeles. Carey McWilliams.

Nation. 168:156-8. F. 5, '49. China: the Communists' plan. Andrew Roth.

Nation. 168:230-3. F. 26, '49. Communists and the right to teach; the case against Communists in the schools. J. L. Childs.

Nation. 168:270-3. Mr. 5, '49. Test of a teacher; the case for Communists in the schools. Carey McWilliams.

National Review (London). 129:476-80. D. '47. Russia, communism and the world. Edward Crankshaw.

Nation's Business. 32:35-6+. Jl. '44. Our Communists' new line. Lawrence Drake.

Nation's Business. 33:80+. S. '45. Our Communists reconvert. Carlisle Bargeron.

Nation's Business. 34:57-9+. S. '46. Red blight in union gardens. J. J. Daly.

Nation's Business. 35:33-5+. Ap. '47. Trained to raise hell in America; International Lenin School in Moscow. J. B. Wood.

Nation's Schools. 40:17-18. N. '47. What is loyalty? A. B. Moehlman.

Nation's Schools. 40:20-1. D. '47. Witch hunters and the schools. Ellis Arnall.

Nature. 161:537-9. Ap. 10, '48. Freedom and loyalty.

New Republic. 114:699. My. 13, '46. Progressives and Communists. James Loeb, Jr.
   Discussion. New Republic. 114:733, 771, 837, 871. My. 20-27, Je. 10-17, '46.

New Republic. 116:12-13. Ap. 14, '47. Bad case of fever. H. A. Wallace.

New Republic. 117:10-14. Ag. 11, '47. State of civil liberties today; symposium.

New Republic. 117:14-15. Ag. 11, '47. Attack on human rights. Henry Wallace.

New Republic. 118:20-1. Ja. 12, '48. Judge declares: that the Thomas Committee subverts the bill of rights; excerpts from dissent. C. E. Clark.

New Republic. 118:22-3. Ja. 12, '48. Norway's solution. Philip Singer and Gilbert Cranberg.

New Republic. 118:15-19+. My. 31, '48. Guilt by gossip. D. S. Gillmor.

New Republic. 118:9+. Je. 14, '48. Mundt bill fight. H. A. Wallace.

New Republic. 119:11. Ag. 9, '48. Witch-hunt in the Northwest.
Reply. W. S. Hopkins. New Republic. 119:28. S. 20, '48.

New Republic. 119:6-8. Ag. 16, '48. Trial by Congress. Michael Straight.

New Republic. 119:14-16. N. 8, '48. Russia and the liberals. L. S. Feuer.

New Republic. 119:5-6. D. 13, '48. Un-American activities.

New Republic. 119:16-18. D. 13, '48. Asia's old order crumbles; flames of communism sweep through southeast Asia. W. L. Briggs.

New Republic. 120:7-8. Ja. 10, '49. Americus and the Kremlin.

*New Republic. 120:7-8. Ja. 31, '49. Liberals and the Communist trial. Morris Ernst; Roger Baldwin.

New Republic. 120:5-6. F. 7, '49. Communist trial.

New Statesman and Nation. 33:331-2. My. 10, '47. Will it happen again? Edmund Penning-Rowsell.

New Statesman and Nation. 34:186. S. 6, '47. Mote and the beam. H. J. Laski.

New York Times. p. 8E. Mr. 23, '47. Rights of Communists. L. H. Eldredge.

New York Times. p. 8E. Mr. 30, '47. Communist party; its suppression advocated. T. L. Anderson.

New York Times. p. 1F+. N. 2, '47. Semantics a red weapon in war on free enterprise. Russell Porter.

New York Times. p. 5E. F. 29, '48. Communist way: how Czechoslovakia was taken over. Albion Ross.
Same abridged with title Iron curtains for Czechoslovakia. Reader's Digest. 52:36-9. My. '48.

New York Times. p. 2. Ag. 7, '48. Text of the Communist party's platform for the presidential election.

New York Times. p. 25. S. 29, '48. Text of President Truman's speech in reply to charges on the Communist issue.

New York Times. p. 8E. Ja. 2, '49. Exposing Communists; committee investigation upheld as safeguard to freedom. Eugene Lyons.

New York Times. p. 8E. Ja. 23, '49. Basic Communist issues involved in trial. Will Lissner.

New York Times. p. 22. F. 21, '49. Soviet system working for own defeat. A. O'H. McCormick.
    Same. Congressional Record. 95:(daily) A1012-13. F. 21, '19.
New York Times. p. 5E. F. 27, '49. Communists claim peak membership; but purges are removing less ardent followers from the ranks.
New York Times. p. 8E. F. 27, '49. Question for Communists.
New York Times. p. 20. Mr. 4, '49. Where communism stands.
New York Times. p. 16. Mr. 5, '49. Teaching by Communists. E. M. Root.
New York Times. p. 10E. Mr. 6, '49. Communism drops the mask.
New York Times. p. 10. Ap. 27, '49. Presentment of Grand Jury warning on espionage.
New York Times Magazine. p. 7+. Mr. 24, '46. Inquiry into the Communist mind. Harold Callender.
*New York Times Magazine. p. 12+. Mr. 30, '47. Report on the Communist party (U.S.A.) A. H. Raskin.
New York Times Magazine. p. 7+. O. 19, '47. Politburo tries a new tack. H. R. Trevor-Roper.
New York Times Magazine. p. 7+. N. 2, '47. What is loyalty? a difficult question. A. M. Schlesinger, Jr.
New York Times Magazine. p. 9+. My. 2, '48. What is a Communist? how can you spot him? Allan Nevins.
New York Times Magazine. p. 10+. Je. 27, '48. French CP, the party and the line. C. L. Sulzberger.
New York Times Magazine. p. 8+. Jl. 18, '48. Everything worth saying should be said. Alexander Meiklejohn.
New York Times Magazine. p. 7+. Ag. 22, '48. Should we outlaw the Communist party? No. H. S. Commager.
    Discussion. New York Times Magazine. p. 2. S. 12, '48.
New York Times Magazine. p. 7+. O. 10, '48. Heresy—the great bogy of the Kremlin. C. L. Sulzberger.
New York Times Magazine. p. 7+. N. 14, '48. Marshall plan is not enough; to meet the challenge of the Communists the non-Communist world needs a real union. Barbara Ward.
New York Times Magazine. p. 7+. F. 27, '49. Should Communists be permitted to teach? Sidney Hook.
New Yorker. 23:25-6. D. 13, '47. Question of the Communist party of America.
Newsweek. 29:28. Mr. 24, '47. Laws to outlaw.
Newsweek. 29:21-3. Ap. 7, '47. Not bombs but a fifth column.
Newsweek. 29:30. Ap. 14, '47. Curran states the case against communism in the NMU. Joseph Curran.
Newsweek. 29:108. Ap. 14, '47. Outlaw American communism. Raymond Moley.
Newsweek. 29:22-9. Je. 2, '47. What Communists are up to.
Newsweek. 29:30-2. Je. 9, '47. How to fight Communism. J. E. Hoover.

Newsweek. 29:46-7. Je. 16, '47. Intrigue in Tokyo: how Russia uses Japanese Communists. H. F. Kern.

Newsweek. 30:24. Jl. 7, '47. Courts and crackdowns.

Newsweek. 30:23. D. 22, '47. Campus cause célèbre.

Newsweek. 31:28-9. F. 16, '48. Seattle coup.

Newsweek. 31:100. F. 16, '48. Can Communist party be outlawed? Raymond Moley.

Newsweek. 31:24. F. 23, '48. Roundup time.

Newsweek. 31:21-2. Mr. 1, '48. Right to investigate; House Committee on Un-American Activities.

Newsweek. 31:26-7. Ap. 26, '48. Movie that hurts.

Newsweek. 31:19-20. My. 10, '48. Into the open; Mundt bill.

Newsweek. 31:88. My. 10, '48. Disclosing the Communists; Mundt bill. Raymond Moley.

Newsweek. 31:23-5. My. 24, '48. Forging and uttering.

Newsweek. 31:24. My. 31, '48. Rider dodgers.

Newsweek. 32:72. Jl. 5, '48. Witch-hunt in Washington.

Newsweek. 32:20+. Ag. 2, '48. Case of Mary and the spy ring shrinks to the case against the reds.

Newsweek. 32:23-4. S. 13, '48. Man from Moscow; two-story enigma.

Newsweek. 32:17-20. D. 20, '48. Is America safe for spies?

Newsweek. 33:30. Ja. 17, '49. Four keys to the Kremlin: new light on Soviet intentions. J. B. Phillips.

Nineteenth Century. 140:302-13. D. '46. Royal Commission. F. A. Voigt.

Nineteenth Century. 143:181-7, 241-8. Ap.-My. '48. Liberalism, socialism and communism. W. L. Burn.

Ohio Journal of Science. 48:169-75. S. '48. Fallacy of communism. A. W. Lindsey.

*Plain Talk. 1:3-4. Ap. '47. Shall we outlaw the Communist party?

Plain Talk. 1:31-4. Ap. '47. 17 ways of spotting the Communist racket. Karl Baarslag.

Plain Talk. 2:32+. Jl. '48. Liberty to destroy liberty. Isaac Don Levine.

Plain Talk. 2:1-5. Ag. '48. Bogota pattern for revolt. Joseph Zack.

*Plain Talk. 2:6-9. Ag. '48. Who's undermining civil liberties? Lawrence Fertig.

Plain Talk. 2:1-5. S. '48. What's wrong with the loyalty program? Federal Employee.

Plain Talk. 3:28-31. O. '48. When is a red herring? Ralph de Toledano.

Plain Talk. 3:48-50. O. '48. Thief at the back door. Willard Price.

Plain Talk. 3:23-5. D. '48. Infection in the colleges. Archie Black.

Plain Talk. 3:26-30. D. '48. Agrarian swindle. Rodney Gilbert.

Plain Talk. 3:37-40. D. '48. Why communism is reactionary. K. E. Boehm.

Political Affairs. 27:207-23. Mr. '48. Role of the Communist party in the present situation. Eugene Dennis.

Political Affairs. 27:773-947. S. '48. 14th national convention of the Communist party, U.S.A., August 2, 1948.

Political Affairs. 27:1006-12. N. '48. Approaching the 30th anniversary of the Communist party, U.S.A.

Political Affairs. 27:1013-37. N. '48. From the briefs on the unconstitutionality of the Smith act; submitted by defence attorneys for the indicted twelve Communist party national committee members.

Political Science Quarterly. 63:45-81. Mr. '48. Position and prospects of the Communists in France. Vernon Van Dyke.

Political Science Quarterly. 63:321-41. S. '48. Democracy losing by default. Nathaniel Peffer.

Progressive. 12:5-8. O. '48. Our lawless loyalty program. L. A. Nikoloric.

Progressive Education. 25:61-4+. Mr. '48. Sword and the shield. W. O. Stanley, Jr.

Public Opinion Quarterly. 12, no. 3:390-8. Fall '48. Why vote Communist? Jan Stapel and W. J. De Jonge.

Publishers' Weekly. 153:2490. Je. 12, '48. Do we fear minority opinions?

Quarterly Review. 286:445-54. O. '48. Anatomy of communism. André Tardieu.

Reader's Digest. 43:1-14. Jl. '43. To collaborate successfully, we must face the facts about Russia. Max Eastman.

Reader's Digest. 45:27-33. O. '44. New Communist conspiracy. Alexander Barmine.
    Same condensed. Time. 44:26. O. 16, '44.

Reader's Digest. 50:140-6. Ap. '47. Truth about Soviet Russia's 14,000,000 slaves; excerpts from Nothing but their chains, by D. J. Dallin and Boris Nicolaevsky. Max Eastman, ed.
    Same. Congressional Record. 93:(daily) A1777-8. Ap. 15, '47.

Reader's Digest. 51:103-7. O. '47. How the Communists took over Albania. Bogdan Raditsa.

Reader's Digest. 53:48. Jl. '48. Death is so permanent. W. H. Chamberlin.
    From * Wall Street Journal. Ap. 7, '48.

Reader's Digest. 53:87-94. Jl. '48. Way to win without war. W. O. Douglas.

Reader's Digest. 53:1-11. N. '48. Fight for Italy. E. L. Palmieri.

Reviewing Stand (Northwestern University). 12, no. 14:3-11. Ap. 10, '49. Should we pass laws to curb communism? radio discussion. W. M. McGovern and others.

Round Table (London). No. 151:627-32. Je. '48. Defence of Europe.

Saturday Evening Post. 219:18-19+. Ja. 25; 24+. F. 1, '47. How the Russians spied on their allies; Soviet espionage network in Canada and its links with the United States. Sidney Shalett.

Saturday Evening Post. 220:18-19+. Ag. 23; 24-5+. Ag. 30; 28+.
S. 6, '47. How the Russians grabbed my government; edited by
Beverly Smith. Ferenc Nagy.
Same abridged. Reader's Digest. 51:80-96. N. '47.

Saturday Evening Post. 220:112. Ja. 10, '48. Have our liberties really
disappeared?

Saturday Evening Post. 220:15. Ap. 24, '48. Is America immune to
the Communist plague? Frederic Nelson.

Saturday Evening Post. 220:172. My. 22, '48. Reds need Wallace as
a people's front. Martin Ebon.

Saturday Evening Post. 220:26-7+. Je. 5, '48. How the church licked
communism in Italy. E. O. Hauser.

Saturday Evening Post. 220:144. Je. 19, '48. Can we protect freedom
without losing it? Mundt bill.

Saturday Evening Post. 221:23+. D. 18, '48. Will Tito's heretics halt
Russia? Edgar Snow.

Saturday Evening Post. 221:104. Ja. 8, '49. Congress must continue
its spy investigation.

Saturday Review of Literature. 28:14-16. S. 1, '45. What makes an
un-American; review of Dies Committee, by A. R. Ogden. M. L.
Ernst.

Saturday Review of Literature. 30:36. S. 20, '47. Phoenix nest; reply
to H. S. Commager. W. R. Benét.

Saturday Review of Literature. 31:11-12. Ap. 24, '48. Communism's
Kampf; review of Lenin, a biography, by David Shub. Asher Byrnes.
Reply, with rejoinder. Saturday Review of Literature. 31:21. Je. 5, '48.

School and Society. 66:177-82. S. 6, '47. Truth will prevail. S. P.
Capen.

School and Society. 67:234-5. Mr. 27, '48. Strategy of democracy.
I. L. Kandel.

School Life. 30:1-7. F. '48. Communism's challenge to American education. J. W. Studebaker.
Same abridged. National Education Association Journal. 37:207-8. Ap. '48.

School Life. 30:28-30. F. '48. Americanism, communism, and fascism; comparative chart.

School Life. 30:35-6. F. '48. Communism in action; study and analysis prepared by Legislative Reference Service of Library of Congress; review. F. L. Hambrick.

School Review. 57:6. Ja. '49. Communism in the schools.

Science News Letter. 54:181-2. S. 18, '48. Smears endanger nation;
tactics of House Committee on Un-American Activities.

Science Teacher. 14:166-7+. D. '47. Scientists want freedom. Joseph
Singerman.

Senior Scholastic. 49:8-10. O. 28, '46. Communist party in America.

Senior Scholastic. 50:7. F. 24, '47. Legislating loyalty. H. S. Commager.

Senior Scholastic. 52:24-5. Ap. 26, '48. Communism in America.

Senior Scholastic. 54:9. F. 9, '49. Communism on trial. H. S. Commager.

Social Service Review. 22:255. Je. '48. Should Communists be barred from teaching positions?

Social Studies. 39:195-200. My. '48. Russia's power of expansion. R. G. Cowherd.

Soundings (London). No. 10:17-22. Ja. '48. Unarmed warfare in South America; in its bid for world conquest the U.S.S.R. has not been slow to foment both strikes and distrust among the workers in Latin America. A. F. Loveday.

Spectator (London). 177:359. O. 11, '46. What communism means. Alan Bullock.

Spectator (London). 177:386. O. 18, '46. Communism in practice. Alan Bullock.

Spectator (London). 180:306. Mr. 12, '48. Communism here. W. J. Brown.

   Reply. A. Watson. Spectator. 180:347. Mr. 19, '48.

*Stanford Law Review. 1:85-107. N. '48. Control of Communist activities.

Survey Graphic. 29:290-3. My. '40. Communists and civil liberties. Victor Weybright.

Survey Graphic. 36:283-7+. My. '47. President's loyalty purge. R. E. Cushman.

*Survey Graphic. 37:366-7. Ag. '48. Great teacher that teaches nothing; can this country afford the cost of heresy-hunting? L. F. Brown.

Talks. 14:6-10. Ja. '49. How can democracy beat communism? Dowdal Davis; Walter Cronkite.

Teachers College Record. 48:295-303. F. '47. USA and USSR. W. F. Russell.

Teachers College Record. 49:1-9. O. '47. Their finest hour. W. F. Russell.

Time. 46:26. Ag. 6, '45. Worst is yet to come.

Time. 47:21. Ap. 8, '46. Red spots; report by Research Institute of America.

Time. 49:25. Ap. 7, '47. Outlaw or curb?

Time. 50:24. D. 15, '47. Black list; Communist or subversive.

Time. 51:36. Ap. 12, '48. Show of force.

Time. 51:14. My. 31, '48. System that works; excerpts from Denver speech. W. O. Douglas.

Time. 51:15-16. My. 31, '48. Logical, but not practical; Mundt-Nixon bill.

Time. 51:22. Je. 7, '48. From the horse's mouth.

Time. 52:11. Ag. 2, '48. Top twelve.

Times Educational Supplement (London). 1750:642. N. 13, '48. Christian and Communist. C. F. Garbett.

Town Meeting (Bulletin of America's Town Meeting of the Air). 10, no. 37:1-22. Ja. 11, '45. Is communism a threat to the American way of life? H. J. Taylor and others.

Town Meeting (Bulletin of America's Town Meeting of the Air). 12, no. 26:1-24. O. 24, '46. Are American Communists a threat to labor unions? Milton Murray and Earl Browder.

Town Meeting (Bulletin of America's Town Meeting of the Air). 12, no. 48:1-23. Mr. 27, '47. How should the democracies meet the challenge of spreading communism? Lawrence Spivak and others.

Town Meeting (Bulletin of America's Town Meeting of the Air). 12, no. 49:1-23. Ap. 3, '47. Should the Communist party be outlawed in the United States? J. R. McCarthy and others.

Town Meeting (Bulletin of America's Town Meeting of the Air). 13, no. 6:1-22. Je. 3, '47. Are communism and Christianity incompatible? W. H. Melish and others.

Town Meeting (Bulletin of America's Town Meeting of the Air). 13, no. 32:1-22. D. 2, '47. Are civil liberties threatened in America? H. L. Ickes and others.

Town Meeting (Bulletin of America's Town Meeting of the Air). 14, no. 4:1-23. My. 18, '48. How should democracy deal with groups which aim to destroy democracy? R. A. Taft and others.

Town Meeting (Bulletin of America's Town Meeting of the Air). 14, no. 20:1-24. S. 14, '48. Are the Congressional spy investigations serving the national interest? Homer Ferguson and others.

United States News. 20:32-3. Je. 14, '46. World revolution and the U.S. David Lawrence.

United States News. 21:26-7. O. 11, '46. Just across the border; report by Royal Canadian Commission reveals Communist fifth column.

United States News. 21:20-1. N. 1, '46. What U.S. Communists face: threats of postwar red hunt.

United States News. 22:34+. Mr. 26, '47. Anti-Communist momentum; growing campaigns in unions and Congress against left-wingers.

United States News. 22:32-3. Ap. 4, '47. Moves to outlaw Communist party; reaction of press.

United States News. 22:58-60. Ap. 4, '47. Representative Thomas's future strategy against Communists.

United States News. 23:20-1. N. 7, '47. Battle over rights of individuals.

United States News & World Report. 24:26-7. Mr. 12, '48. How Communists take over.

United States News & World Report. 24:28-9. Mr. 26, '48. How a nation is sovietized.

United States News & World Report. 24:30. Ap. 2, '48. British aim in loyalty test: security, but no witch hunt.

United States News & World Report. 24:13-14. Ap. 23, '48. Bogota: warning to Americas.

United States News & World Report. 24:22-3. Ap. 30, '48. Setback for Russian strategy.

United States News & World Report. 25:38-9. Ag. 13, '48. Pitiless publicity. David Lawrence.

United States News & World Report. 25:24-5. Ag. 20, '48. Peacetime spying: Soviet methods.

United States News & World Report. 25:15-16. Ag. 27, '48. Is FBI's anti-spy evidence wasted?

United States News & World Report. 25:40-1. Ag. 27, '48. Spy hunters.

United States News & World Report. 25:18-19. S. 10, '48. Communist-control plans.

United States News & World Report. 25:15-17. O. 1, '48. Soviet's rising power in Asia.

United States News & World Report. 25:40+. O. 8, '48. Shift in Communist strategy; concentration of effort on key industries.

United States News & World Report. 25:68-71. O. 22, '48. U.S. talks bluntly to Russia; speech delivered at Paris. W. R. Austin.

United States News & World Report. 25:11-13. D. 17, '48. Soviet's 30-year rise to empire: grabbing a fifth of the earth.

United States News & World Report. 25:26. D. 17, '48. Communists' new drive in Italy.

United States News & World Report. 25:18-19. D. 24, '48. Hunt for war and postwar spies.

United States News & World Report. 26:36-40. F. 18, '49. How to meet Soviet challenge: steadfast pressure by prosperous U.S. the policy of George F. Kennan.

United States News & World Report. 26:46-7. F. 18, '49. British strategy on Communists.

University of Chicago Round Table. 533:1-44. Je. 6, '48. Mundt-Nixon bill. Charles Kersten and Malcolm Sharp.

Vital Speeches of the Day. 11:647-9. Ag. 15, '45. America and world communism. C. B. Luce.

Vital Speeches of the Day. 13:17-19. O. 15, '46. Capital and labor are natural allies. B. J. Sheil.

Vital Speeches of the Day. 13:358-62. Ap. 1, '47. Red fascism. E. McK. Dirksen.

*Vital Speeches of the Day. 13:460-3. My. 15, '47. Communist creed; the basis of Communist action. W. C. Bullitt.
    Same. Congressional Record. 93:(daily) A2142-4. My. 1, '47.

Vital Speeches of the Day. 13:612-14. Ag. 1, '47. America versus communism in one world; address, July 14, 1947. H. E. Stassen.

Vital Speeches of the Day. 14:80-4. N. 15, '47. Twentieth century threats to liberty. M. K. Hart.

Vital Speeches of the Day. 14:366-8. Ap. 1, '48. Case of Czechoslovakia; address March 22, 1948. Alexander Cadogan.

*Vital Speeches of the Day. 14:482-9. Je. 1, '48. Should the Communist party in the United States be outlawed? H. E. Stassen; T. E. Dewey.

Vital Speeches of the Day. 14:495-7. Je. 1, '48. While Rome burns. C. B. DeMille.

Vital Speeches of the Day. 14:503-5. Je. 1, '48. Fundamental defenses; women's responsibilities. F. P. Bolton.

Vital Speeches of the Day. 14:555-60. Jl. 1, '48. Mundt-Nixon bill. K. E. Mundt.

Vital Speeches of the Day. 14:620-3. Ag. 1, '48. My commitments; betrayal by old parties. H. A. Wallace.

Vital Speeches of the Day. 14:628-30. Ag. 1, '48. Communism sets a trap. C. W. De Kiewiet.

*Vital Speeches of the Day. 14:645-9. Ag. 15, '48. Our political competence; fundamental differences between communism and democracy. W. O. Douglas.
  Excerpts. Time. 51:14. My. 31, '48.

Vital Speeches of the Day. 14:706-8. S. 15, '48. Moral leadership. J. F. Dulles.

*Wall Street Journal. p. 6. Ap. 7, '48. Gresham's law in politics. W. H. Chamberlin.
  Abridged with title Death is so permanent. Reader's Digest. 53:48. Jl. '48.

World Report. 2:24-5. Ap. 1, '47. World strength of Communists.

World Report. 2:12-13. Je. 17, '47. Communists win Hungary by infiltration.

World Report. 3:20-1. Jl. 22, '47. How strong are the ties? voting strength of Communists in Europe.

World Report. 3:18. N. 25, '47. Why British government leaves Communists alone.

World Today (London). 4:523-30. D. '48. Czechoslovakia under Communist rule. G. L.

*Yale Law Journal. 58:1-143. D. '48. Loyalty among government employees. T. I. Emerson and D. M. Helfeld.

Yale Review. n.s. 37, no. 3:411-27. [Mr.] '48. Tolerance and treason. D. C. Coyle.